THE HORSE
FROM CONCEPTION
TO MATURITY

Peter D. Rossdale
M.A., Ph.D., D.E.S.M., F.A.C.V.Sc., F.R.C.V.S.

J. A. ALLEN
London

ISBN 0–85131–546–1

Second edition, completely revised and re-set, published
in Great Britain in 1993 by
J. A. Allen & Company Ltd
1 Lower Grosvenor Place
London SW1W 0EL

First published by The California Thoroughbred
Breeders Association 1975

First J. A. Allen (cased) edition published 1975

Reprinted 1977

First J. A. Allen (paperback) edition published 1985

Reprinted 1986

Reprinted 1989

Reprinted 1997

British Library Cataloguing in Publication Data.

A catalogue record for this book is available from the
British Library.

Production editor: Bill Ireson
Typesetter: Fakenham Photosetting Ltd, Fakenham, Norfolk
Printed by Dah Hua Printing Press, Hong Kong

THE HORSE
FROM CONCEPTION
TO MATURITY

CONTENTS

INTRODUCTION

A horse for all seasons

In this book Part I describes the life of the foal from the time of its conception to weaning. It looks at both sides of the coin. Internally, the way in which the organs, glands and tissues contribute to the function of the living organism; and externally, the results of these functions in terms of everyday experience of how the foal is conceived, develops in the uterus of the mare, is born, adapts to the environment and grows to become fully independent of its mother.

Part II covers the anatomy of the limbs with particular reference to the way the muscles, tendons, ligaments and bones are arranged to meet their special functions in supporting the body and enabling the horse to achieve, despite its size, the speed for which it is renowned. Inevitably, the limbs are prone to injuries and these are considered under the heading of lameness with a discussion of their diagnosis and treatment.

The problems which confront horse owners and veterinarians can be properly understood only if we possess a knowledge of the horse's body and the manner in which it functions. It is necessary to have a grasp of anatomy in order to appreciate the limitations and capabilities under various conditions.

This book presents an account of the various structures of the horse's body, the manner in which they function and how this knowledge can be used in day-to-day management.

Climate, soil and management of horses differ according to region, for instance, as between the western seaboard of the United States, Australia, and the United Kingdom and we can benefit from a comparative approach. For example, by highlighting differences in methods, customs and results, we can seek to provide answers to important questions, such as why a particular system of management may be adequate for one environment but not for another, why disease or injury is prevalent under certain circumstances but avoided in others, or why horses are reared more easily in one climate than another.

Evidence derived from this type of inquiry may sometimes form the basis for changes in traditional techniques; the need for which might not be apparent from a purely parochial study.

A product of evolution

If we consider, first, the purpose for which we use horses in the modern age, we may find we are so accustomed to assuming the rights of mastership over this particular species that we almost believe the horse's body was evolved for riding and racing, and that the ability of mares and stallions is measured in their capacity to produce the end product of our choosing. This attitude is far from correct and puts the cart before the horse in no uncertain manner. In fact, the structure of the horse's body and the way in which it functions is directly related to its evolutionary history extending over many millions of years.

It is only recently (on the evolutionary scale) that mankind has harnessed the horse for his own special purposes and by careful selection of breeding stock has been able to exaggerate certain qualities, obtaining ponies for children to ride, heavy draft horses for work and ultrafast breeds for racing. But while the structures of the body may differ in degree, basically they remain the same; in other words, every horse is built to an identical design, moving and responding to its surroundings in a similar manner.

The horse in perspective

In whatever part of the world horses are kept for racing and breeding, mankind's efforts are governed by certain fundamental factors, such as body structure, inheritance, environment and the type of work to which the horse is put. These factors also dictate the limits of success that can be achieved in any particular sphere, and before embarking on any detailed examination of the horse they must be brought into perspective.

We may influence conformation but we cannot change the inherited material to the extent of affecting the body's blueprint; for example, by breeding a two- or three-toed horse. Therefore, if we are to understand the body of the horse, we must appreciate the extent to which it has been moulded by evolution.

Specialisation for speed

The horse has acquired certain specialised features, primarily concerned with the species' survival. For example, the limbs have become lengthened and simplified, the digits of the hands and feet reduced, so that the horse of today stands virtually on the tips of four toes.

These limb changes were accompanied by a perfection of form in head, neck and body; the net result being an animal of considerable size but great speed. In fact, speed is the horse's defence in the wild state. It has survived by running away from danger, unlike species such as the cat which faces its enemies and fights.

In addition, the horse acquired definite methods of eating and digesting its food, the teeth and gut becoming developed to assimilate the fibrous food of the plains on which it lived.

Herd behaviour

It was not only changes in structure, however, which helped the horse to survive in the wild state; instinctive patterns of behaviour were also formed. Horses became grouped in herds displaying characteristic social and sexual attitudes to one another. For instance, by developing a limited season for mating they ensured that conception occurred at a time of year which would result in their foals being born when food and climate were optimum. The 'habit' of foaling during darkness presumably had some adaptive significance in survival, perhaps enabling mares to produce their young unseen by predators and to afford the maximum amount of daylight in which to become established in the herd.

Whatever the reasons for the formation of these and other behavioural patterns, they remain today and we must accept them with the structural changes.

The point which requires emphasis is that the horse of today was not evolved to meet our needs; that it serves its modern function as well as it does is a remarkable tribute to its versatility. In this century we are placing the horse in an increasingly artificial environment and subjecting its body to ever-greater stresses. Small wonder, therefore, that we encounter problems on the studs and in the racing stables.

The environment

The environment in which horses live is of course greatly affected by the human element which we call management. Whether, for example, horses are kept in looseboxes or turned out onto paddocks, the way they are fed, the amount of exercise they receive and the weight of their rider all differ from one area of the world to another.

Perhaps the most notable difference in the man-made (compared to the natural) environment is the fact that mares are kept separate from stallions. This segregation has profound effects on breeding programmes: it forces management to decide when a mare is in oestrus and when mating shall take place; makes necessary the ritual of teasing the mares and is responsible for so-called abnormal states of behaviour known as 'silent heat'. In the covering sheds matings must be performed with the mares placed under some form of restraint; a twitch attached to the upper lip and perhaps ropes around the legs. Some might think the necessity of such restraint a sad commentary on a system which prevents the male and female of the species from freely exercising their most natural of prerogatives!

The custom of confining horses to looseboxes is another disturbing element, disrupting the social patterns of the herd by alternately isolating individuals and remixing them into arbitrarily selected groups. The stresses which these daily arrangements produce may give rise to abnormal behaviour traits and vices.

The loosebox itself places the horse in an environment which is not only foreign to its free-living nature but also subjects it to such physical insults as a dust-polluted atmosphere, draughts, extremes of temperature and interference with natural lighting. Horses are, in consequence, predisposed to such conditions as 'broken wind', allergies and, in young horses, diarrhoea.

Chronic obstructive pulmonary disease (COPD) is the term used to describe broken wind. This is a condition of allergy or hypersensitivity of the small airways of the lungs. These airways contain very small muscle layers around the tubes and these go into spasm due to a reaction between certain elements in dust (such as fungal spores) and the animal's defence mechanism. The reaction may be likened to abnormal intensity of a normal control mechanism; the condition may be likened to asthma.

Fresh air is the chief element of therapy and prevention. Mouldy hay or straw are the most common contributors to the condition.

Straw bedding is a particular challenge to horses susceptible to or suffering from broken wind. Such an individual, if it is necessary to bring them into looseboxes, should be bedded on woodshavings, paper or peat moss. It is also sensible to feed good quality hay – which may have been immersed in water for several hours – or proprietary equivalents.

The foaling box may also bring special risks to the mare and her offspring at a time when both are vulnerable to infection; the mare to the entry of bacteria into her uterus, the foal to infections of the lungs and umbilicus.

In addition, looseboxes are costly items as far as overheads of the stud farm are concerned, requiring litter for bedding and man-hours for cleaning out. More attention is now being paid to the construction of looseboxes to eliminate the more obvious disadvantages, while in many breeding centres of the southern hemisphere, where the climate is favourable, they have been dispensed with altogether. Perhaps there would be less need to rely on buildings to protect horses in the United Kingdom if, in 1833, the decision had not been taken to change the registration date of Thoroughbreds from 1 May to 1 January. It would have been possible to select 1 March as a practical alternative.

The racehorse is subjected to extremes of environmental stress. It is broken and ridden when barely 18 months old, which tests the tissues of the body to the utmost under the most unnatural conditions. Injuries to bone, ligaments, tendons and joints are relatively common and bear witness to the frailty of the body structure when subjected to the type of work for which we rear our horses. However hard breeders may try, they cannot arrange matters so as to produce a 'machine' which is certain to function just as we would wish.

In many respects the environment in which we keep our horses is so convenient that it will not be altered merely because it involves certain risks to the horse's health. In fact, if we compare conditions in which horses are reared and used in Europe, the United States, Australia, South Africa and New Zealand we find considerable differences in management and climate. It is remarkable that despite this diversity the results obtained appear very similar. For instance, it seems, as far as accurate data can be obtained, that there is no great variation in fertility rates among Thoroughbred broodmares; or unsoundness in racehorses.

Vaccination

Vaccines are special preparations which stimulate an immune response of the individual into which they are administered (in horses, usually by injection).

They are made up of bacteria which have been treated in such a way as to retain their immune-stimulating properties but which makes them innocuous as far as side-effects are concerned. This process consists either of treating the microbe and attenuating its virulent powers while retaining it alive or, more often, of killing the microbe to produce a dead vaccine.

More recently, particularly with viruses, microbiological engineering has enabled scientists to identify specific parts which stimulate immunity and those which are responsible for virulence. The immune-stimulating part is then separated and used in the vaccine leaving behind the harmful fragments of the virus.

At present there is a search for an effective herpesvirus vaccine for horses to prevent virus abortion and catarrhal bronchitis. Up to now vaccines against herpesvirus have consisted of killed virus, or live virus that has been altered in the laboratory to remove virulence. In both these types of vaccine the immunity achieved is relatively short lived and vaccines today contain only sub-type 1, the abortion strain of the virus.

Vaccines against influenza are in daily use and are compulsory under the rules of racing in the United Kingdom and in Ireland. It is hoped that shortcomings in existing vaccines (principally short-lived protection) will be offset by the advent of newly-available ISCOM (Immune Stimulating COMplex) vaccines. These vaccines consist of inactivated antigens of the important viral strands; an antigen being that part of an organism that provokes antibody formation in the vaccinated animal, hence protection from future infection.

Horses are routinely vaccinated against tetanus.

Part I

CHAPTER ONE

FUNCTIONS OF BROODMARES

Breeding organs of the mare

The breeding organs (Figures 1.1 and 1.2) consist of two ovaries, the uterus, cervix and vagina; and the pituitary gland.As far as function is concerned, one cannot regard these structures as isolated from one another, or from the rest of the body. A complicated and delicately balanced relationship exists between the various parts. This sometimes makes it difficult to interpret the cause and effect of various problems of infertility or dysfunction of the breeding organs.

Ovaries

The ovaries of the mare (Figures 1.3 and 1.4) are roughly bean-shaped. Their size varies in different individuals and in the same mare at various times of the year. On average, they measure about 7 cm × 4 cm. Each ovary consists of a fibrous-like mass (stroma) containing numerous sacs of fluid (follicles) in which an egg (ovum) is to be found. Every individual is born with a complement of many thousands of eggs and does not produce more during her lifetime. In addition to the follicles and their eggs, the stroma may contain one or more structures, each known as a 'yellow body' (corpus luteum). How they come to be formed and their function will be discussed later.

Fallopian tube

The Fallopian tube (Figures 1.1 and 1.5) or oviduct lies in the membrane which supports the ovaries and the uterus. Each tube is coiled and measures about 25 cm in length. It is open at one end and enters directly into the uterus at the other.

Uterus

The uterus (Figures 1.1, 1.2 and 1.6) is a hollow organ with muscular walls lined on the inside with a layer of cells containing numerous small glands. It is roughly T-shaped and composed of a body and two horns; the horns are joined to the Fallopian tubes and the body communicates with the exterior through the cervix and vagina.

The uterus is capable of undergoing profound changes during pregnancy when it accommodates the growing foetus, besides acting as a surface for attachment of the placenta. It also acts as a gland by secreting prostaglandins and is involved in the production of hormones.

Cervix, vagina and vulva

The interior of the uterus is connected to the outside through the cervix. The cervix forms a highly muscular neck to the uterus and, like the uterus, is able to change under varying circumstances; these include a capacity to dilate to facilitate passage of the stallion's semen and at the termination of pregnancy to allow passage of the foal during birth.

The vagina is also capable of undergoing certain changes which will be described when we come to consider the reproductive cycle. Together with the vulva, the vagina acts as a vestibule of protection between the outside world and the interior of the uterus; the im-

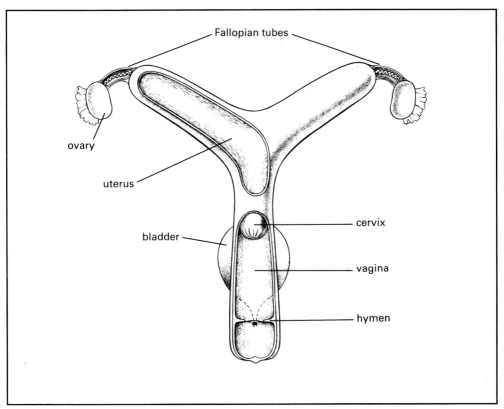

Figure 1.1 Diagram to show the mare's breeding organs, viewed from above with sections exposing internal structures

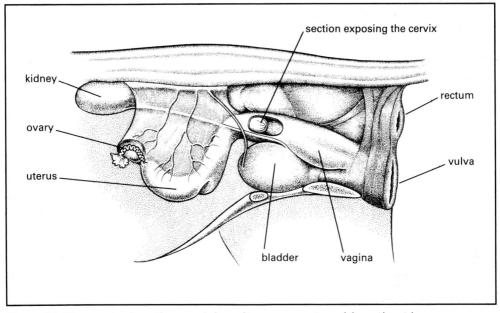

Figure 1.2 Diagram to show the mare's breeding organs, viewed from the side

3

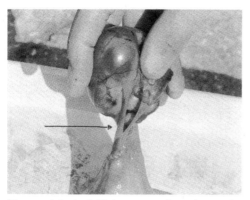

Figure 1.3 A follicle protruding from the ovary's surface (between the thumb and finger). The arrow points to the ligament which connects the ovary to the horn of the uterus

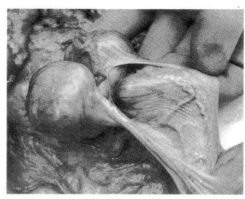

Figure 1.5 The Fallopian tube can be seen as a tortuous tube running in the membrane which joins the ovary (left) to the horn (right)

Figure 1.4 An ovary cut in half to show a recently-formed 'yellow body' (A) and an unripe follicle (B) probably in the process of being resorbed; (C) reveals a 'yellow body'

portance of which will be discussed in relation to the problems of infection.

Pituitary gland

The pituitary gland is a very small body situated immediately beneath the brain in the skull. It produces a wide range of hormones. A hormone is a substance produced by a gland and which passes in the bloodstream to have its effect on a distant part of the body. To clarify this statement we can take three examples of pituitary hormones: follicle sti-

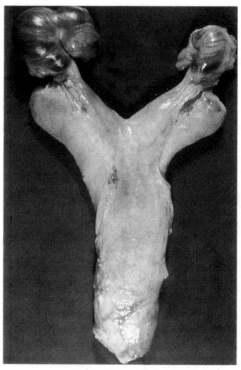

Figure 1.6 The uterus and ovaries. The left horn shows follicle development in the ovary

mulating hormone (FSH); luteinising hormone (LH); and prolactin. The function of these will be placed in perspective later but, for the present illustration, it is sufficient to say that FSH and LH emanate from the pituitary and travel in the bloodstream to the ovaries, on which they exert their effects. Growth hormone is also produced which affects most tissues in the body.

Hypothalamus

The hypothalamus is part of the brain which tells the pituitary to release certain hormones including oxytocin; a hormone important in parturition and lactation.

Pineal gland

The pineal gland is very close to the hypothalamus and responds to light falling on the back of the eyes and, in consequence, to daylight length.

From the foregoing we are now in a position to discuss the ways in which hormones contribute to the sexual signs and changes occurring throughout the oestrous cycle of the mare (Figure 1.7).

Oestrous cycle

There are two phases of the cycle: oestrus and dioestrus.

Each is characterised by:
1. Inner changes occurring in the sex organs and glands.
2. Psychological changes manifested by alterations in behaviour and temperament.
3. The functional aspects of the cycle involving the act of coitus (mating), fertilisation of the egg, followed by pregnancy.

The physiological changes occurring during the oestrous cycle are complex and not all of them are fully understood. However the broad pattern of events is well known and proceeds as follows.

Oestrus

Oestrus is the phase of the cycle where the female is receptive to the stallion and allows him to approach, mount, enter and achieve ejaculation.

The state of oestrus lasts, on average, five days and is associated with an outpouring of FSH from the pituitary. This hormone stimulates a small number of follicles already present in the ovaries to grow in size; they increase from microscopic proportions to attain a diameter of several centimetres (see Figure 1.6).

Although several follicles develop in this fashion, one will usually outgrow the others. When it has reached between 4 cm to 5 cm in diameter, it will rupture. This event is called ovulation and is brought about by the action of pituitary LH.

Ovulation always occurs through a certain place in the surface of the ovary known as the ovulation fossa. The contents of the follicle, including the egg, escape and the egg passes into the Fallopian tube. If the egg becomes fertilised in the tube it will continue on its way to the uterus where it arrives on the fifth day after ovulation. If the egg is not fertilised it becomes resistant to sperm entry after a few hours. It then remains in the tube and disintegrates.

Any other follicles which have been growing in either of the two ovaries usually undergo a process of resorption (atresia). Their lining walls become thickened and the fluid they contain is resorbed.

The follicles developing in the ovaries during oestrus produce the hormone oestrogen. This causes specific changes in the genital passages. The lining of the vagina becomes moist, reddened, and lubricated by mucus of low viscosity; the cervix is relaxed and the folds of its rose-like structure are puffed and oedematous (full of fluid). The uterine wall loses its tone and the lining of the uterus, cervix and vagina become flushed with blood.

Oestrogen is also largely responsible for changes in the mare's behaviour which occur during oestrus and which will be described later.

Dioestrus

The period of rejection of the male which follows oestrus is called dioestrus, namely the

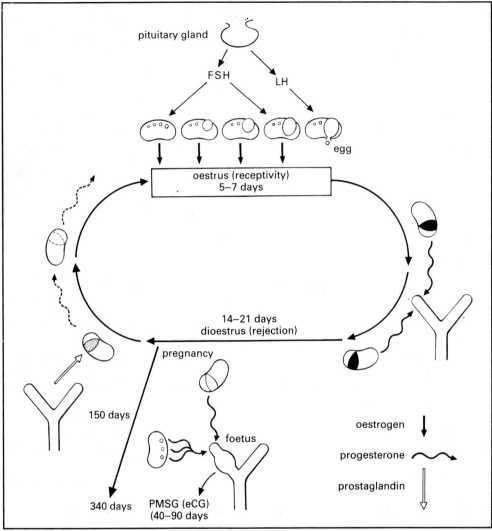

Figure 1.7 Diagram to show the oestrous cycle of the mare. FSH = follicle stimulating hormone; LH = luteinising hormone. Circles in the ovary represent follicles one of which enlarges and ruptures to release an egg at the ovulation fossa. The black wedge is the yellow body that secretes progesterone until it is broken down (or affected) by the hormone prostaglandin

time between successive oestrus periods. Dioestrus lasts typically (atypical patterns are described below) 14 days. The mare then returns into oestrus and so the cycle continues. A further period of oestrus ensues, followed by a further dioestrus; and so on throughout the breeding season.

The state of dioestrus is initiated by the secretion of LH from the pituitary gland causing ovulation. The rupture of the follicle is accompanied by a breakdown of the blood vessels in its lining causing membrane haemorrhage into the cavity previously occupied by the fluid and egg. A blood clot forms and special cells in the lining membrane then grow into the clot and complete the yellow body.

The yellow body acts as a gland and

produces the hormone progesterone. This body continues to act as a gland for about 15 days, after which time it ceases to secrete progesterone and gradually becomes smaller. Prostaglandins are substances produced by the uterus which cause this destruction (luteolysis) of the yellow body (literally breaking down, or lysis, of luteal tissue). Finally, all that remains is a small white scar (corpus albicans) in the substance of the ovary.

Progesterone is responsible for changes in the genital tract which include a closing down of the blood vessels in the lining membrane, the surface of which becomes pale and sticky. The cervix is made to constrict and the wall of the uterus becomes turgid. Progesterone prepares the uterus for the reception of the fertilised egg and plays a major role in the maintenance of the foetus in the uterus during pregnancy.

Hormonal control of cycle

The hormonal control of oestrus and dioestrus is based on a series of changes that might be likened to switches. Each switch has an effect on the next in the series until the last turns on or off sexual activity. In this analogy, the last switch of the series produces oestrogen, the hormone accounting for the behaviour of oestrus with its associated changes in the genital tract, and progesterone, the hormone of dioestrus.

Both these hormones are produced by the ovaries. Oestrogen from the lining of the follicles and progesterone from the yellow body.

The oestrous cycle is, therefore, an alternating dominance of oestrogen (heat) and progesterone (dioestrus).

The switches that control the alternate production of these two hormones are to be found in the pituitary gland. Here, the hormones FSH and LH are produced. FSH, as its name implies, causes follicles to develop in size. It is secreted in two surges, one midway in the cycle and another at the start of oestrus. The mid-cycle surge causes several follicles to enlarge but it is only the oestrous surge which takes these follicles to the stage of ovulation. In practice, it is only one or two follicles out of the crop that have been produced during each oestrous cycle which ultimately ripen for ovulation. LH causes the follicle to rupture and promotes the forming of the yellow body (Figure 1.8).

In order to discern the control of FSH and LH secretion, we have to go one stage further back. This switch lies in a special area of the brain, the hypothalamus. It is here in certain nerve cells that gonadotrophin-releasing hormones (GnRH) are produced. These act specifically on the pituitary to cause the release of either FSH or LH. At the level of this switch, rhythmic alternating patterns

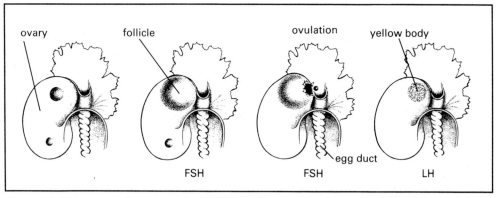

Figure 1.8 Diagram to show (from left to right): the ovary in dioestrus; follicle development; oestrus with ovulation; and development of the yellow body. The influence of pituitary hormones FSH and LH is also shown

drive the release of FSH and LH, which, in turn, promote progesterone or oestrogen. This rhythmic pattern is partly inherent and basic to the reproductive cycle of the mare; partly influenced by the season of the year and partly by environmental factors such as quality of feed and climatic conditions.

The influence of season (seasonality) is mediated through a higher switch, namely the pineal gland, situated in the brain. This produces the hormone melatonin, thereby controlling the switch within the hypothalamus and the secretion of GnRH. Melatonin levels increase during darkness and decrease in the light. The first switch in the chain is, therefore, the eyes. Light falling on the back of the eye (retina) initiates a signal that passes along the pathway of the optic nerve into the brain itself. It is this message which makes the individual aware of light and, particularly, of the number of hours of daylight at any given time of the year.

It is the length of daylight which triggers the onset of oestrous cycles when the period of daylight is 12 hours or longer; the mare's hormonal system recognises the onset of spring. And it is this switch that can be triggered by providing artificial daylight to promote the onset of cycling early in the year by, for example, placing a 100 watt lamp in the loosebox.

Having described the hierarchy of control from the eyes to the ovaries let us now bring the system into practical perspective.

Mares recognise the time of year through the eyes and pineal gland. At the appropriate season, when daylight has been increasing substantially, oestrous cycling starts. Up to this time, sexual activity has been quiescent and no heat cycles would have been evident, a state known as anoestrus (literally, no oestrus). The onset of cycling may be preceded by an indeterminant pattern of oestrous behaviour known as transitional oestrus.

Once true cycling has been triggered, the process continues in a series of cycles throughout the summer and early autumn when decreasing daylight hours shuts down the system and the individual returns to anoestrus. The situation is notably affected by early grass growth.

During oestrous cycling, the follicles produce oestrogen under the influence of FSH; and oestrogen concentrations increase in the bloodstream. The hypothalamus reacts by turning the switch that releases the GnRH to promote the release of LH from the pituitary. As the concentrations of LH rise in the bloodstream this in turn triggers the switch resulting in the forming of a yellow body and the production of progesterone. At the same time oestrogen levels decrease following rupture of a follicle and the dual effect of increasing progesterone and decreasing oestrogen turns off the switch of LH and turns on the switch of FSH.

There is, however, a further step required before the mare can return to oestrus. This is the need for some action to be taken to end the life of the yellow body and thereby decrease progesterone levels in the blood. Progesterone blocks the onset of oestrus and maintains the individual in dioestrus. The hormone responsible for breaking down the yellow body is prostaglandin. This is produced in the uterus at about day 14 after the previous ovulation. Within 24 hours the yellow body stops producing progesterone and the falling levels are recognised by the hypothalamus which promotes the production of FSH through the secretion of GnRH, thereby starting a further cycle of hormonal events.

Differing patterns of oestrous cycle

We have seen that oestrous cycles may be absent in winter (anoestrus). Levels of GnRH and therefore LH are insufficient during this period to sustain sexual activity. The ovaries are inactive and, often, small and hard. The mares will not accept the stallion even though they have zero levels of progesterone.

On the other hand, the usual 14-day period of dioestrus may be prolonged by the persistence of a yellow body beyond its normal lifespan. The long dioestrus may occur at any season of the year and last for weeks or, even, months. This state may be distinguished from anoestrus by measuring progesterone concentrations in the bloodstream. In anoestrus they are zero and in prolonged dioestrus they will be above a minimal value. Prostaglandin injections may be used to end the state of prolonged dioestrus but is, of course, of no benefit in true anoestrus because this state is not dependent on an active yellow body.

In the early spring, hormonal levels may be sufficient to promote sexual activity and the onset of oestrus but without promoting ovulation. Periods of oestrus lasting several weeks may then occur. The mare is receptive but is unable, of her own accord, to pass into a state of dioestrus. Eventually, this period ends with an ovulation and this then starts proper cycling activity.

Short cycling (i.e. oestrus occurring at intervals of less than 12 days) may be the result of uterine infection or other inflammatory conditions of the uterine lining. This results in the release of prostaglandin prematurely and therefore the breaking down of the yellow body with the consequent return of the individual to oestrus.

In pyometra (pus in the uterus) the lining of the uterus may be damaged to the extent that prostaglandin is not released and a state of prolonged dioestrus occurs. However, most cases of prolonged dioestrus are the result of a more physiological effect that stops the uterus from producing prostaglandin. This condition is usually overcome when the mare is brought back into oestrus by a prostaglandin injection or through the spontaneous resumption of cyclical activity on the part of the uterus.

Lactational anoestrus is the term given to describe an absence of cycling in a mare with a foal at foot. This is thought to be the result of the hormone associated with lactation, namely prolactin. The block is believed to occur at the level of GnRH secretion but the exact mechanism is unclear.

Variations in the oestrous cycle may be apparent or real. Apparent states may be related to our misinterpretation of the sexual signs, the so-called silent heat for example. In this the mare is actually in heat but does not display the usual signs when presented to a male teaser. She will usually accept the stallion when presented; her failure to display appropriate signs may be a side-effect of the artificial conditions under which she was bred, with the male separated from his harem.

Artificially high levels of protein in the diet and the warmth of stables are other factors which may help mares to become sexually active in winter. In all these instances we are conditioning the pituitary to accept that spring has arrived and with it the natural breeding season of the species.

The oestrous cycle is also suppressed during pregnancy. When conception occurs, the fertilised egg passes into the uterus and initiates a series of changes. The yellow body continues to function instead of declining on the 15th day after its formation.

The presence of a developing foetus stimulates the formation of ulcer-like structures in the uterus. Since the 1930s it has been known that these structures produce enormous quantities of a hormone known as pregnant mare serum gonadotrophin (PMSG). It is not clear exactly what the function of the hormone is but it has been shown to consist of a mixture of FSH and LH. Dr W. R. (Twink) Allen, Scientific Officer to the Thoroughbred Breeders' Association (TBA) Equine Fertility Unit at Newmarket, has renamed PMSG. It is now known as equine Chorionic Gonadotrophin (eCG) because one of its functions is to cause follicles to develop and ovulate in the ovary from about day 42 onwards, thereby producing yellow bodies to supplement and replace the yellow body formed at the time of conception. These ulcer-like structures, which are present between the 35th and about the 100th day of pregnancy, are called endometrial cups. Their exact function and that of the hormone they produce are not fully understood.

Oestrous cycle and behaviour

The characteristic feature of the mare's be-

9

haviour (Figures 1.9 and 1.10) during the oestrous cycle is the alternating period of oestrus, when the mare will accept the stallion, and of dioestrus when she rejects him. In the jargon of stud staff, the terms 'in heat', 'in season' and 'showing' may be used to describe oestrus, and 'out of heat' and 'gone off' to describe dioestrus. This behavioural pattern is based on corresponding physiological changes already described and the alternating dominance of the hormones oestrogen and progesterone.

At the teasing board the mare in heat leans towards the teaser, straddles her hind legs, raises her tail and everts the lips of the vulva (winking), so exposing the clitoris. In the paddock the mare may be stimulated to show signs of oestrus when in contact with other members of the group or when other horses pass nearby. A mare in oestrus may urinate frequently and void a yellowish, viscous, sweet-smelling urine. A marked change in temperament may be apparent, especially in mares which are normally aggressive or difficult to handle; they may be more easily caught and less resentful of handling. If approached by attendants or rubbed over the

hindquarters, they respond as if they were at the teasing board.

The signs of dioestrus are to a large extent the converse and the mare will not accept the stallion. There is a reluctance to approach the teasing board, resentment of handling, and kicking when approached by a male horse. She displays obvious signs of rejection (ears back, biting, kicking) and her genital tract becomes dry, sticky and the surface of the cervix and vagina appear white. The cervix itself becomes tightly constricted compared with the relaxed state of oestrus. During anoestrus and pregnancy, most mares show behavioural patterns similar to those exhibited in dioestrus.

Functional aspects

In both physiological and behavioural effects, oestrus provides the mare with an optimum chance of conception at a time of year that will ensure her foal is born when climatic conditions are favourable (i.e. after 11 months' gestation). The time the mare will accept the stallion is limited to a matter of

Figure 1.9 A mare displaying characteristic oestrous behaviour, relaxed to teasing, and showing

Figure 1.10 This mare displays typical dioestrous behaviour at the teasing board, rejecting the teaser, kicking out

days and because she ovulates during that period it ensures that the sperm, which have a limited lifespan in the female tract, will have the best chance of fertilising the egg. This means the stallion's services will not be squandered during periods when ovulation is unlikely to take place.

Once the sperm have entered the female tract, their ability to fertilise the egg lasts, on average, two to three days. There are exceptions at either end of the scale, and the spermatozoa of some stallions live for seven days, while other sires' sperm appear to lose their capacity for fertilisation within 24 hours. The egg will itself lose the capacity to be fertilised and die within about 48 hours of ovulation.

In the practical world of horse-breeding programmes we must aim, therefore, at utilising to the best advantage our knowledge of the physiological and behavioural components of the oestrous cycle. In effect this requires that we should arrange the mating of mares 24 to 48 hours before they ovulate.

A typical cycle has been described but unfortunately, under the conditions in which we breed Thoroughbreds, such an ideal seldom exists and we are faced with a variety of problems.

Problems associated with breeding programmes

In 1975 the national average conception rate among Thoroughbreds in the United Kingdom was about 70 per cent. This figure was obtained from returns on about 11,000 mares in the General Stud Book. More recent statistics show that there has been some subsequent improvement. Results may be bettered by some 10 per cent, or even 20 per cent, among small groups such as on studs which cater for two or three stallions and 80 to 120 mares. It is claimed, with some justification, that where non-thoroughbred horses are bred under more natural conditions (and the stallion runs free with his mares) that the rates of fertility are nearer to 100 per cent. For this reason, the relatively poor results obtained in Thoroughbreds is a source of criticism. It is instructive, however, to examine some of the factors which may account for this relatively poor performance.

Selection
Thoroughbred breeding stock, as opposed to non-thoroughbred stock, is selected with nearly all the emphasis on racecourse performance; the better the record, the less chance that a mare or stallion will be culled. In other words, if a Thoroughbred mare goes barren for, say, two years in three she may still be retained in the breeding stock simply because she had won a valuable stakes race, whereas a non-thoroughbred would be put down or used only for riding.

Fecundity (i.e. the ability to conceive, carry a foal to full-term, deliver and rear it) is usually not given sufficient consideration in the selection of broodmares and this is bound to be reflected in subnormal breeding performances.

Season
Another adverse influence stems from the necessity to mate Thoroughbreds outside their natural breeding season of April to August as a result of the registration date of 1 January. It is of course possible to achieve conception in any month of the year, but outside the months mentioned it is, on the whole, more difficult; the oestrous cycle is less regular; ovarian activity, as measured by follicle development and ovulation, is reduced; the sexual behaviour of the mare is more difficult to interpret and the stallion's libido and quality of semen decreases. To a certain extent, management is able to offset these inherent biological disadvantages by such measures as artificial light in the stable, the provision of special diets and shelters for warmth. In addition, veterinarians perform routine examinations of the mares, an aspect of management dealt with later.

The habit of breeding Thoroughbred mares before April is largely the consequence of a decision taken in the United Kingdom by the Jockey Club in 1833. It was decided to change the registration date of Thor-

oughbred horses from 1 May to 1 January. This was considered necessary because the former date fell during the Flat racing season and it was not convenient to have horses changing their ages at this time. The Jockey Club's choice of 1 January, subsequently set the pattern throughout the world; it was unfortunate in many respects that 1 March was not chosen instead.

During evolution, horses were naturally selected by the survival of those who were able to breed only in the spring and summer thereby ensuring the foals were not delivered in the autumn and winter when food was in short supply and climatic conditions were not conducive to survival of the newborn foal. Those members of the herd that displayed this breeding pattern survived and passed their genetic material to subsequent generations, whereas those that did not conform failed to do so.

Today's conditions of management have largely removed the pressures towards seasonal breeding. In many ways, selection is based on the capacity of the mare to conceive and deliver her foal in any month of the year, including the winter. In Thoroughbreds, the winter months are favoured by breeders in order to get early (more valuable) foals.

Management
Not only are the limits of the stud season arbitrarily placed so that they do not coincide with the natural breeding season, but the length of the season is curtailed. The number of ovulations which can occur in the season is, in consequence, limited and the chance of conception correspondingly lessened. Since ovulations tend to occur less frequently before April, some individuals undoubtedly have an effective breeding season of less than two months. In addition it is customary to limit the number of services in each oestrus, which further restricts the chance of conception, especially if for any reason the stallion's ejaculate is sub-fertile.

Segregation
Segregating the stallion from his mares raises

a further problem because stud workers are required to diagnose the behavioural signs of oestrus. Under natural conditions the stallion would interpret these signs. The ritual of teasing overcomes this problem to a limited extent though some mares are not sufficiently stimulated by the teaser to show that they are in oestrus. In these cases the term mentioned earlier, silent heat, is often used: a mare shows dioestrous behaviour at the teasing board although she is in a state of physiological oestrus (i.e. with a follicle developing in the ovary and a relaxed, moistened cervix).

The dichotomy between physiological and behavioural oestrus is becoming an increasingly common problem and one cannot help wondering if some individuals are not conditioned by the teasing ritual to show 'abnormal' behaviour at the teasing board. Such behaviour is not, of course, really abnormal in the pathological sense; it may even be considered natural under the artificial conditions at the teasing board.

Irregular cycles

If silent heat is the failure of a mare in physiological oestrus to show oestrous behaviour, conversely there are mares who display strong oestrous behaviour but at the same time fail to produce follicles or to ovulate. This type of problem is most frequently encountered outside the months of the natural breeding season (i.e. in February, March and early April). Once again, we cannot say this divergence is pathological, unless perhaps it occurs persistently in the spring and summer.

Mares who display irregular cycles do so more commonly in the months outside those of April to August. The term 'transitional oestrus' is used to describe the type of oestrous periods we expect the mare to experience as she passes from winter anoestrus (no heat periods) to summer cycling (regular heat periods of 5 days, followed by dioestrus of about 15 days).

Transitional oestrus is often prolonged, occupying 10 to 30 days or more. The ovaries develop follicles which either fail to ovulate, and the mare stops showing oestrous signs for a further period before starting true oestrus, or ovulation eventually occurs in the normal fashion at the end of the heat. Again, it is only when this state persists in the natural breeding months that we can ascribe it to pathological causes.

The anoestrous state occurs naturally in the winter months. Sometimes it affects mares in the stud season and presents one of the most frustrating problems known to management. Anoestrus is perhaps more commonly found in mares with a foal at foot. Whether it is considered to be a natural or pathological condition depends to a great extent on definition.

It is well recognised that some forms of anoestrus are the result of a foetus dying after a matter of days or weeks, or of the breeding organs remaining in a semi-pregnant state even though the conceptus has gone.

Behavioural signs

In some instances mares show signs of behavioural oestrus although physiologically in dioestrus, or even pregnant. It is rare, however, for these individuals to accept the stallion and the condition is usually rather one of erroneous diagnosis on the part of the observer.

CHAPTER TWO

MARES IN BREEDING SEASON

Detection of the mare's sexual state

Under natural conditions where the stallion runs free with his mares, it is he who interprets the sexual state of the mare at any particular time. In most systems of Thoroughbred management, however, the stallion is kept separate from his mares except when mating takes place. Both mare and stallion are led in hand so that the timing of the occasion becomes one of managerial decision.

If, under these circumstances, a mare is presented in a non-receptive state, the stallion may receive crippling injuries. For this reason management must take stringent measures to ensure that each mare is receptive before mating is attempted. In addition, management must decide the timing of the event with a view to achieving the maximum chance of conception in each oestrous period.

There are two methods by which the exact sexual state of a mare is determined and these, broadly speaking, consist of:
1. The observation of the mare's behaviour.
2. Veterinary examinations of the breeding organs conducted at appropriate times during the oestrous cycle.

Observation of the mare

It is necessary here to discuss the manner in which we treat mares to stimulate them to show these signs, a process commonly known as 'trying', or 'teasing'.

The teaser

It is usual for studs to keep a male horse especially for the purpose of teasing mares (Figures 2.1 to 2.12). This may be a Thoroughbred horse or belong to another breed; for instance, pony stallions are a popular choice. Some horses become too aggressive when used as teasers while others do not display enough vigour. The ideal teaser does not abuse the mares but exhibits sufficient interest to stimulate them to show signs of oestrus.

Methods

The most common method is to hold the teaser behind a board, covered on the front by a bristle or rubber mat and placed near the stables. Then each morning the mares are led to the board in turn and presented head on or sideways. A variation of this method, favoured in many European and southern hemisphere breeding centres, is to run or lead mares through a crush with the teaser on the outside.

Teasing mares while they are at grass is often performed with a permanent or movable board hung on the paddock's rails. In this case mares may be observed as a group; individuals in oestrus usually approach the teaser but 'shy' mares should be led in hand to the board.

OPPOSITE PAGE
Figures 2.1 to 2.8 The mare is led into the teasing board, on the other side of which the teaser is held by a groom (2.1, 2.2 and 2.3); rejection is evident from tail swishing (2.1), the attitude of the mare's ears (2.4, 2.5 and 2.6) and her final refusal of the teaser (2.7 and 2.8)

14

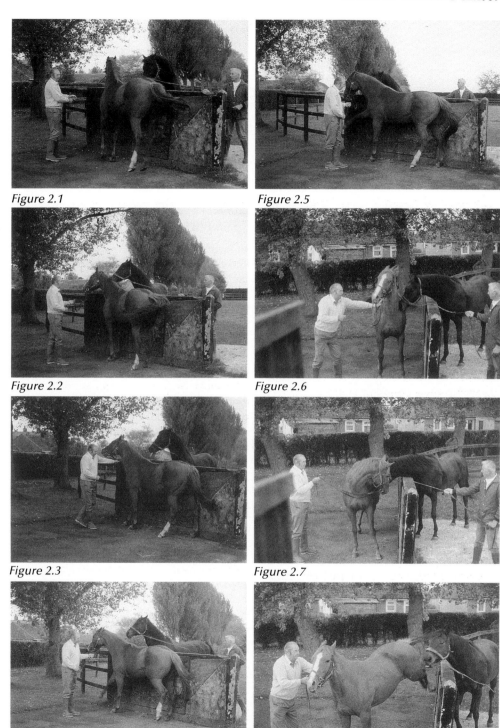

Figure 2.1

Figure 2.2

Figure 2.3

Figure 2.4

Figure 2.5

Figure 2.6

Figure 2.7

Figure 2.8

Figure 2.9 The teaser is led to a group of mares

Figure 2.10 The teaser is separated from the group of mares by a fence. Receptive mares may approach and show

In addition, it is customary on many establishments to exercise the stallions by walking them along the outside of paddocks in which mares are grazing. The handlers can then watch for signs of oestrous behaviour.

Some studs have a specially boarded or railed area strategically placed so that it abuts several paddocks and in which a male horse is tethered or allowed to run free. This arrangement permits partial contact of mares and teaser over many hours each day instead of the few minutes that is usual in the 'in hand' method of teasing. Less usual teasing programmes include the running of a small pony stallion among the Thoroughbred mares or the inclusion in the group of a male horse who has been vasectomised (i.e. the sperm ducts have been severed so that conception cannot follow coitus).

Results

When a mare is brought into contact with a male horse in one of the methods described above, the display of sexual behaviour usually conforms to patterns which make it obvious to the onlooker whether or not the mare is in a receptive state.

However, individuals may show idiosyncracies. Before considering some of these, it cannot be too strongly emphasised that it is solely for our own convenience that mares should be stimulated into showing sexual signs. When a stallion runs with his mares

and is their constant companion, he is then the sole arbiter of their state at any particular time. This is a most important point to grasp lest we fall into the error of regarding any individual's behaviour as abnormal merely because, under the methods which we choose to stimulate her, she fails to show expected signs. The stallion most probably relies more on a sense of smell than signs to evaluate a mare's sexual state and the visual signs are of only secondary importance (Figure 2.13).

Idiosyncratic behaviour includes silent heat and 'shy breeders'. The latter are mares who show dioestrous-type behaviour when they are in an oestrous state. They do not exhibit strong signs of sexual behaviour when brought in contact with the male and may stand meekly at the trying board or appear reluctant to approach it. Among the contributory causes of this unusual behaviour is the habit of teasing mares without allowing their foals to accompany them to the board. However, some mares are so foal-proud that in attempting to guard their foal they fail to show the usual sexual signs. Another factor in mares confined to looseboxes at night is that their eagerness to be turned loose in the paddocks may mask the signs of oestrus at the trying board. Mares in this category may respond better if they are teased later in the day or when on the way back from the paddocks in the afternoon or evening.

It seems probable that some mares show

Figure 2.11 The mare has initially rejected the teaser but now is becoming receptive

Figure 2.12 Especially in the early stages of oestrus a mare may accept the teaser's approaches, as is happening here

fierce behaviour at the board even during oestrus because of the repetitive habit of presenting them to the teaser, day in and day out, when they are in dioestrus. The same behaviour may be induced by some previous unpleasant experience or it may be the result of an inherent trait in a particular individual.

Many of those mares who exhibit silent heat or are shy breeders may display signs of oestrus when turned out in the paddock, perhaps stimulated by other mares or even by their own foals at play; or they may show some slight signs of oestrus when confined to the stable. Alternatively their only external evidence may be a lengthening of the vulva and a slight raising of the tail.

It is not unknown for individuals to show signs of oestrus only when in the company of a particular male horse or even another mare. Lesbian-type relationships have been reported in which two mares form a close association and are inseparable in the paddock. In these cases they may show oestrus only in the presence of one another and may even appear jealous of an approach by another horse.

If an individual shows none of the signs of oestrus, either at the trying board or in the paddocks, she may give a show when taken to the covering yard. Here the ritual associated with the act of coitus (placing of protective boots and hobbles on the limbs, etc.) may produce the typical signs even though the

stallion is absent from the yard. Placing a twitch on a mare may also induce oestrous-type behaviour.

In contrast, there are mares who may show signs of oestrus when they are in a state of dioestrus or even pregnant. However these mares rarely accept the stallion and therefore

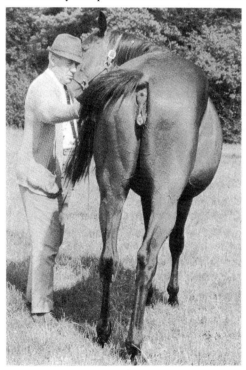

Figure 2.13 Mares in oestrus are docile, they squat and show winking of the vulva

present management with a dangerous problem.

Because so many mares display behaviour which does not allow for a true assessment of their sexual state, it is not surprising that veterinarians have been called upon to help in diagnosis. Veterinary examinations of mares prior to mating are now routine on most studs in the United Kingdom as well as those in many other parts of the world.

Veterinary examinations

Veterinary examinations fall under roughly four headings:
1. Palpation of the ovaries and the uterus through the wall of the rectum.
2. An examination of the cervix and vagina including bacteriological and cytological techniques.
3. Ultrasound examination (scans).
4. Hormonal assays.

The purpose of the examination is:
a) to confirm the observed signs of sexual behaviour, i.e. to determine whether the mare is in an oestrous, dioestrous or pregnant state;
b) to correlate ovarian activity with oestrus so that with a knowledge of follicular development and time of ovulation, mating may be arranged at the optimum time;
c) to detect infection and other pathological causes of infertility so that they can be treated.

Examinations are conducted as follows.

Restraint may be necessary in the form of a twitch, but more often all that is required is for one attendant to hold the head and one the tail. As is generally the case in the handling of horses, the ease with which they are restrained is usually directly related to the type and amount of handling the animal has previously received. In Newmarket and other major breeding centres where all mares are regularly subjected to veterinary examinations the cooperation of individual mares is

of a much higher order than might be expected elsewhere.

Another form of restraint which is sometimes helpful is to grasp a fold of skin in the neck region of the horse and hold this tightly while the examination is in progress (Figure 2.14). In exceptional cases a tranquillising drug may have to be administered. Mares with foals undoubtedly stand better if allowed to see and smell their foals.

Some operators, for their own protection, prefer to have mares placed in stocks while others work around a door post (Figure 2.15) or with bales of straw placed between themselves and the mares.

Rectal palpation

A rubber or plastic glove is generally used in order to protect the operator and reduce the chances of injury to the mucosal lining of the rectum. The glove is well lubricated with soap or other substances and the operator may use either the left or right arm (Figure 2.16).

It is a comparatively simple matter to feel the ovaries through the wall of the rectum and to pick them up between thumb and fingers. In this way the size and position of any follicle may be recorded, together with

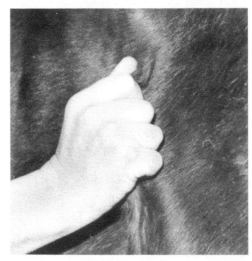

Figure 2.14 In lieu of a twitch, a firm hand-grasp of a fold of skin on the neck has a remarkably effective restraining influence

Figure 2.15 For his own protection, the veterinary surgeon stands to one side of the stall's door post as he proceeds with the examination

other valuable information concerning the state and activity of the ovaries.

The results obtained from ovarian palpation are helpful in regulating the mating programme. For example, when there are no follicles palpable in the ovary, conception is impossible and mating should be witheld until ovarian activity develops. In this way it is possible *to reduce the number of services of the stallion* and, more important, the act of coitus can be concentrated into the most fertile part of oestrus (i.e. when there are follicles about to ovulate).

There are, of course, limits in the interpretation of what one feels at these examinations and what is in fact present. For instance, it is sometimes difficult to differentiate between follicles and cysts (hollow cavities containing liquid) which may be present in the supporting membrane of the ovary.

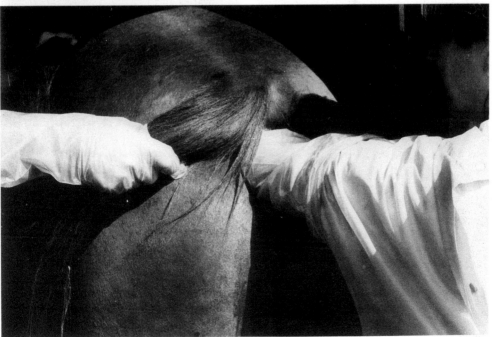

Figure 2.16 Rectal palpation. A disposable glove is used to protect both mare and examiner

Also, one cannot distinguish between a follicle destined to undergo degeneration and one that is haemorrhagic and distended by blood-stained fluid; in both cases they may, on palpation, be diagnosed as true follicles (i.e. ones destined to ovulate).

When the veterinarian palpates the ovaries he is also able to feel the uterus. This is helpful as the consistency of the uterine wall changes during the oestrous cycle and helps the veterinarian to distinguish between dioestrus, silent heat and pregnancy.

Vaginal examination
Examination of the vagina is performed with an instrument known as a speculum (Figure 2.17) which is lubricated and placed in the vagina. There are a variety of these in general

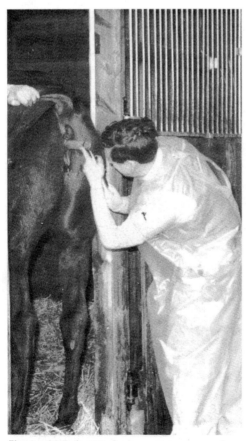

Figure 2.17 A veterinary surgeon examines the cervix with the aid of a speculum

use (the most important being the disposable type), but the principle behind each is to provide an illuminated view of the cervix. In this way the veterinarian can appraise the state of the cervix and vagina and determine the particular point of the oestrous cycle. Changes which normally occur have already been described but bear repetition because of their importance in the diagnosis of oestrus. During the latter state the cervix is moist and relaxed with its folds swollen or oedematous; the lining of the cervix and vagina have a reddened appearance. As soon as ovulation occurs the cervix becomes paler, its folds firmer and it is inclined to protrude in a definite shape into the vagina. In dioestrus these changes become more marked so that the cervix is white, firm and usually covered with a sticky mucus. The latter appearance will also apply in anoestrus or pregnancy.

At the time of a visual inspection of the cervix other diagnostic techniques may be used. For example, material can be collected from the cervix and uterus to provide additional information of infection.

Ultrasound
Ultrasound (scanning) is based on a technique developed in the first part of the century and used notably in the detection of underwater objects such as submarines. It was adapted for medical purposes of diagnosis some years ago and more recently has formed a routine part of veterinary investigations.

The technique enables the interior of the body to be viewed on a screen without the need for invasive methods. It therefore forms a humane and non-painful way of seeing below the surface of the skin.

Thus ultrasound diagnosis of the mare's sexual activities is possible. Ultrasound is a beam of high-pitched sound waves which is reflected by objects of different densities in its path (e.g. bone and muscle). The reflected waves are picked up and displayed on a television screen where a picture of the examination site can be built up.

The traditional method of examining the

mare's ovaries and uterus has been per rectum. The feel of these discloses the presence and size of follicles in the ovary, consistency of uterine tone and presence or absence of pregnancy.

By ultrasound the size and number of follicles present in the ovary can be established with a high degree of accuracy. The presence of a pregnancy can be observed from as early as 12 days from ovulation and the pregnancy monitored up to full term. This not only ensures a greater accuracy of pregnancy diagnosis than can be achieved by the means of rectal palpation or blood or urine testing, but also provides the means whereby twins can be diagnosed at an early stage.

The following advantages over more traditional methods of examination are provided by ultrasound scanning:

a) the size and number of follicles in the ovary can be seen at any given time of the cycle;

b) a better prediction can be made, therefore, of when follicles are about to ovulate;

c) the time and occurrence of ovulation – diagnosis is more accurate than by rectal examination alone;

d) excessive accumulation of fluid and the presence of cysts in the uterus can be seen directly and do not have to be interpreted on the basis of feel alone;

e) the size, shape and position of the pregnancy may be determined with accuracy from a much earlier stage than is possible by rectal palpation. Further, from about 25 days onwards the foetal heartbeat may be seen thereby providing some insight into the health status of the conceptus. The only comparable method previously was the electrocardiograph (ECG) and this method is not effective until about 120 days of pregnancy;

f) twins may be identified and a programme of action adopted from an early stage. The most popular approach is to view the uterus 17 days after the last mating. If twins are identified in separate horns of the uterus one may be squeezed and ruptured allowing the other to develop normally.

This is a highly successful procedure and may be 90 per cent effective in practice.

When twins are developing in the same horn of the uterus, however, the success rate of rupturing one, with the other developing to term is not so high. It is possible in these instances to separate the adjacent sacs by gentle pressure providing the conceptuses have not become fixed as is normal from about day 17 onwards. If the twins can be separated one can then be squeezed successfully. If they cannot be separated, they should be left alone and observed in order to determine whether or not one of the two may die. It is estimated that about 50 per cent of these early adjacent twin pregnancies do resolve into single pregnancies by 40 days. Some veterinarians claim that starving the mare may help but there is no objective evidence that this is the case and studies that have been performed have not defined exactly what is meant by starvation in these circumstances.

Alternative options available are to abort the pregnancy with prostaglandin and have the mare remated, or to allow the two foetuses to develop to about 90 days and then kill one by injecting it with potassium chloride via a needle inserted into the heart, under ultrasound control, transabdominally (i.e. with the needle inserted through the abdominal wall and *not* per rectum). Other methods have been tried, such as surgery or by inserting a video endoscope through the cervix puncturing one of the two foetal sacs. In most of these cases the result has been loss of both pregnancies.

The decision as to what approach should be made in any particular instance must depend on the dialogue between the attending veterinarian and the owner. The only hard-and-fast guideline is that a mare that is pregnant beyond 35 days from conception develops eCG and is not likely to return to heat for a fertile mating until a further 80 days have elapsed and the endometrial cups have ceased to function. The other well-established fact is that the majority of twin pregnancies are either aborted or carried to term with one or both twins being delivered dead. If born alive, twins may survive but are usually uneconomic either in size, strength or substance of their skeleton.

Hormonal assays

The introduction of methods employing antibodies in the laboratory has enabled measurement of hormone levels in the bloodstream. These tests are also referred to as assays and, because the antibodies are labelled with radioactive substances, the term radioimmunoassay (RIA) is often heard in scientific circles.

For practical purposes the tests provide a means of measuring very small quantities of various hormones, even to the level of a nanogram (ng) which is one-thousand-millionth of a gram!

The most commonly used test is for progesterone and other sex hormones. However, we have to be careful about interpreting the results because we are measuring only the levels in the blood; and the blood is but a means of transport from the gland producing the hormone (e.g. the ovary or pituitary) to its site of action (e.g. the uterus).

The interpretation of levels is further complicated by the fact that the action of the hormone on the target depends on its ability to lock onto the tissue on which it has an action. This locking device is known as a receptor and the action of the hormone, to a large extent, depends on the number of receptors. These numbers can be influenced by the hormone itself or by other hormones and may therefore vary in number from time to time.

Although this may sound a complicated concept, it may be easier to understand from the following example. The pituitary gland produces LH that causes the follicle in the ovary to ovulate. However much LH is produced by the pituitary it will only cause ovulation if there are sufficient receptors present on the lining of the follicle. These receptors are increased by the action of oestrogen and therefore increase during the period of heat (oestrus).

Once ovulation has occurred, the yellow body produces progesterone and this is carried in the bloodstream to the uterus where it locks onto receptors causing the uterine muscle to become inactive in a state of contraction. Again, it is the number of receptors present in the uterine muscle as much as the level of progesterone which results in the effect of progesterone on the uterus.

Progesterone levels above 1 ng/ml indicate a functioning yellow body whereas those below 1 ng/ml suggest that no yellow body is present and that the mare is either in oestrus or anoestrus.

During dioestrus, levels are just above 1 ng/ml at the end of oestrus, when levels are rising rapidly, or at the end of dioestrus when they are falling. In between, levels vary from day to day within a range of about 4 ng/ml to 20 ng/ml.

During early pregnancy, levels vary between about 4 ng/ml and 30 ng/ml. Other hormones are not usually measured in practice except in exceptional circumstances (such as a disease).

There is a considerable variation between individual mares and the degree to which they display typical changes during the oestrous cycle. Therefore, one cannot rely solely on behaviour, ovarian activity or the state of the cervix and uterus when deciding the stage they are at.

Finally, mention must be made of the routine use of the hormone LH. If this is injected intravenously into a mare in oestrus, it will promote ovulation within 48 hours, providing a ripe follicle is present in one of the ovaries. In this way it is possible to cut short an oestrous period and reduce the number of matings.

CHAPTER THREE

THE STALLION

Stallions are the pride of any stud at which they stand. Housed in special boxes often of palatial proportions, turned into paddocks reserved entirely for their use, they are the central attraction. More often than not they are placed in the full-time care of grooms who ensure that their every need is met even more meticulously than are those of horses in training. All this because they are considered too valuable a risk to be allowed to roam free as is their natural inclination.

Breeding organs

The genital organs (Figure 3.1) consist of two

glands (testes) which are responsible for the male gametes (spermatozoa). To each testis is attached a structure, known as an epididymis, in which the sperm are stored. The epididymis is connected with a single tube (ductus or vas deferens) which in turn joins with its opposite number to form the urethra. This is a single duct providing a common outlet for urine and semen. Semen consists of spermatozoa together with fluids and substances secreted by the accessory sex glands.

Testes
The two testes are oval structures contained in folds of skin (scrotum). Each has flattened sides presenting two surfaces, two borders

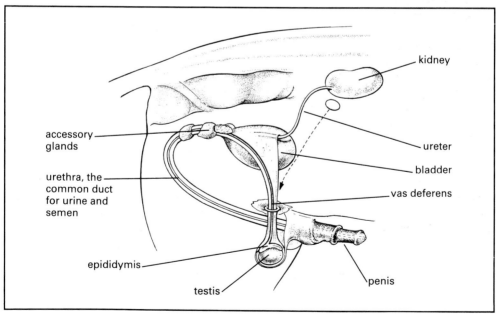

Figure 3.1 Diagram to show the stallion's genital organs (from the right side). The dotted line indicates the route taken by the testis in its descent from the abdomen to the scrotum

23

and two extremities. The free border is below and convex. The upper border is the one by which the testis is suspended in the scrotum and to which the epididymis and spermatic cord are attached. In an adult stallion each testis will be about 12 cm long and weigh about 300 g. The left gland is usually larger than the right but both vary in size from stallion to stallion.

The testis is covered by a strong fibrous capsule and the gland substance is soft and reddish-grey in colour. It is sub-divided into lobes by fibrous tissue and muscle and composed of minute tortuous tubes which, as they unite with other tubes of similar kind, form larger, straighter tubes (Figure 3.2). These converge toward the front part of the gland and pass through the tough fibrous coat to enter the epididymis.

The spermatozoa develop from round cells lining the coiled tubes of the gland. These round cells become elongated as they grow towards the central lumen of the tube in the centre of which are the fully-formed mature spermatozoa. On the outside of the tubes there are special cells (interstitial) which are responsible for the production of the hormone testosterone (Figure 3.3).

Descent of the testes

In the foetus the testes are found close to the kidneys but towards the end of pregnancy they migrate and pass through an opening in the abdominal muscles – the inguinal ring – and from there through a canal into the scrotum. The mechanical factors which bring about migration of the testes are largely unknown but increasing pressure of the abdominal contents may play a part.

In some cases one or, more rarely, both testes may fail to pass through the abdominal opening and are left inside the abdomen. Such a horse is known as a cryptorchid – colloquially, a 'rig'. The retained testis is usually small, thin, soft and not productive of sperm. However, the retention of one testis in the abdomen does not prevent the individual from being fertile and it may be associated with aggressive behaviour. In some cases of hind limb lameness, the testis retained in the inguinal canal may be blamed and the individual therefore subjected to castration. A

Figure 3.2 Diagram of the testis showing divisions into areas containing coiled tubes in which the sperm develop. Straighter tubes eventually enter the epididymis

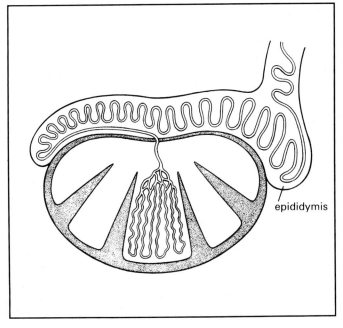

epididymis

24

Figure 3.3 Diagram of a coiled tube of the testis cut in section: A and B are cells which are the precursors of sperm C; D is a special cell (Sertoli) to which the sperm become attached before breaking loose and travelling in the tubes leading to the epididymis; E are interstitial cells which produce testosterone

testis frequently remains in the inguinal canal until the horse is a 3- or 4-year-old after which it completes its descent into the scrotum. This condition is not true cryptorchism but one of relatively late maturity. Once the abdominal ring closes, as it normally does soon after birth, only those testes which are already below the ring can enter into the scrotum. They otherwise become retained in the abdomen.

Epididymis

Each epididymis attached to the upper border of the testis stores the sperm and consists of a head, a body and a tail. The head is composed of a dozen or more coiled tubes which unite to form a single tube known as the duct of the epididymis. This duct with its complex coils, forms the body and tail of the epididymis and terminates in the ductus deferens along which the sperm are eventually transported to the urethra at the time of ejaculation.

Excretory ducts

The ductus or vas deferens extends from the tail of the epididymis to the urethra. It ascends in the spermatic cord enclosed in the inguinal canal to the opening (inguinal ring) in the abdominal muscles. Here it runs backwards and towards the midline of the abdomen to the pelvic cavity. Each duct opens into

the urethra close to its origin with the bladder and at a point beneath the prostate gland.

The urethra is a long tube which extends from the bladder to the glans penis. The duct can be divided into the pelvic and extra pelvic parts. In addition to the vas deferens it receives openings from the accessory sex glands. The urethra is enclosed in a layer of muscle which plays an important role in the ejaculation of semen and evacuation of urine.

The penis

The penis is the male organ of copulation, composed of erectile tissue enclosing the extra-pelvic part of the urethra. The glans penis is the enlarged free end of the organ and its base is surrounded by a prominent margin, the corona glandis, through which the end of the urethra projects for about 25 mm. The penis becomes erect when its veins become engorged with blood. The veins are arranged as relatively large spaces forming a network of vessels in the dorsal part of the penis.

The prepuce

The prepuce, popularly known as the sheath, is a 'pocketing' of the skin which covers the free portion of the penis when it is not erect. The skin of the prepuce contains a double fold so that there is an internal and an external portion. The internal layers are hairless and supplied with large numbers of seba-ceous glands which produce a fatty smegma, a continual secretion with a strong, unplea-sant odour.

The spermatic cord

The spermatic cord consists of structures carried by the testis in its migration from the abdominal cavity to the scrotum. The cord contains arteries, veins, lymphatics, nerves, the vas deferens and the cremaster muscle which is capable of lifting the testis from the scrotum into the lower part of the inguinal canal.

The accessory glands

The accessory glands are the seminal vesi-cles, the prostate and the bulbo-urethral glands.

The seminal vesicles. These two elongated sacs lie on either side of the urethra close to its origin at the bladder. They are about 15 cm long and some 5 cm in diameter and each has a duct which opens into the urethra.

The prostate gland. Placed at the junction of the bladder and beginning of the urethra, into which it opens through about 15 ducts. The secretion of the prostate gland is milky in appearance.

The bulbo-urethral glands. There are two, situated on either side of the urethra. They are about 5 cm in length and each has about six to eight ducts which open into the urethra.

The function of the accessory glands is to secrete seminal plasma.

Semen

Semen consists of spermatozoa and seminal plasma (Figure 3.4). The average volume of ejaculate is 40 ml to 120 ml, containing some 100 to 150 million spermatozoa per cubic millimetre.

Spermatozoon

The spermatozoon (pl. spermatozoa) is the male sex cell (gamete). It is very different in character from the egg oecause it is a highly motile cell capable of swimming relatively great distances in the female genital tract, seeking the egg and combining with it to achieve fertilisation. The spermatozoon is made up of a head, middle piece and tail (Figure 3.5). Its size is about one-hundredth that of the egg which is no more than the size of a grain of sand.

The head contains the nucleus which forms the greater part of this region and which is capped by the acrosome.

The sperm are formed by the multipli-cation of cells which line the coiled tubes in the testis. During this process of multipli-cation the number of chromosomes con-tained in the cell nucleus are reduced by half, the mature spermatozoon containing, there-

Volume of semen	40-120 ml
Number of sperm	100-150 million per cu mm
Abnormal spermatozoa (coiled tails and protoplasmic drops)	about 16%
pH	average - 7.330 pH units
Seminal plasma	
Specific gravity	1.012
Ergothioneine*	7.6 mg /100 ml
Citric acid*	26 mg /100 ml
Fructose*	15 mg /100 ml
Phosphorus*	17 mg /100 ml
Lactic acid*	12 mg /100 ml
Urea*	3 mg /100 ml

Figure 3.4 The constituents of semen. (Asterisks denote average values)

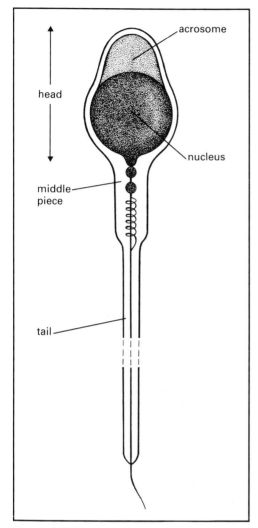

Figure 3.5 Diagram of a spermatozoon

but once in this organ it is thought that the sperm separate from the plasma as they make their way to the Fallopian tubes. It has been suggested that the plasma nourishes the sperm and even that it may eventually kill them off to prevent them from ageing. Sperm age rapidly, and it seems that the longer sperm reside in the female's genital tract before conception the greater the proportion of foetal abnormalities. This phenomenon has not been demonstrated in horses but is known to occur in other species.

The characteristic components of equine semen are fructose, ergothioneine, citric acid and sulfhydryl. The fructose content, considered so important in the semen of many species, is, in fact, scarce in that of stallions. The significance of this is not known. Some work has been carried out on the sulfhydryl content of plasma because this substance, present in highest concentration in the last portion of the ejaculate, is known to be toxic to sperm. Attempts have been made to correlate fertility with sulfhydryl content but the results have been inconclusive.

Seasonal variations in semen quality can be judged from the fact that citric acid, ergothioneine and the numbers of spermatozoa decrease from February to June and then show an increase. Ejaculate volume is low until April and increases greatly in May and June during which months the concentration of sperm may be increased as much as seven times.

Once in the uterus the spermatozoa (Figure 3.6) swim to the opening of the Fallopian tubes at the tips of each uterine horn. From here they travel up the tube to meet the egg which one of them will enter and fertilise.

The capacity of any semen sample to fertilise the egg decreases with the age of the sample. In practice it is reckoned that two days is an average period during which a horse can be fertile from a mating. Cases have, however, been recorded where fertilisation has occurred seven days after coitus.

In general the more dilute the semen sample, in terms of numbers of spermatozoa per millilitre, the less fertilising capacity it

fore, half the amount of inherited material present in each body cell. At the time of fertilisation the egg supplies the other half to the new individual. Body cells are said to contain the haploid number of chromosomes and sex cells the diploid number; in the horse that is 64 and 32 chromosomes, respectively.

Seminal plasma

The exact function of seminal plasma is not known. It certainly provides a vehicle in which sperm may be carried into the uterus

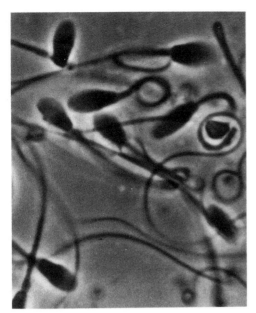

Figure 3.6 A highly magnified view of equine spermatozoa, some of which have straight and some coiled tails

possesses and there is a critical point below which it entirely loses its fertility. It is curious that although many million spermatozoa are placed in the uterus there may be too few for the one that is required to achieve union with the egg. The reason may be that conception is a cumulative effect. For instance, spermatozoa are retained at the junction of the uterus and Fallopian tube and travel up the tube in relatively small numbers. Then, before fertilisation can occur, the spermatozoa must remove the debris around the egg by secreting an enzyme known as hyaluronidase; the number of sperm required to achieve this is not known. In addition, the sperm probably have to go through a process of ripening (capacitation) before they are capable of fertilising the egg. If for any reason they do not undergo this ripening process the number of live active sperm in a semen sample is not related to their fertilising power.

Some stallions' semen seems to lose its fertilising power more quickly than others. A great deal more research is necessary before we can understand why this is so or whether

there are measures we can take to improve matters in any particular case.

As far as individual mares are concerned, conditions in the uterus are likely to influence the fertilising power of semen. Infection and perhaps immune reactions between the mare's cells and spermatozoa are two major considerations. Again, more research is required before we can understand and overcome these problems.

Hormonal control

The production of sperm and the sexual behaviour of the stallion are controlled by hormones secreted by the pituitary and testes. The pituitary hormones (FSH and LH) are similar to those produced by the same gland of the mare. FSH stimulates the growth and formation of spermatozoa in the testes while LH causes the interstial cells to liberate testosterone into the bloodstream. Testosterone promotes the male characteristics and sexual drive (libido).

The activity of the pituitary tends to vary with the seasons and it is affected by the amount of daylight just as is the case with the mare. The quality of semen and sexual drive of the stallion is thus greatest during late spring and summer which coincides with the natural breeding season.

Artificial insemination

For years farmers have accepted the usefulness of artificial insemination in cows and sows but the Thoroughbred breeding industries of the world have been reluctant to introduce this technique. It is not allowed in Thoroughbred breeds due to political and economic considerations, but is now being practised more frequently in other breeds.

The technique consists of collecting an ejaculate from the stallion by means of an artificial vagina. The sample may be treated in different ways:

a) the whole sample is used;
b) the sample is divided into 10 or 20 'doses' depending on the quality of the sample.

There are two methods of handling the semen sample:
1. When insemination is to take place within minutes or hours of collection, the sample is maintained at body temperature and used untreated or together with special nourishing and protective substances contained in extender fluid.
2. Deep freezing the samples divided into doses – usually referred to as 'straws' because of the capillary-like tubes in which they are stored in a deep-frozen condition. These are subsequently thawed before use. Both the freezing and thawing have to be conducted under special cir-

cumstances in order to maintain the viability of the sample. The semen samples, whether used fresh or following freezing, are inseminated through a long pipette inserted through the vagina and cervix of the mare just prior to the expected time of ovulation.

Mating

The rituals arbitrarily imposed on mares and stallions at mating are bound to influence their sexual behaviour (Figures 3.7 to 3.20). The normal period of courtship is reduced, disturbed by handling or disallowed depending on managerial decisions. Most studs allow the stallion time to tease his mare before mounting. He is then held behind

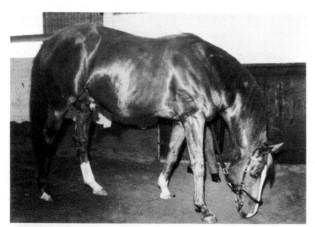

Figure 3.7 The stallion sniffs the ground where a mare has urinated . . .

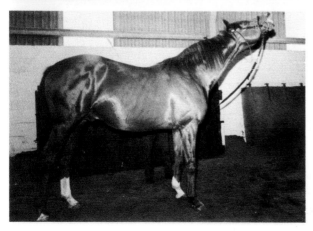

Figure 3.8 . . . this causes the stallion to show the typical flehmen attitude. This action is a response to a pheromone, a substance secreted by one animal and which produces changed behaviour in another

29

Figure 3.9 The mare is restrained with a twitch, her hind feet are fitted with felt boots to protect the stallion

OPPOSITE PAGE
Figure 3.10 (top) The stallion is allowed to tease the mare, ensuring she is fully receptive before any attempt is made to cover her. Note the mare's tail, bandaged for hygienic purposes and held out of the stallion's way

Figure 3.11 (bottom) Having teased the mare the stallion is now led forward to cover her

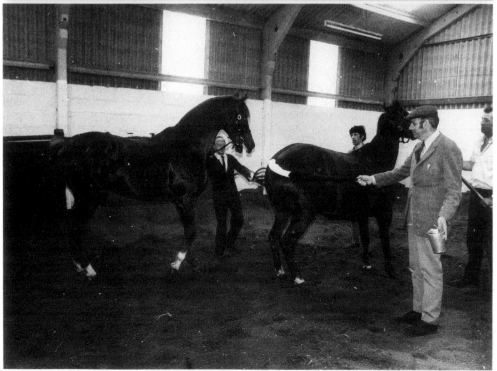

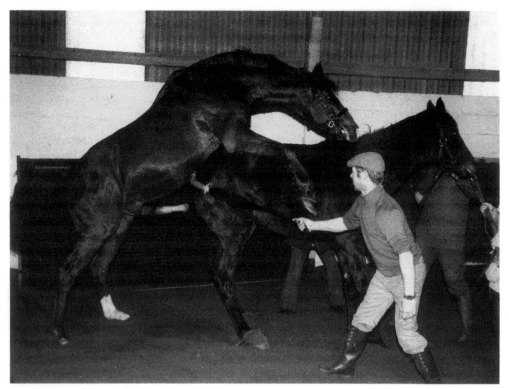

Figure 3.12 The mare's stance when mounted is defensive. It is at this stage that the stallion is most exposed to a kick

OPPOSITE PAGE
Figure 3.13 (top) The groom leading the stallion watches for tail movement and pulsation of the penis which will indicate that ejaculation has occurred

Figure 3.14 (bottom) The stallion withdraws when the mare is covered. However, withdrawal does not always mean an ejaculation has occurred; the stallion may have been unable to ejaculate and withdraws of his own choosing

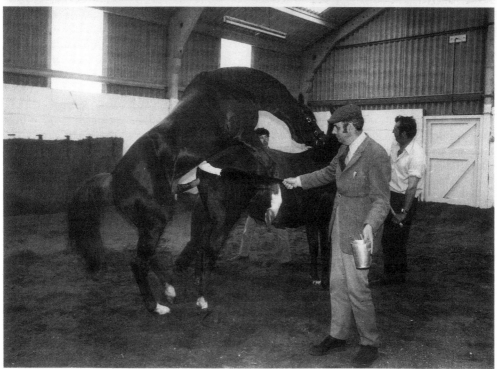

the mare, allowed to smell and 'taste' her, and restrained until he is ready to mount. These procedures interfere with natural courtship but may not have any practical significance as far as conception rates are concerned. In some cases though, either the mare or the stallion may be affected even to the extent that the stallion will not complete the sexual act or the mare will not allow him to do so.

Further evidence that breeding in hand is unnatural is found in the various forms of restraining the mare, considered necessary to protect the stallion. The mare is 'twitched', one foreleg is held up and fractious mares may be blindfolded. On some studs hobbles are applied to the hind legs. Another precaution is to place felt boots on the mare's hind legs to reduce the risk of damage to the stallion.

Thoroughbred mare fertility

In preparing this section I am indebted to Sidney Ricketts, B.Sc., B.V.Sc., D.E.S.M., F.R.C.V.S. for permission to quote from text and to reproduce charts published in his research work on mare fertility.

He demonstrated a trend by analysing Thoroughbred mare fertility returns sent to Weatherbys over the period 1970 to 1989 from owners based in the United Kingdom and Eire.

These returns show encouraging improvements in the general level of Thoroughbred mare fertility achieved under conditions of natural mating and under management conditions which vary widely in terms of degree of intensity and sophistication.

Mr Ricketts comments on this:

It is only possible to speculate on the probable multifactorial cause of the improvement in these measures of equine population fertility, but one must hope that improvements in standards of stud farm management and progress in veterinary medicine have at least played useful parts. The halving of the barren mare rate is particularly encouraging as it is generally accepted that 'problem' mares are less aggressively culled now than was the case previously, leading to their increased proportion in the population. One must assume that greater knowledge and application of technical aspects, by stud grooms, managers and veterinary surgeons have made a significant contribution.

The analysis showed that there was an increase of 41 per cent in the number of mares covered in the period under examination (Figure 3.15). This trend continued in 1990 but has been on a downward spiral since.

The overall increase of 75 per cent in live foals born (Figure 3.16) is suggestive of improved fertility.

The conception rate figures, including mares that produced live foals or aborted (Figure 3.17), improved 11.2 per cent, an encouraging trend.

The live foal rate (Figure 3.18) improved by 13 per cent with most of that improvement in the last decade.

The barren mare rate (Figure 3.19) was reduced by 10 per cent – from 21.9 per cent in 1970 to 11.7 per cent in 1989.

The gestation rate failure (Figure 3.20) decreased by 2.2 per cent.

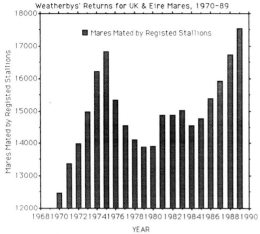

Figure 3.15 Mares mated by registered stallions

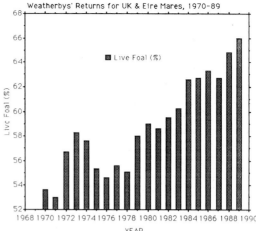

Figure 3.18 Live foal (%)

Figure 3.16 Live produce

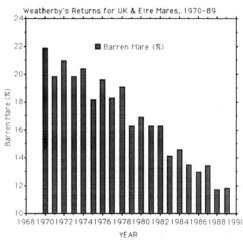

Figure 3.19 Barren mare (%)

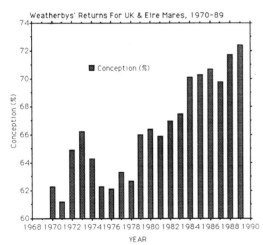

Figure 3.17 Conception (%)

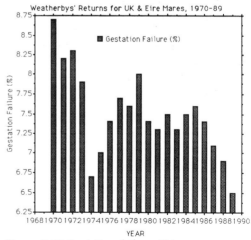

Figure 3.20 Gestation failure (%)

35

CHAPTER FOUR

INFERTILITY IN MARES AND STALLIONS

The annual conception rate among Thoroughbreds varies from about 60 to over 70 per cent. Any figures referring to national statistics form only a rough guide because of variations in management, climate and other circumstances in which horses are bred. For example, the percentage may exceed 80 in small groups of mares where there is careful selection of breeding stock and good management. Conversely, low rates may be recorded for exceptional reasons such as infertility in the stallion or venereal spread of infection.

The Thoroughbred breeding season is arbitrarily defined as 15 February to 15 July in the northern hemisphere. In the southern hemisphere it is August-December and each year at least 30 per cent of mares end the season barren. National conception rates do, therefore, give some indication of the loss incurred by the Thoroughbred breeding industry. The important question is to what extent it is due to faults in management, to disease or to inherited factors and whether we can reduce the loss.

Infertility in mares

The term 'infertility' has no precise definition with respect to mares or stallions. It varies according to the user. In general it is applied to a mare or a stallion based on relative breeding performance rather than, as is sometimes the case, employed as meaning an inability to breed. In the latter event the term 'sterility' may be applied.

A mare that is said to be infertile may have been pregnant in the past or capable of being pregnant in the future but having difficulty in conceiving in a particular year. The term 'subfertility' is therefore often used in these circumstances.

When applied to a mare, subfertility may mean that the individual returns to oestrus more frequently than average before conceiving or, more commonly, that she is barren in a higher proportion of years than average; the average being about one barren year in four or five. However, the ease with which a mare conceives in any particular year or in a series of years may depend upon the corresponding fertility (subfertility) of the stallion to which she is mated. Also important is the efficiency of management in terms of the recognition of whether or not the mare is in heat, the day within the heat selected for mating and control of the stallion with reference to successful ejaculation.

It must be recognised, therefore, that there is a managerial component of subfertility. To this must be added the physiological (normal) variations in the mare's sexual behaviour according to climate, time of year, age and nutritional status. These variations are found in such states as prolonged dioestrus, anoestrus, oestrus without ovulation, prolonged oestrus, etc.

The third cause of subfertility is one usually referred to as pathological. This infers that the individual has some disease, such as an infection or inflammation of the uterus, a tumour of the ovary, abnormal conformation of the genital tract, etc.

Finally, there are conditions causing sterility (i.e. absolute infertility including sex chromosome abnormalities).

Management

Many individuals fail to get in foal because they are mated too soon before or after ovulation. If mated too soon the sperm lose their capacity to fertilise the egg while waiting in the Fallopian tube. On the other hand, if the mare is mated after ovulation the egg itself loses the capacity to become fertilised (i.e. its outer membrane resists penetration by the sperm). There is an increasing resistance from immediately after ovulation to 24 hours when, in most cases, it is complete. Management has to use the ideal fertilising opportunity, which exists between about, on average, 48 hours prior to 12 hours following ovulation. By controlling the time of mating, the management's decisions can influence the success or failure of particular matings. Veterinary supervision can aid these decisions to a marked degree so mating can be synchronised with ovulation.

Other decisions of management which are crucial for high levels of fertility in any given period include an accurate teasing programme; veterinary assistance with this is often helpful through gynaecological examinations of the cervix and ovaries. Ensuring that a stallion actually ejaculates at the time of mating is another way in which management contributes to fertility percentages. There may be difficulty in certain individual stallions in determining whether or not ejaculation has occurred at any given mating.

The second level of treatment for subfertility is associated with pathology or disease in the individual. This is of course a veterinary matter and owners should be expected to understand but not to initiate such treatment. In fact, the decision on what form of treatment is appropriate depends very much on the diagnosis of the condition. The

veterinarian uses a range of investigations based on establishing the normality, or otherwise, of ovarian and uterine function.

Treatments consist of administering special substances, fluids and antibiotics into the uterus to combat infection, suturing the vulva to overcome any deficiency which allows air into the genital tract abnormally, and hormone treatment where indicated. Removal of a diseased ovary is sometimes performed where tumours occur. However, the main contribution that can be made by veterinary science is to ensure that the timing and conditions of mating are appropriate for the mare and the stallion. Some stallions have semen which is less fertile than others in terms of number of sperm contained, activity of the sperm and length of fertilising capacity. These stallions should be used closer to the time of mating than those with higher quality semen.

Normal variations or physiology?

We must accept that it is not natural for every mare to produce a foal each year. Many individuals are every-other-year producers. This is because mares have a relatively long pregnancy together with only seasonal breeding activity – normally late April to August – and opportunities for annual conception are consequently limited. The uterus needs time to recover after foaling and a mare has only to carry late into the summer to reduce the possibilities of successful conception to, at best, two or three heat periods.

These difficulties are greatly increased because mankind has arranged the Thoroughbred breeding season so that it is out of phase with the natural season. Data collected in Australia by Dr Virginia Osborne indicates that the peak period for ovulation occurs after the end of the stud season (Figure 4.1). Since the shedding of an egg is a prerequisite for conception – and failure to ovulate is rarely caused by disease – a substantial proportion of mares are barren simply because they fail to ovulate when mankind wants to breed from them.

Outside the natural breeding season mares

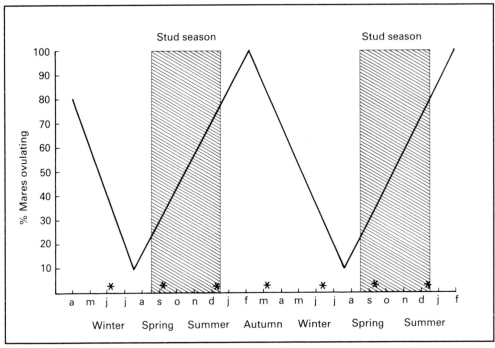

Figure 4.1 The chart summarizes data collected by Dr Virginia Osborne of Sydney University. It shows the percentage of mares ovulating during different months. Asterisks mark the solstices

undergo a state of anoestrus, that is, their oestrous cycle is suppressed and their ovaries become inactive so that no eggs are shed. A variation of this condition is a mare who shows signs of oestrus while her ovaries are quiescent. The reasons for inactivity can be traced to the pituitary gland. As we learned earlier, this small organ, situated beneath the brain, produces a large number of hormones including FSH and LH that control many activities of the body.

A mare cannot conceive when the pituitary is inactive and is producing minimal levels of FSH and LH. The gland can be stimulated by the increased daylight hours in late spring and summer. It may also be affected by warm surroundings and high levels of nutrition such as provided by spring grass. These conditions can be simulated early in the year by use of artificial lighting, warm stabling and diets rich in protein. By increasing the activity of the pituitary in winter and thereby providing more frequent opportunities for concep-

tion through the induction of oestrous periods and ovulation, mankind has been able to overcome some of the physiological causes of infertility.

Pituitary gland activity may be affected by lactation as well as by winter conditions. The gland controls mammary development and milk secretion and while it is producing the hormones necessary for these it may reduce output of FSH and LH. Prolactin is a hormone produced by the pituitary gland which is associated with the production of milk although, in the horse, its role in this respect may be complemented by another hormone called growth hormone.

Prolactin is thought to be associated with lactational anoestrus which can occur in mares that are suckling their foals. However, it has not yet been established that this relationship actually exists in the horse although it does occur in other species. Normally the interval between oestrous periods is 17 days, on average, but mares with foals at foot may remain sexually quiescent for several months or until the foal is weaned.

Pathology or disease?

A substantial proportion of mares who fail to breed for more than one stud season show evidence of uterine infection but in most cases some accessory factor is necessary for infection to become established. Infection limits the chance of conception because it reduces the sperm's survival time and increases the risk of the fertilised egg dying soon after it reaches the uterus.

Infection causes inflammation of the mucous-membrane lining of the uterus, cervix and vagina. It usually produces a catarrhal discharge which may escape from the vulva and collect on the hairs of the tail, thighs and inner aspect of the hocks. The signs are most obvious during oestrus when the cervix is relaxed and the secretions of the uterus are more fluid. These so-called 'dirty' mares are well recognised by stud staff because of the visual evidence. Many such

mares, however, may be detected only by the veterinarian's clinical examination and the swab test (i.e. the collection of material from the uterus and cervix for laboratory study) (Figure 4.2). Bacteria grown from uterine infections include *Streptococci, Coliforms, Staphylococci, Klebsiella, Pseudomonas* and, less commonly, varieties of fungus which are important because of their capacity to cause abortion.

As the part played by infection is not clearly defined it is frequently difficult to determine whether it is a cause of infertility in its own right or merely a symptom of some other abnormality; a case of which comes first, the chicken or the egg? Any one of a number of factors may make the genital tract more susceptible to infection.

Conformation

The genital tract may be predisposed to infection by poor conformation of the vulva and pelvis. Normally, these form a valve (Figure 4.3) which prevents air entering the

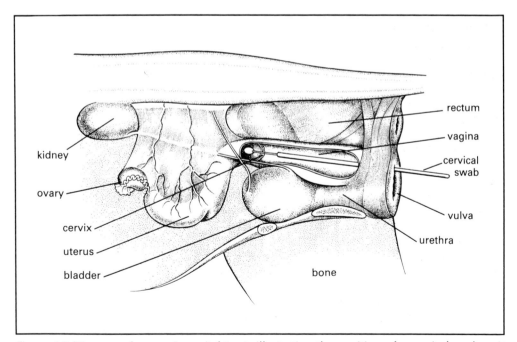

Figure 4.2 Diagram of a mare's genital tract, illustrating the position of a cervical swab as it penetrates the cervix to collect material from the posterior part of the uterus

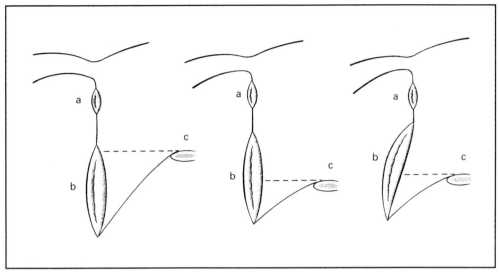

Figure 4.3 Diagram to show the arrangement of the mare's anus (a), vulva (b) and floor of the pelvis (c). It also shows: (left) good conformation, with the majority of the vulva below the level of the pelvic floor; (centre) poor conformation; leading to a situation where (right) the upper part of the vulva is tending to sink forward, allowing air into the tract

vagina, its walls being collapsed so that they press against each other. However, air may enter the vagina if the valve is breached, for example, by a speculum, through a fault in conformation, or after foaling when the after-birth is hanging from the uterus.

During oestrus, slack or elongated vulval lips will allow air into the vagina but if a mare has poor conformation air will enter whether or not she is in oestrus. The level of the brim of the pelvis in relation to the opening of the vulva seems to play an important part in the efficiency of the valve. If a substantial pro-portion of the vulvar lips is above the level of the pelvic brim, there is a tendency for the perineum to sink forward and part of the vulva comes to lie horizontally. Air is sucked into the vagina, which becomes ballooned, and may penetrate into the uterus. The presence of air, together with contaminating dust and microorganisms predispose to chronic inflammation and infection of the genital tract (Figure 4.4). This cannot be cured unless the valve is restored by stitching the upper part of the vulva together. This operation is often referred to as a Caslick, after its pioneer Dr E. A. Caslick, a Kentucky

veterinarian. In some individuals the vulval conformation (Figure 4.5) becomes so bad that the Caslick operation (Figures 4.6 and 4.7) cannot be successfully completed to a level which allows a sufficient aperture below the level of suturing. In France, Dr Edward

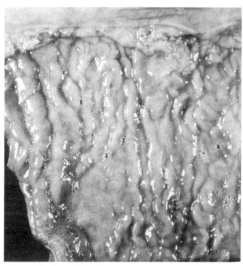

Figure 4.4 Chronic inflammation and infection of the genital tract

40

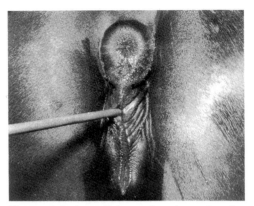

Figure 4.5 A well-formed vulva, showing good conformation

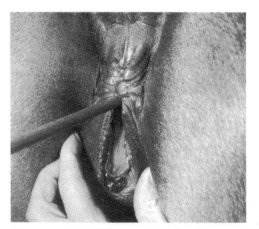

Figure 4.6 A Caslick operation has been performed on this vulva

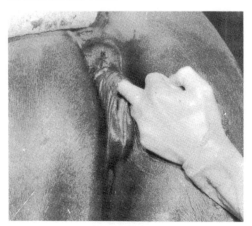

Figure 4.7 The effect of the Caslick operation showing a reduction of the vulvar opening by joining the lips surgically

Pouret introduced an operation to deal with these cases, separating the floor of the rectum and roof of the vagina surgically under appropriate anaesthesia. This allows the vagina to move in a caudal direction and the vulval aperture, therefore, to descend below the brim of the pelvis.

Pregnancy and birth

The passage of the foal through the birth canal stretches the tissues and this reduces the effectiveness of the valve between the vulva and pelvis. Air may enter the genital tract for at least several hours after birth and the presence of the membranes increases the chance of this happening. It is therefore most important that mares should be left undisturbed after foaling so that they remain lying down, preferably until the afterbirth is ready to come away.

In addition, every effort should be made to avoid stirring up dust, such as follows the shaking of straw or hay and only the best bedding should be used in the foaling box. The genital tract's resistance to infection is reduced by pregnancy and birth. The lining of the tract is damaged and a residue of blood and other matter is inevitably left behind after foaling. However, the uterus contracts quite rapidly following birth and any foreign matter is expelled by the time the foaling heat occurs, that is five to 18 days later.

Poor results are obtained from mating in this particular heat period and usually the mare fails to conceive or the foetus is subsequently aborted. This illustrates that more time is often required for complete recovery of the tract. The oestrogen produced during oestrus helps to mobilise the defences of the uterus against infection. It may even be that nature intends the foaling heat to cleanse the uterus, rather than allow a new pregnancy.

For reasons which are not clear, some individuals take weeks or months before they recover from the effects of pregnancy and birth. During this time mating may be positively harmful since it helps to introduce bacteria into the uterus. It is surprising how often we find that mares who have bred regularly become infertile as a result of a birth which may not have appeared abnormal but which leaves the individual predisposed to infection.

Pregnancies which have ended in abortion, or in which the foal or its membranes are infected, are invariably followed by problems of infertility. There is a close relationship between the effects of birth and subsequent breeding results. Conception in maiden mares is in the region of 90 per cent but the rate is considerably lower in foaling mares and it appears that the older a mare the greater the risk of infection. This may be the result of repeated pregnancies not only on the uterus but on the conformation of the vulva and perineum.

Coitus

Coitus may contribute to, or be the cause of, infection in a susceptible mare. The stallion's penis always carries germs such as *E. coli* or *Streptococci* which are transmitted to the mare at the time of mating. In addition, before the mare is mounted her vulva will often lengthen and her vagina become so relaxed that air is drawn into the genital tract. Therefore, measures should be taken to ensure that the atmosphere of the covering yard is as free from dust as possible. For this reason sand is a much better base than straw.

A swab test is often useful if taken two days after service. A healthy mare should be clean at this time but those susceptible to infection may well give positive growths, especially of *Streptococci*, and it is then advisable to treat with antibiotics. Because coitus exacerbates infection, chronicallly infected mares are best treated out of the breeding season.

Venereal spread (i.e. infection transmitted from one mare to another by way of the stallion) is common. There is inflammation of the uterus and a catarrhal discharge from the genital tract. Affected mares are unlikely to conceive until the infection is cleared. The stallion may become infected and then act as a mechanical carrier, carrying the germ in the urethra, urethral fossa and/or sheath smegma. While any organism can be passed in this way, *Klebsiella* is the most dangerous because it is capable of becoming established in a healthy genital tract (as opposed to one that is suceptible to infection) and also because it is the one most able to infect the stallion's genital organs. *Pseudomenas* and *Streptococci* are frequently transmitted by venereal spread but their ability to become established depends on the susceptibility of the mare's genital tract.

Contagious equine metritis (CEM) is a venereal infection of mares and stallions caused by a bacteria known as *Taylorella equigenitalis* which was first identified in the 1970s. The stallions act as carriers but do not show symptoms. The condition has been largely eradicated in the United Kingdom and elsewhere due to strict control measures which includes regular swabbing of the cervix and clitoris. However, CEM is thought to occur widely in non-thoroughbred horses in some mainland European countries. The clitoris, occupying as it does a position at the end of the genital tract harbours any bacteria that may be present in the more forward parts (i.e. the vagina and uterus). Swabbing from this position therefore provides an overall determinant of the presence of venereal bacteria. The clitoral swab is therefore an important part of screening mares for the presence of venereal disease.

Hormonal imbalance

In the past people have referred to hormonal imbalance as a cause of infertility, but it is now seen to be more a matter of effect rather than cause; the effect of natural variations in sexual activity rather than a fundamental imbalance of glandular function. Nowadays, measurements of hormones in the bloodstream can be performed by highly sophisticated tests. Changing levels of sex hormones can thereby be identified and this has resulted in a much improved means of diagnosing the hormonal status of the individual.

Pathological causes of hormonal imbalance include the granulosa cell tumour of the ovary, tumours of the pituitary or extreme conditions of the uterus such as pyometra when the uterus is full of pus.

Hormones such as oestrogen play a significant part in the uterus's resistance to infection. Their exact actions are not known but it is probable they cause increased blood flow to the mucous membrane lining where the bacteria are. Oestrogen also increases the mobility of the white blood cells, some of which (phagocytes) kill bacteria or limit their spread. Local immune responses of tissues may also be involved but as yet we know little about this aspect.

Early abortion is a common reason for temporary infertility. Infection and other factors may cause death of the foetus at any time; if this occurs after about the 35th day of the pregnancy the mare goes into a pseudopregnant state and will not return into oestrus for some weeks or months. Should this happen after the middle of the breeding season it may well mean that the mare goes barren for that year.

Besides infection and hormonal problems there are a number of specific conditions which cause infertility.

Ovarian tumours

Tumours occasionally grow in an ovary. Granulosa cell types, derived from the cells of this name which line the follicles, are the most common. The ovary becomes enlarged and honeycombed with cyst-like spaces containing bloodstained fluid (Figure 4.8). The

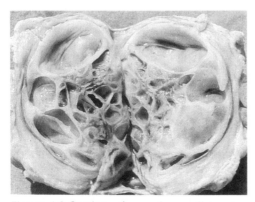

Figure 4.8 Section of granulosa cell tumour showing the cystic spaces which are fluid filled in life

mare cannot breed unless the affected ovary is removed but once this is done her fertility is restored and she can function quite adequately with the remaining ovary.

Blocked oviducts

One or both oviducts (Fallopian tubes) may become blocked in old mares. At ovulation the egg passes into the tube but unless fertilised does not descend into the uterus. Therefore, if conception does not take place the egg stays in the tube and slowly disintegrates. Some of the lining and contents of the follicle also enter the tube (Figure 4.9) and this debris may cause blockage, eventually

Figure 4.9 A highly-magnified view of debris collected from a Fallopian tube, consisting of the lining of a follicle discharged at ovulation and eggs that have not been fertilised

preventing the passage of the fertilised eggs, a condition which will obviously cause infertility if it affects both tubes. Infection ascending from the uterus may also cause inflammation of the tube and result in obstruction, but the condition does not appear to be as common as in the human female and is probably not a significant cause of equine infertility.

Failure to ovulate

Failure of a follicle to ovulate so that an egg is not produced during oestrus will obviously result in a sterile heat. Follicles may fail to develop or, once formed, bleed from their lining without ovulation, or they may develop to a certain size and then regress. These events – or non-events – are probably the result of insufficient FSH and LH being produced by the pituitary. They fall into the group of physiological rather than pathological causes of infertility. It has been suggested that structural alterations in the substance of the ovaries may prevent ovulation in a proper manner, i.e. through the ovulation fossa. These cases are of pathological origin.

Sterility

Sterility caused by a variety of conditions can result in absolute infertility, e.g. sex chromosome abnormalities.

Treatment

Diagnosis of the cause of infertility is obviously the key to successful treatment but, as already indicated, there are many gaps in our present knowledge. The incidence of physiological infertility may be reduced by veterinary examinations in which ovarian function is correlated with oestrous behaviour. Mating can then be synchronised with ovulation. The intravenous injection of LH to stimulate ovulation is helpful in this connection.

Injection of oestrogens and irrigation of the uterus with warm fluid may induce signs of oestrus in mares that are not coming into season. The Caslick operation, sexual rest and the administration of antibiotics into the uterus are useful to treat infections.

Infertility in stallions

As with mares, the term infertility is a matter of degree. Complete infertility or sterility is a comparatively rare phenomenon but conception rates do vary from horse to horse and for this reason it is said that one horse is more fertile than another. Before condemning any particular stallion, allowances must first be made for deficiencies in management as well as for his mares. A horse with a high proportion of problem mares, such as those suffering from infection or foaling late in the season, is likely to return relatively poor figures.

Theoretically a fertile horse should be capable of obtaining 100 per cent conception among 40 or 50 mares. We must, however, accept that about 20 per cent of mares will be barren for reasons not associated with the stallion. Stallion infertility should therefore be measured by conception rates between zero and 80 per cent. A stallion obtaining 70 per cent conception must be regarded as having satisfactory figures but those with 60 per cent and less should be suspected of being sub-fertile.

The reasons for subfertility or sterility can be discussed under the headings of lack of libido and semen quality.

Lack of libido

Lack of libido may be manifested in various ways. The horse may show no interest in his mares, he may try but fail to mount, or go through the whole process of mating without ejaculating. Lack of sexual drive may be due to insufficient production of LH by the pituitary and/or testosterone by the testes. Because the sexual drive is based on testosterone it is this hormone which plays a decisive role. Psychological factors and painful lesions of the back or hind limbs are other factors which may interfere with the normal sequence of sexual behaviour and prevent the completion of the ejaculatory process.

Failure to recognise ejaculation may also contribute to infertility. Those responsible usually decide that ejaculation has taken place on seeing the tail flag or feeling the urethra pulse. The latter method is probably the more reliable, but in some cases seminal plasma may be ejaculated without sperm and the horse is then led away from his mare in the erroneous assumption that a successful mating has taken place.

Recognising ejaculation is usually simple, but some stallions can be extremely deceptive and without experience of their behaviour

traits management may find recognition difficult.

When we consider the relatively few ovulations which occur within the arbitrary limits
of the breeding season and the fact that it is
the general aim to mate mares only once in an
oestrous period, even one missed opportunity
may have great significance for a particular
mare.

Semen quality

The quality of the semen can be measured by
the number of sperm present and percentage
of those living per millilitre of sample, their
activity (motility) and morphology.

There is general agreement now that for a
stallion to approach normal fertility he should
have the following minimum values:

Total volume	35 ml
Gel-free volume	25 ml
Sperm concentration	20 × 10,000,000 per ml
Total number of sperm	1.5 × 10,000,000,000
Total number of live sperm	1 × 10,000,000,000

Mention has already been made of the fact
that in any given sample the fewer the sperm
the less chance of conception and that
motility and a capacity for fertilisation are
necessary. Motility is simple to measure but
laboratory techniques to assess the fertilising
power of sperm have yet to be developed.

Morphology may be measured in terms of
the percentage of abnormal forms. These
include defects in the head or tail which may
be of an acquired or inherited nature. The
proportion of abnormal sperm varies according to the season and the amount of use made
of a horse; the first ejaculates in a breeding
season usually contain a higher proportion of
abnormalities than those later in the season.
Illness, especially if associated with fever,
may cause a deterioration in semen quality
and render a stallion temporarily infertile.

Infection of the horse's urethra or accessory sexual glands with organisms such as
Klebsiella or *Streptococci* may result in partial
or complete infertility. These infections are
usually the result of venereal spread and
although uncommon should never be disre-
garded. For this reason it is important that
mares should be inspected from a bacteriological viewpoint before service.

CHAPTER FIVE

LIFE BEFORE BIRTH

The foal, or the foetus as it is usually called in its life before birth, develops within the uterus of the mare for an average of 340 days. During this period, known as pregnancy or gestation, it not only takes on the form of a new individual, but also grows to a size and maturity that enables it to survive in the outside world.

The foetus, as far as clinical observation is concerned, is largely hidden throughout this period of gestation. We have little first-hand knowledge of its wellbeing and most of the knowledge about its basic function has come from experimental rather than clinical means.

There is, therefore, a scarcity of information about the way a pregnant mare should be managed in relation to the progress and development of her foetus. In recent years, however, some progress has been made. We are now able to visualise the foetus by means of ultrasound scanning. In the early stages of pregnancy the contents of the uterus may be visualised by inserting the scanning head per rectum. From about the 80th day until full term, the optimal approach is to apply the scanner head to the mare's abdomen.

Nevertheless, despite the drawbacks of inaccessibility, we have a considerable amount of information about the development and growth of the foetus, much of which has come from experimental studies.

Conception

The egg consists of a single cell about the size of a grain of sand. The spermatozoa are even smaller and many millions are contained in each ejaculate of a stallion. After coitus the spermatozoa travel rapidly up both horns of the uterus and into each of the Fallopian tubes. In these tubes they await the descent of the egg after it has been expelled from the ovary (ovulation).

The egg is fertilised by the entry of one spermatozoon and subsequently is resistant to the entry of any other male cell; it cannot be fertilised a second time. The union of the egg cell (ovum) and the sperm cell (spermatozoon) 'activates' the egg and the inherited material (chromosomes and genes) combine to form a single cell.

This single cell then divides repeatedly, so that at first two cells, then four, then eight, then 16 are formed. At this early stage the term 'embryo' is often used instead of foetus. The term 'blastocyst' is also used to describe the hollow ball of cells in which the fertilised ovum enters the uterus from the Fallopian tube.

Embryo transfer

The fertilised egg can be collected and transferred to another mare by a technique called embryo transfer which is, like artificial insemination, prohibited for use in Thoroughbred horses. However, it is being used with increasing frequency in many non-thoroughbred breeds.

The mare is mated in the usual way and the fertilised egg is obtained and may be transferred to a recipient, again under special conditions which allow the transferred egg to develop in the recipient.

The technique consists of collecting eggs from the Fallopian tube or uterus by special techniques of flushing. The egg enters the uterus on the fifth day following ovulation and it may be flushed from the uterus by surgical or nonsurgical means.

The objective of the technique is primarily to enable a mare of choice to be used for the production of many offspring concurrently employing surrogate mothers. The eggs can be transported over long distances within and between countries which, therefore, has the advantage of convenience; the recipient mares can stay at home rather than be transported to where the donor mare resides. It is necessary for the recipient mares to have their sexual cycles coordinated in such a way that they have a yellow body present at the time of transfer, enabling the uterus to prepare for implantation.

Development and growth

In the uterus the egg cells continue to multiply but at the same time certain cells become differentiated into organs, blood, muscle, skin, etc. By about the 20th day an outline of the foal has appeared in miniature.

From the 20th day onwards the organs and tissues that have been formed start to grow.

Of course not all the tissues will be fully formed in the first 20 days (e.g. hair does not appear until about the seventh month). The organs will not necessarily mature until a much later stage, the lungs, for instance, grow as an organ from an early stage of pregnancy but cannot function normally until about the 300th day after conception. For this reason a foal born in a very premature state cannot survive.

Just as the young need body-building substances, so the foetus depends on an adequate diet to meet its demands for growth. In addition, it must receive the vital gas oxygen and dispose of waste products (carbon dioxide, ammonia, etc.) which are potentially poisonous if allowed to accumulate in the body. These processes, which in the outside world are carried out by the lungs, kidneys and digestive tract, are performed for the foetus by the placenta, an organ developed especially for the purpose.

By ultrasound scanning we can visualise foetal structure as well as activity and heart rate. We are thus able to obtain some valuable clinical information about foetal development and its health status. This is a progressively expanding subject to which has been added the means of measuring blood flow in the foetus through the expertise known as Doppler ultrasound. This is based on the understanding that sound is altered as it travels away from or towards a fixed point; and the variation of speed may also be assessed.

An older and still employed means of measuring heart rate is through the electrocardiogram. The electrodes are attached to the surface of the back and abdomen and the foetal heartbeat may be distinguished from that of the mare.

Nourishment of the foetus

Yolk sac placenta

In the early stages of growth the foetus is nourished from fluids which surround it in the Fallopian tube. Once inside the uterus, it develops a special outgrowth from its body containing numerous blood vessels. This structure is known as the yolk sac placenta. Although the foetus normally develops at a definite point in the left or right horn of the uterus, it has no firm attachment to the uterine wall before the 25th day.

True placenta

By the 25th day from conception, a membrane has grown from the body of the foetus. This is the true placenta which is connected to the foetus through the umbilical cord. The cord carries blood between the foetus and the placenta, besides allowing for removal of urine from the bladder.

The true placenta is filled with fluid (allantoic fluid) in which the foetus floats like a small splinter of wood. The placenta soon becomes firmly attached to the uterine wall, the surface of each interlocking by the formation of millions of minute finger-like projections, each containing very small blood vessels or capillaries.

In this way the blood vessels of the mare and the foetus are brought into very close apposition (Figure 5.1) and substances such as protein, sugar, fats, etc., can pass from the mother's bloodstream into that of her foal. In addition, waste materials travel in the reverse direction and gases can be exchanged.

In recent years, research has shown that there is a close relationship between some hormone levels in the bloodstream of the mare and the health or otherwise of the placenta. In particular, the metabolites of progesterone (usually referred to as progestagens) may increase markedly in late pregnancy if the placenta is diseased. Increases occur normally near to full-term (i.e. at about 320 days gestation) but the abnormal increases may occur as early as 200 days.

The increase is often associated with premature mammary development and milk secretion. Mares with a damaged placenta may run milk for days, weeks or months starting as early as 250 days gestation.

Foetal health and wellbeing may also be judged by the content of calcium, sodium and potassium in the milk. Full-term values are reached normally just before foaling.

Amnion
A further membrane, the amnion, is developed at the same time as the placenta. This is a fine transparent sheet which entirely encloses the foal, separating it from the fluid of the placenta on the one side and keeping it bathed in its own fluid on the other (Figure 5.2).

The fluids of the placenta and amnion
The placenta contains a yellow or yellowish-brown fluid, formed partly by the placenta and partly from waste liquid produced by the foetus. This allantoic fluid, as it is called, can be seen gushing from the vagina when the placenta ruptures at the time of birth.

The foetus is able to pass urine through a special duct known as the urachus which connects the bladder and the placenta

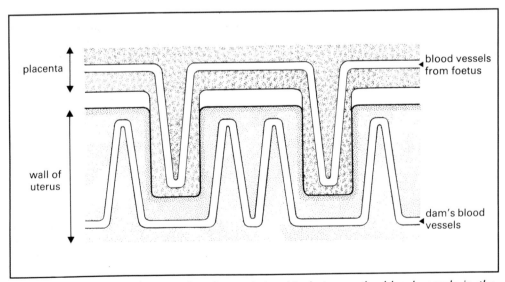

Figure 5.1 Diagram to illustrate the close relationship between the blood vessels in the placenta and the wall of the uterus

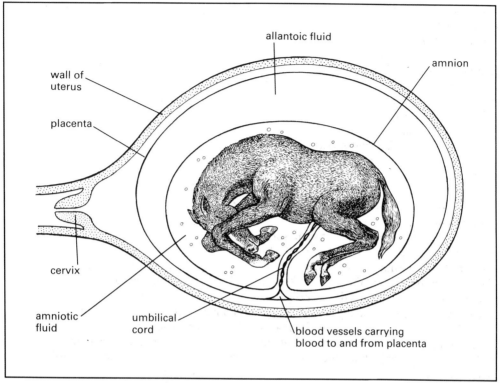

allantoic fluid

amnion

wall of uterus

placenta

cervix

amniotic fluid

umbilical cord

blood vessels carrying blood to and from placenta

Figure 5.2 Diagram showing the relationship between the amnion, the placenta and the wall of the uterus

through the umbilical cord. The urachus is open only during foetal life and closes when the cord breaks soon after the foal is born.

A curious pad-like structure called a hippomane (the literal meaning of which is 'horse madness'), is formed in the allantoic fluid. This structure – peculiar to the horse family – is composed of a conglomeration of salts and cells which crystallise to produce this characteristically rubber-like object which is often found on the loosebox floor after a mare has foaled.

The foetus is bathed in the straw-coloured, slimy amniotic fluid, which, although entering the nostrils and mouth, does not normally penetrate into the lungs but is swallowed and passes into the stomach.

Indications of foetal health and wellbeing have already been mentioned, and there are other avenues of investigation being explored at the current time. These relate mostly to obtaining amniotic fluid (amniocentesis) by inserting a needle transabdominally into the amniotic sac (aided by ultrasonic guidance). However, at present this is not without some risk and it cannot be used in practice. It may become a means of diagnosis as well as therapy, but this is for the future.

The maintenance of pregnancy

The maintenance of pregnancy, that is the continuing presence of a foetus in the uterus, is under hormonal control. Progesterone plays a dominant role, although other hormones are also involved, notably oestrogen.

Even though the foetus starts its life micro-

49

pic in size for the first week or so of development, its presence in the Fallopian tube and subsequently in the uterus is sufficient to initiate a series of changes in the latter organ and the ovaries.

These changes are best explained by describing them as they occur during the 340 days which separate conception from birth (Figure 5.3).

Ovulation, followed by the formation of a yellowish body, occurs in the ovary towards the end of oestrus and the egg is immediately shed into one or other of the Fallopian tubes. By some unknown process, only an egg which has been fertilised can pass down the tube into the uterus, where it arrives on about the fifth day following ovulation.

From the 11th day there is a considerable difference in the tone of the uterus and it becomes thicker than in the non-pregnant state.

By day 17, if fertilisation had not taken place, the yellow body would end its functional life and an oestrous period would be about to commence; in the pregnant state the yellow body continues and oestrus is suppressed.

Between day 17 and 22 several follicles increase in size and a small percentage of pregnant mares show some signs of oestrous behaviour at this time.

At about day 35 the hormone eCG is produced by the endometrial cups that develop in the lining of the uterus adjacent to the placenta. These form a string of saucers encircling the developing foetal membranes and remain for up to the 90th to 100th day. This circle is found in the pregnant horse at the junction between the uterine horn and body, just where the young foetus is developing.

In recent years, the work of Dr Allen in Newmarket has revealed through careful observation and experiment that the hormone eCG is actually secreted by foetal cells that pass from the foetal membranes into the uterine wall around day 37 following conception. These cells are foreign to the mare and

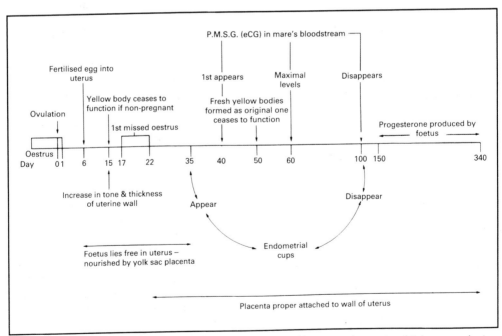

Figure 5.3 Diagram to illustrate the various changes and hormonal events which occur during pregnancy

evoke an immune response which eventually terminates their existence at about day 90 of pregnancy. Once embedded in the wall of the uterus the cups continue to produce the hormone even if the foetus is subsequently aborted; eCG enters the bloodstream and is present between day 40 and day 100, attaining a maximum concentration at about day 60.

The original yellow body of pregnancy, that is the one produced at the time of ovulation and prior to fertilisation, ceases to function at about day 50. It is replaced by the ovulation of the follicles which started to appear in the ovary between day 17 and 22.

These accessory yellow bodies, as they are called, continue to produce progesterone until about the 150th day when they too cease to function. From this time onward the foetus secretes the progesterone necessary for the continuance of pregnancy and the ovaries are no longer a factor. In fact, after the 150th day, pregnancy would continue even if the ovaries were removed.

Stud management and pregnancy

The practical considerations of the events described include:

1. The tendency of some mares to show oestrous behaviour even though they are pregnant. This does not mean that all of these will accept the stallion if presented to him; it requires that management should be aware of the possibility of pseudo-oestrus, which may best be diagnosed by a veterinary examination.
2. Experimental evidence indicates that when a foetus dies in the early stages of development, the mare may not return into oestrus because of the continuing presence of a functional yellow body in the ovary. In these cases it may be helpful to flush out the remnants of the dead foetus with a saline douche.

   Dr Allen's work shows that even if the foetus is aborted (Figure 5.4), its presence in the uterus after about the 40th day may

Figure 5.4 Mid-term aborted foetus with the amnion removed

programme the 'cups' and that they will then continue to produce eCG until the 100th day. The effect of this phenomenon may result in a state of pseudo-pregnancy and the mare will not return into oestrus for many weeks or even months. At present there is no known treatment which can be used to induce the mare to return into oestrus when she is in this type of condition.

3. Because the foetus and not the ovaries produce progesterone after day 150, the hormone disappears from the bloodstream of the mare and is found only on the foetal side of the placenta. After day 150 any attempt to prevent abortion by injecting progesterone into the mare will place the hormone on the 'wrong side' of the placenta; for this reason some doubt must be thrown on the effectiveness claimed for this therapy.

Pregnancy diagnosis

The diagnosis of pregnancy plays a highly important part in stud management during the mating season. For instance, it is necessary, once a mare has been covered by the stallion, to know whether subsequent oestrous periods are missed because of pregnancy, because the mare has gone into a prolonged period of dioestrus or is undergoing silent heat.

Because of the limited duration of the stud season, the earlier the diagnosis the better. In

51

practice, the manual examination (that is, the palpation of the uterus through the wall of the rectum) is used routinely for this purpose. However, it is not possible to be sure of the results and is more customary to examine mares between 25 and 42 days from the time of last service. Ultrasound scanning can now be used for accurate diagnosis as early as 15 days after mating.

If a mare is found to be barren, there are certain measures which may be taken in attempts to hasten the onset of a further oestrous period. (See Chapter Four.)

Even when a mare has been found to be pregnant at 40 days, it is advisable to have her rechecked at about the 60-day stage, since in about 10 per cent of cases the foetus dies during the intervening time.

In the manual rectal examination, the veterinarian relies on feeling two changes in the uterus, namely, the increased thickness of the walls and the presence of the fluid swelling produced by the foetus at the junction of the horn and the body. These changes are quite readily palpated and there is no evidence that the examination produces any undesirable effects.

Another means of diagnosis is based on the fact that between the 40th and 100th day of pregnancy there are large quantities of eCG in the mare's bloodstream. Therefore, if a sample of blood is analysed the hormone may be detected and the pregnant state revealed.

The MIP (Mare Immunological Pregnancy) test employed by laboratories to assay the blood levels of this hormone is, as its name implies, now performed by immunological methods and carried out in a test tube. The older method involved injecting a small portion of mare's blood into an immature female mouse. After two days the mouse was killed and positive results were indicated by characteristic changes in the ovaries and uterus.

The disadvantage of pregnancy diagnosis involving either of these laboratory tests is that they cannot yield accurate results before the 45th day of pregnancy. In addition, as already mentioned, recent work has shown that under certain circumstances the hormone may be present in the bloodstream even though the foetus has died. However, since these cases are comparatively rare, a blood test may be considered adequate in practice if used between the dates mentioned.

Finally, large quantities of oestrogen-like hormones appear in a pregnant mare's urine from the 100th day until the end of pregnancy. Laboratory tests for this hormone (Cuboni test) provide a reliable diagnosis, although there is the disadvantage that early detection of a foetus is impossible and urine collection may be a tedious process.

Feeding the pregnant mare

The principles of feeding pregnant mares may be summarised as follows. Experimental work performed in South Africa has shown that if the mare is given insufficient protein between day 25 and 32 of pregnancy, the foetus may be aborted. Under general farm management the degree of starvation may rarely, if ever, approach the levels in the experiment. Nevertheless, the foetus of a mare mated early in the year may be at risk if additional rations are not provided.

If a pregnant mare is fed on a sufficient diet, her foetus will come to no harm even though she is exposed to a very cold climate. In fact, rather than confine a mare to a stable in order to keep her warm, it is probably more necessary to ensure that she receives adequate daily exercise. Unfortunately, we are not in a position to know for certain what will be the consequence on the foetus of various procedures to which mares are subjected; the stress of travelling by road or air, for example.

Twins

It is well known that if twins are conceived, the resulting pregnancy will frequently be terminated by abortion, or if they are carried to full term, each individual will be too small for economic value (Figure 5.5). The horse appears to be the only mammal whose uterus

Days from conception	Approximate length from head to tail	Approximate weight
56	10 cm	9 g
112	28 cm	70 g
224	56 cm	9 kg
280	84 cm	19 kg
340 (full term)	97 cm	45 kg

Figure 5.5 Chart showing the length and weight of a foetus in relation to stage of pregnancy

cannot successfully rear two young at the same time. The reason may be in the size of its placenta, which is diffuse (i.e. it covers all the uterine wall), in contrast to that of the pig (e.g. where it occupies only a small portion of the total surface area). It seems, therefore, that in the horse there is just not room for two placentae and after a certain stage of pregnancy one competes against the other to the extent that one of the foals will die and cause an abortion.

CHAPTER SIX

ABORTION

A foal born before the 300th day of pregnancy has little chance of survival because many of its organs, especially the lungs, are not mature enough to sustain life in the outside world. Such a foal may be delivered with a beating heart and attempt to breathe but it will usually die. In scientific parlance it is non-viable, and is termed an abortion.

On the other hand a foal born between the 300th and 320th day will have a reasonable chance of survival, much depending on the nursing that it can be given. These foals are usually of relatively low birth weight and called premature. Births occurring after 320 days are described as full-term.

Abortion (Figures 6.1 and 6.2) may occur at any stage of pregnancy although the terms embryonic and early foetal death are sometimes applied to abortions in the first 100 days.

The foetus may be likened to a parasite living in the mother's uterus. While alive it receives nourishment and is tolerated; but once it dies it represents a foreign body and is soon rejected from the uterus. In these cases the most logical method of disposal is through the cervix and vagina. The foetus and its membranes may not actually be observed at the time of abortion. This may happen because of their small size, coupled with the fact that the mare may be in the paddock and the evidence therefore remains unseen. Not all mares show a discharge after abortion and this too may make the abortion

Figure 6.1 The amnion cut away showing the foetus and umbilical cord

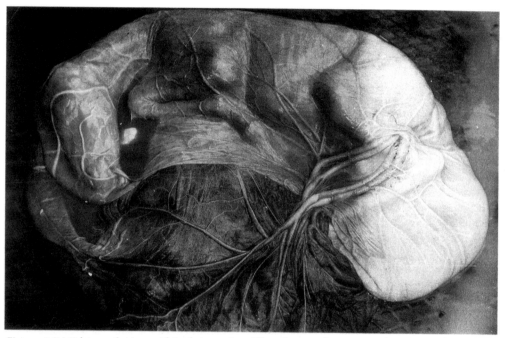

Figure 6.2 Mid-term foetus within the amnion. The placenta is separated and lies in the lower part of the picture

inapparent. Resorption of the foetus (i.e. its return into the mare's bloodstream) is another synonym for early foetal death. All these terms are used to describe a pregnancy known to have started because of a positive test (rectal or biological) before about 40 days, but for which there is no produce and no evidence of abortion. In practice, the mare returns unexpectedly into heat or is examined subsequent to an earlier examination (say at 40 days) and the loss of a pregnancy is identified. Mummification occurs occasionally in a foetus, particularly a twin. The tissues lose their water and become hardened. A twin that is mummified may be delivered with the normal member at full-term or can cause a problem and affect the other member. However, there is really no biological difference between an early and a late abortion. Once pregnancy has been confirmed its loss may be diagnosed in that individual and may occur at any stage. It is true that the earlier the first diagnosis the higher the proportion of pregnancies that will be lost in any given population of mares. This is because there is a steady loss throughout the whole of gestation. The earlier the first diagnosis the more chance there is of that pregnancy being lost.

In the mare, estimates vary from 10 to 15 per cent throughout pregnancy starting from day 17. This is now the occasion when pregnancies are routinely established by means of ultrasound diagnosis. Prior to ultrasound, 42 days was generally the starting point for positive pregnancy diagnosis.

About 1 in 20 pregnancies are lost between day 17 and 40. A further 1 in 20 are lost between day 40 and 150; and another 1 in 20 between days 150 and 300.

The causes of this loss are described below.

Causes of abortion

The causes of abortion can be listed, as:
1. Twin pregnancy.
2. Infection with bacteria, virus or fungus.

3. Hormonal failure.
4. Errors of development and implantation.
5. Influence of management.

Twins

Twins are included as a cause of abortion because the great majority are either aborted or born prematurely without a chance of survival (Figures 6.3 and 6.4). Russian workers reported that in 266 twin pregnancies 199 aborted, 16 produced two foals and 13 a single foal which could be reared. The remainder were born dead or were either too small or too weak to survive. In the United Kingdom and Ireland the incidence of twins

in Thoroughbreds is about 1 per cent of all pregnancies. Other breeds appear much less affected and this might relate to the selection of broodmares on the grounds of racing performance. Such selection does not account for a paticular tendency towards conceiving twins.

Twins represent the largest single group of aborted foetuses. At some time after the fourth month one twin often dies but may be retained in the uterus where it undergoes a certain amount of decomposition. Eventually both twins are aborted, the dead one perhaps causing the rejection of the second which is always in a much better state of preservation

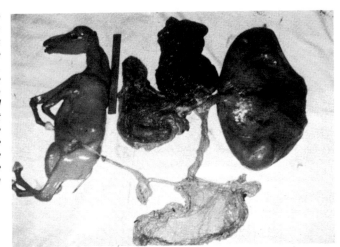

Figure 6.3 When twins are aborted one has usually been dead for sometime and has started to degenerate, the other may be well preserved. Here, twin foetuses are shown, aged about seven months. A ruler has been laid against the one on the left which died sometime before abortion. The foetus on the right is still enclosed in the placenta and was living at the time of abortion

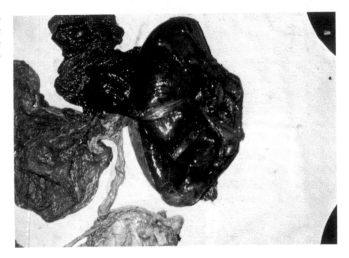

Figure 6.4 Here, the placenta of the well preserved twin has been removed. The foetus is still within the amnion

and may die only a short time before abortion.

Equine twins arise from the fertilisation of two individual ova. Twin ovulations are more frequent in mares than is generally realised. Presumably there is some biological mechanism within the mare which normally eliminates twin conceptions. This seems a reasonable theory in view of the fact that the species cannot normally carry twins to full-term.

Infection

The effect of infection may be:

a) indirect, where there is destruction of large areas of the placenta causing foetal death through starvation and toxaemia;

b) direct, where the microorganisms invade the foetus.

Bacterial causes

Bacterial infection is a common cause of abortion (Figure 6.5). The germs involved are the same as those associated with infertility. They include *Taylorella equigenitalis*, *Streptococci*, *E. coli*, *Klebsiella* and *Staphylococci* in roughly that order of incidence.

Bacterial infection may cause abortion at any stage of pregnancy. There is no hard and fast rule but in general *Streptococci* are responsible for abortions up to about 150 days whereas *E. coli* are more often the cause during the last half of pregnancy.

Bacteria are frequently present in the uterus at the time of conception and this is the most common way microorganisms come to cause abortion. A mare that has a chronic infection of the uterus, or in which the genital tract is for any reason less capable of resisting infection, will be more likely to suffer an abortion than a completely healthy mare. Infection may enter the uterus through the cervix if the mare takes in air through the vulva or may be carried there in the bloodstream of the mare once she has become pregnant.

Viral causes

In the 1930s it was well-recognised in Kentucky that an infectious type of abortion occurred, sometimes affecting one or two mares and on other occasions causing abortion in large numbers of mares stabled on a particular premises.

This infectious abortion became known as viral abortion. The pioneering work of Dr Roger Doll of the University of Kentucky provided much of the basic information regarding this disease. Subsequently, as modern techniques for virological examin-

Figure 6.5 A foetus with its membranes aborted on the 120th day of pregnancy. It is approximately 18 cm long. The normal size at this stage would be approximately 20 cm. This foetus is undersized for its gestational age, probably as a result of the infection which caused the abortion

ation in the laboratory became perfected, the causal agent was identified as a herpesvirus and provided with the designation Equid herpesvirus 1 (EHV-1). Other herpesviruses were identified as EHV-2 and EHV-3, the latter causing coital exanthema (spots) and the former being ubiquitous and not thought to cause disease, although the last word has probably not been said on this subject.

EHV-1 was found to have two types: subtype 1 and subtype 2. Both subtypes cause respiratory disease but subtype 1 was mainly responsible for abortion.

More recently, virologists have come to describe EHV-1 subtype 2 as EHV-4. There are now, therefore, four known strains of herpesvirus: EHV-1, EHV-2, EHV-3 and EHV-4. EHV-1 and EHV-4 are essentially causes of respiratory infection, snotty nose, catarrh, slight fever and coughing in young horses and a more insidious and asymptomatic condition in older horses, although infection may always predispose (make more susceptible) an individual to bacterial infection of the upper airways and lungs.

Abortions occur from about the fifth month of pregnancy and reach a peak at about seven to nine months. Occasionally an affected foetus will reach full-term and be born alive but they are usually weak and die within the first few days.

There are not usually lesions on the membranes of aborted foetuses and the abortion occurs without warning. Externally, the visible mucous membranes of the foetus may be jaundiced and internally there may be oedematous fluid in the thorax. Characteristic lesions include focal necrosis of the liver (i.e. small areas of dead cells which contain viral inclusion bodies).

The reasons why the virus sometimes, but not always, crosses the placenta and infects the foetus causing abortion, remain unclear. The evidence suggests that pregnant mares can be infected without necessarily aborting. It is thought that the immune status of the individual may be part of the explanation. For this reason, vaccines have been developed. The most commonly used is Pneumabort-K

containing killed virus particles that are injected intramuscularly at five, seven and nine months gestation according to the instructions of the manufacturers. Other vaccines, such as Rhinomune, contain live virus that has been modified by laboratory processes so as to retain immune-stimulating properties without causing disease.

Arteritis is another virus which may cause abortion. Unlike EHV-1 the virus causes obvious signs of illness in an affected mare, including discharges from the eyes and nose and filling of the limbs (oedema). Up to 50 per cent of affected pregnant mares may abort. There are no other known viruses which cause abortion and the one which so commonly causes influenza appears not to harm the foetus and certainly does not cause abortion.

Fungal causes

Abortion due to infection of the placenta by various types of fungi has been known in the United Kingdom since 1962. The number of fungal (mycotic) abortions usually exceeds those caused by herpesvirus.

Fungi probably enter the uterus during the heat period at which conception occurs or, in the case of foaling mares, shortly after birth. The causal relationship between uterine infection and dust-contaminated air in foaling boxes or covering sheds has been emphasised in previous chapters. Fungi may become established following antibiotic treatment and the incidence of mycotic diseases among all domesticated animals has risen since antibiotics have been used routinely.

Fungi grow on the placenta and cause substantial thickening and degeneration of its uterine surface. In a proportion of cases there may be lesions on the amnion and in the foetus. Fungal infections do not cause immediate abortion but spread slowly, thus reducing the nourishment available to the foetus.

For this reason the aborted foetus is often small and only a fraction of the normal weight for its gestational age. If abortion does not occur the foal may be carried to full-term and be born in a reasonably vigorous, but undersized and undernourished, state. Most mycotic abortions occur during the second half of pregnancy.

Hormonal failure

In practice we recognise a category of abortions in which the foetus appears normally developed and there is no evidence of infection or other explanation as to the cause of the abortion. We assume therefore that the reasons are hormonal.

The hormone progesterone plays a dominant role in the maintenance of pregnancy, preparing the uterus for reception of the fertilised egg and the attachment of the placenta. In summary: it is responsible for the necessary changes in the uterus for the continuance of pregnancy and nourishment of the foetus. Other hormones such as oestrogen and cortisone are also involved in this process. The maintenance of pregnancy should therefore be regarded as a matter of hormonal balance.

Another part of the equation is that these hormones may be produced on either side of the placenta, that is by the mare and/or foetus. For example there are good reasons for believing that progesterone is produced by the mare only during the first 150 days of pregnancy and thereafter by the foetus. Evidence from other species suggests that cortisone and adrenocorticotrophic hormone (ACTH) secreted by the foetus, are closely associated with the biological mechanism which determines when pregnancy shall end in birth.

If this mechanism is upset birth is likely to be provoked prematurely.

Similarly, it is reasonable to suppose that abortion may be brought about by failure in the glands that control hormonal balance. In our present state of knowledge we can only guess at the reasons why these failures occur or what hormone levels are affected. There are so many gaps in our basic knowledge of this particular field of biology that the horse owner and his or her veterinarian are faced with a certain number of inexplicable happenings as far as aborting mares are concerned.

Errors of development and implantation

This is another area about which we have little understanding. In other species we know that abortions may be the direct consequence of defective genetic or chromosomal material in the newly-formed individual. It has been postulated that the abortion of a foetus with malformations may be one way in which nature controls the genetic health of the species. In other words, serious abnormalities are not allowed to live and reproduce themselves. Not all deformities are eliminated by abortion and some foals are born with such abnormalities as cleft palate and parrot jaw.

Failure of the placenta to become attached (implanted) to the uterus is commonly put forward as a reason for abortion in the first 30 days of pregnancy. Even at the 35th day, the foetus is lying free in the uterus and its membranes are not firmly attached to the uterine wall. It has been suggested that the foetus is particularly vulnerable at this stage.

Any disturbance of the intricate mechanisms maintaining pregnancy may pose a threat to the safety of the foetus. We cannot hope to explain many of the noninfective causes of abortion nor to take measures to prevent them until we know more of the actions of eCG and the factors which control the attachment of the placenta to the uterus.

Influence of management

The question must be asked – to what extent can management be responsible for a mare aborting? This is largely a theoretical consideration because it is extremelty difficult to relate cause and effect in any particular individual. For example, if pregnant mares are subjected to abnormal stresses such as being transported by air or road, put through the sale ring, handled roughly or excited by unusual events (e.g. low-flying aircraft or hounds in the vicinity of their paddock), we might expect an abortion. However, a statistical approach would be necessary to determine if any of these happenings are really significant and this study would have to involve large numbers rather than individuals.

The habit of confining mares and foals to boxes to shelter them from the intemperate winter and then galloping the mare in a paddock separate from her foal, so that she does not harm it, might be harmful to a foetus in the early stages of growth. Again, this is theoretical because no study of this aspect has been made.

Some owners worry that manual examinations for pregnancy are harmful. There is really no evidence that this is so. In fact, it is surprisingly difficult to cause a mare to abort a twin foetus when, as is sometimes the case, a veterinarian attempts to squeeze one of the two foetal sacs at about 40 days when a mare is twinning. Even this measure may not dislodge the foetus. There are cases in which mares have been operated on for a twisted gut when they are 40 days pregnant and have carried their foal, normally, to full-term.

The older a mare the more likely she is to abort and therefore vigorous culling of these mares and those with bad breeding records might make a significant contribution to the abortion problem.

Faulty nutrition is unlikely to cause abortion unless levels fall below certain minimum requirements of quality and quantity, which they rarely do.

Symptoms of abortion

As already mentioned, abortions can occur at any stage of the pregnancy. Early abortions, that is up to the 40th day after conception, may merely prevent the mare undergoing oestrus. For example the egg may be fertilised and pass in the normal way into the uterus, triggering off the changes in the mare's glands and uterus which normally occur at conception. We do not know how the mare's body recognises the difference between a fertilised and nonfertilised egg, but that it does so at an early stage is indicated by the knowledge that fertilised eggs pass down the Fallopian tube and arrive in the uterus five days later, whereas eggs which are not fertilised remain in the tube and do not enter the uterus.

One of the changes as a result of conception is that the yellow body produced at the time of ovulation continues to produce progesterone beyond the usual 16 days. It thereby suppresses the oestrous period which would normally occur in a nonpregnant mare 16 days after the end of the previous heat.

It seems that a foetus which dies within 16 days of conception might, despite its brief sojourn in the uterus, set off the unknown mechanism which allows the yellow body to continue. This causes the mare to miss one or sometimes a number of oestrous periods.

If pregnancy has reached the 35th day then, if the foetus dies, the mare will probably not return into oestrus for a considerable time. The reason is that by this stage the endometrial cups are producing eCG and will continue to do so for a further 60 days, whether or not the foetus stays in the uterus.

Later in pregnancy (Figures 6.6 and 6.7) the foetus and its membranes are more substantial and there will be evidence of a discharge or of the placenta hanging behind the mare after the abortion. In the second half of pregnancy abortions may be preceded by development of the mammary glands and the excretion of milk. In the case of twins, the mare may run milk when one twin dies and continue for days, weeks or (more rarely) months before the abortion finally occurs. It is thought that the foetus in some way inhibits development of the mare's udder until it is nearly ready to leave the uterus. After the foetus dies this inhibiting influence is removed and the mare therefore springs her bag.

Abortions rarely affect the general health of the mare except in as far as they may be followed by a condition of retained placenta and infection of the uterus. There is a very definite relationship between abortion and subsequent failure to get in foal not only in the same year, but in the future. This re-

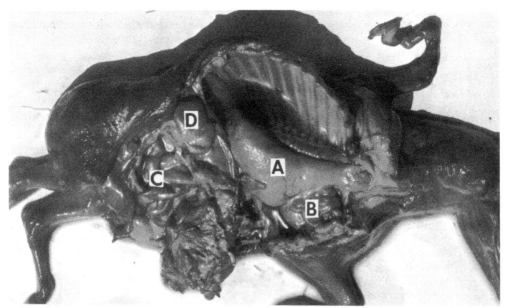

Figure 6.6 This 120-day-old foetus has been opened at the chest and abdomen to reveal: lungs (A), heart (B), intestines (C) and ovary (D)

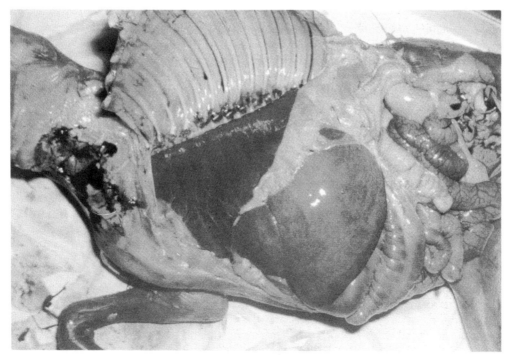

Figure 6.7 A foetus aged about five months, opened to show (from top left to bottom right) rib cage, lungs, liver and intestines

lationship appears to apply to abortions at any stage of pregnancy.

Prevention of abortion

The success of any particular measure to prevent abortion is difficult to assess. In view of the small number of abortions that occur each year the chance of one particular mare aborting is relatively small. Although, as already mentioned, she may be more difficult to get in foal there is no evidence to suggest she is more likely to abort in subsequent pregnancies than any other mare. It follows that the success of any treatment can be judged only against failure. In other words if a mare is treated in a certain way and aborts we know that a particular treatment has not been of any consequence but, conversely if she does not abort, we are left wondering if what we have done has affected the issue at all.

The most favoured preventative method is to administer varying doses of progesterone on the assumption that because this hormone is necessary for pregnancy it may be deficient. Injections used to be given but nowadays there are powerful progesterone-like substances which may be administered by mouth on a daily basis. There are several grounds for doubting the efficacy of this treatment:

1. Claims of success have been made for a dose rate which is so small that it is unlikely it could make a significant contribution to the hormonal status of an animal the size of a mare.
2. As already mentioned, beyond 150 days of pregnancy the hormone is produced by the foetus and not the mare. In fact it is not present in the mare's bloodstream after this time. One wonders, therefore, if the administration of progesterone to the mare can get across to the foetus.
3. There is no evidence that abortions are related to progesterone deficiency in the mare. Here it must be admitted that there is equally no evidence that it is not. Only future research can resolve the question

and this sentiment really sums up the whole problem of prevention.

In general terms measures to avoid abortion should include an adequate diet, in quantity and quality, at all times of the year. Mares should, as far as possible, be kept in the same environment and left as undisturbed as is reasonably possible. In the commercial hurly burly where mares are dispatched to different studs at various stages of pregnancy, transported by road, rail and air over long distances, put through sales rings, confined to boxes and galloped away from their foals, it would be surprising if some of these actions did not result in abortion. There is therefore a case for avoiding intemperate actions as far as possible but one must recognise the fact that horses are bred at our convenience and the consequences of our actions have at times to be accepted for this convenience.

The use of vaccines such as Pneumabort and Rhinomune has been mentioned briefly as a means of preventing viral abortion. These vaccines do not prevent respiratory infection (they do not contain EHV-4), and are not 100 per cent effective against the abortion form. It is thought that they may prevent abortion storms but not individual incidents occurring.

It is to be hoped that a new generation of vaccines will appear on the market resulting from current research that uses the high technology of identifying and isolating pieces of virus and combining them with suitable carriers (vectors). Such carriers may in the future be used as a vaccine in a much more effective manner than is available at present. They may also combine EHV-4 with EHV-1, thereby making the protection more complete against the respiratory disease.

Two major problems that must be faced with herpesvirus infection, in contrast to infections such as influenza, is that the virus may remain in a latent form. Latency is the term used to describe the capacity of a virus to lie dormant in the body for many months or years and then become active due to circumstances such as those associated with stress, or the result of a separate infection by another virus or, even, bacteria. Comparatively little is known about latency in equine herpes infections but this is a subject which is currently receiving much attention from research workers.

Another feature of herpesvirus infection is the relatively short immunity which a natural infection bestows upon the individual. Even natural infection may stimulate immunity lasting only a matter of a few weeks and this weak immune response increases the difficulties of producing effective vaccines.

The two problems of latency and poor immune response combine to cause an individual to be susceptible to repeated attacks of viral infection, both from a recrudescence of a previous infection that has laid dormant in the individual and from renewed challenge from other individuals, perhaps those which are experiencing a fresh awakening of an infection which has been latent from a previous occasion in which symptoms were apparent.

An essential feature of good management is that an aborting mare should be isolated, her box disinfected, bedding burnt and those in attendance suitably clad for easy disinfection of boots, clothing, etc., until a veterinary examination of the foetus and its membranes can eliminate the possibility of an infectious cause of the abortion.

A Code of Practice exists for the control of diseases such as Equine Herpesvirus Abortion (caused by EHV-1), Equine Viral Arteritis (EVA) and Contagious Equine Metritis (CEM). (Copies of the Code are available from the Horserace Betting Levy Board, 52 Grosvenor Gardens, London SW1W 0AU.) The Code also covers prevention of other bacterial diseases such as *Klebsiella* and *Pseudomonas*.

Post mortem examination

The foetus and its membranes should be placed in a plastic bag and despatched as soon as possible to a laboratory under the direction of the veterinarian in charge. A bacteriological examination of the mare's genital tract may also be helpful in cases of bacterial or mycotic abortion.

Conclusion

Abortion is a problem which can never be entirely eliminated. In fact the more efficient the methods of attaining conception, the more mares will tend to abort. In many cases of mares that are difficult to breed from, nature has the last laugh; after several barren years a mare may be made to conceive, only to abort a single foetus or even twins.

CHAPTER SEVEN

BIRTH OF A FOAL

The period of development during which the foal develops in the uterus is one of preparation. When it is completed the foetus is said to have reached maturity.

The length of pregnancy is relatively constant for each species, although its duration varies between individuals. In the Thoroughbred horse pregnancy lasts, on average, 340 days, with a normal spread of about 20 days above and below this figure. Pregnancy is terminated by birth or parturition, which means literally 'a bringing forth'.

Whose finger on the trigger?

For years scientists have been trying to discover the exact mechanisms which initiate birth. Does the mother or the foetus decide the date; is increased concentration of the hormones oestrogen, oxytocin or cortisol responsible; or decreased levels of progesterone?

Oxytocin is produced by the posterior lobe of the pituitary gland, acting upon the muscle of the uterus causing it to contract. It therefore forms an integral part of the birth process and of the expulsion of the afterbirth. Oxytocin may be administered by the veterinarian to aid the involution of the uterus and to induce parturition in certain circumstances.

A great deal has been learned in modern times about the hormone substances known as prostaglandins. These cause contraction in certain types of muscle such as those making up the wall of the uterus. As they cause abortion in some species, prostaglandins have

been studied in connection with contraception, but they are also of interest from the point of view of whether they might play some part in initiating normal birth. Prostaglandins were first identified during the early 1930s as substances present in human semen. Following their discovery they were not considered to be biologically important until they were rediscovered in the 1960s. Eventually they were used in equine veterinary medicine because of their proven ability to destroy the yellow body in the ovary.

Prostaglandins are composed of a number of different components: PGE, F2d, PGE2 and others. These are hormones with actions on the yellow body. They are also products of the inflammatory process and are often produced at the site of injury.

Evidence obtained from cross-mating horses and donkeys suggests that the genetic make-up of the foetus influences the duration of pregnancy, while recent work on sheep indicates that in this species at least, the foetal hormones play a dominant role.

It is well known to breeders of horses that the majority of mares give birth during darkness, or at least between 7 p.m. and 7 a.m. (Figure 7.1). Since the act of birth is not voluntary, the most likely explanation is that the decreasing intensity of light at nightfall provides a stimulus which is mediated through the eyes and pituitary gland of the mare. A similar sensitivity to light on the part of the pineal gland has been observed in connection with the stimulation of sexual activity in the spring and summer months.

As far as horses are concerned, the conclusion is, therefore, that although the foetus

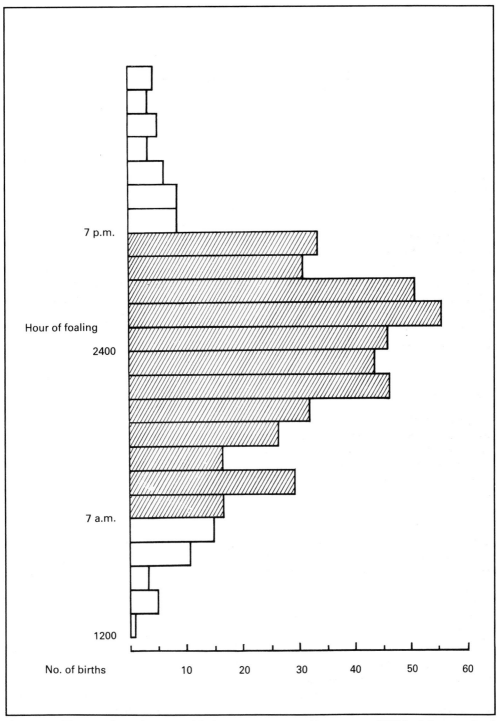

Figure 7.1 Chart to show the time of foaling in 501 mares: 90 per cent of 501 foals born arrived between 7 p.m. and 7 a.m.

controls the overall length of pregnancy, it is the mare who decides the actual hour of birth.

Birth canal

For 11 months the foetus has resided inside the uterus surrounded by fluid and membranes; now it has to journey to the outside world. It makes this journey through what is commonly referred to as the birth canal. This consists of the soft structures of the cervix, vagina and vulva, surrounded by the bones of the maternal pelvis. The latter forms an unyielding ring of bone through which the foal must pass. For this reason it is essential that the various parts of the foal lie in such a way that they facilitate, not impede, its passage by becoming lodged. In practice there is only one correct position, posture and presentation in which the foal may be born. While these terms are the technical jargon of veterinarians they are useful to a proper understanding of normal and abnormal delivery (Figures 7.2 and 7.3).

The term 'position' refers to the alignment of the backbone of the foal relative to that of its dam. The only normal position is with both backbones in the same plane and in close apposition to one another (dorsal position). It is perhaps easier to understand this point if we consider some abnormal positions, namely, with the foal lying on its back (ventral position) or lying across the birth canal (transverse position).

Posture refers to the disposition of the limbs, head and neck. Here again there is only one normal posture; that is with the forelegs and head extended in front of, and the hind legs extended behind, the foal.

Presentation refers to whether the foal is coming forward or backward; that is, with the head and forelegs first (normal and anterior presentation) or tail and hind limbs first (abnormal and posterior presentation).

We might liken the position, posture and presentation of the foal during the second stage to a person diving through a hoop.

During the last third of pregnancy the foetus lies on its back with its head directed towards the birth canal and its forelimbs flexed (that is, in a ventral position, flexed posture and anterior presentation). During the early part of birth the body rotates and the limbs extend so that the foetus is aligned for delivery.

Forces of birth

Birth is accomplished by a process in which the foal is pushed through the pelvic hoop and along the birth canal. The forces involved are brought to play by the muscles of the uterus and those that form the belly, or abdomen, of the mare. The foal is squeezed out of the mare and it is only the fluid content in the placenta and amnion which makes this process possible (Figure 7.4).

We might regard the abdominal cavity as a cone-shaped box which contains the guts, together with the uterus and its contents. The blunt end of the cone is formed by the diaphragm (the membrane which separates the abdominal cavity from the chest); the sides of the cone are formed by the muscles of the back, above, and the belly muscles below. When the mare strains to deliver her foal the diaphragm and back are kept fixed while the belly muscles contract, thus transmitting pressure to the contents of the box. It should be apparent that the efficiency of the muscles will be enhanced if the mare is lying on her side, since by this action the pressure will be increased. In fact, we shall see that the mare spends most of second-stage labour lying down.

The act of birth can be most conveniently described under the headings of first, second and third stage labour.

First stage labour

The first stage of labour is characterised by rhythmic contractions of muscles in the uterine wall. These contractions pass in waves from one end of the organ to the other. In this way pressure is exerted on the contents of the uterus and the placenta is pushed with increasing force against the cervix; as the latter opens, the membranes rupture and some of the fluid contents gush through the

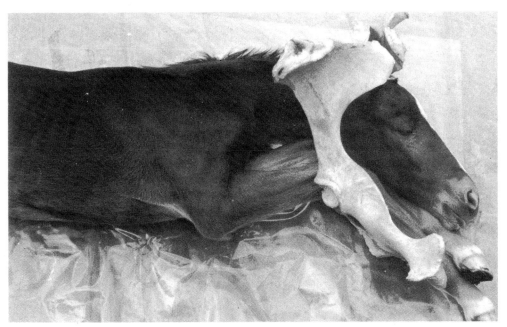

Figure 7.2 Normal posture, presentation and position of the foetus passing through the 'hoop' formed by bones of the pelvis

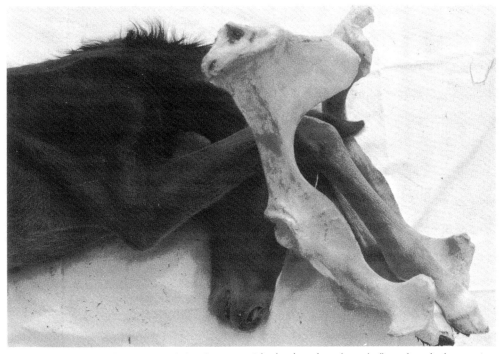

Figure 7.3 Abnormal posture of the foetus, with the head and neck flexed and obstructing passage through the pelvic outlet

67

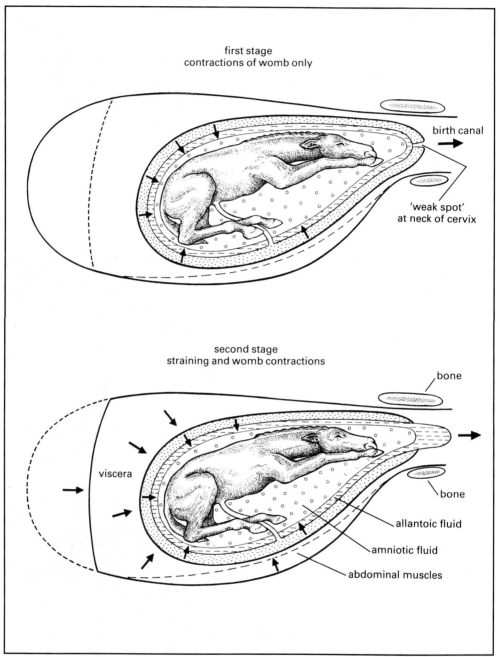

first stage
contractions of womb only

birth canal

'weak spot'
at neck of cervix

second stage
straining and womb contractions

bone

viscera

bone

allantoic fluid

amniotic fluid

abdominal muscles

Figure 7.4 Diagram showing the forces of birth which push the foal from its position in the uterus through the birth canal which is bounded by the bony hoop formed by the pelvis. In first stage labour the muscles of the wall of the uterus contract and exert pressure (small arrows) on the contents, eventually causing the placenta to rupture at a weak spot close to the cervix which at this time is dilating. In second stage labour the contractions of the uterus are supplemented by those of the abdominal muscles (large arrows) and the diaphragm is fixed at the position of inspiration (breathing in)

vagina and emerge through the vulvar lips. The rupture of the placenta marks the end of first stage and beginning of second stage labour.

We recognise the signs of first stage labour by the way the mare behaves when she feels the pain of her contracting uterus. These signs include uneasiness (walking around the box and pawing at the ground), profuse or patchy sweating, retraction of the upper lip (the flehmen posture) (Figure 7.5), lengthening of the vulva (Figure 7.6), signs of maternal instinct such as licking the coat (Figure 7.7), and milk squirting from one or both teats of the udder.

These signs may last for several hours or be present for only a short time before the second stage arrives. In rare instances they may be absent altogether so that second stage begins without any premonitory signs. The pain that mares feel during first stage appears to vary in intensity and generally occurs in waves. For this reason the mare alternately exhibits signs one moment and then rests or returns to the manger to eat food or nibble at straw the next.

Second stage labour

The second stage of labour starts with the dilation of the cervix and the rupture of the placenta; it ends when the foal has been completely delivered. It covers the period of explusion or delivery of the foal from the uterus to the outside world. The main feature of second stage is the powerful expulsive efforts by which the mare supplements the forces exerted on the uterine contents and which are initiated by the muscles in the uterine wall.

The great majority of mares spend most of the second stage of labour lying on their sides and over 95 per cent of them do so during the final stages of delivery. It is also noticeable that mares who are confined to looseboxes will often lie with their backs pressed against the partitioning wall or manger. This may help to fix the back while the abdominal muscles are contracting.

Second stage labour lasts for periods rang-

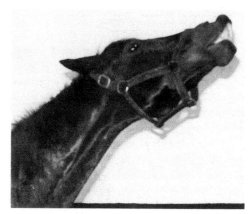

Figure 7.5 The flehmen posture. Head raised and upper lip retracted

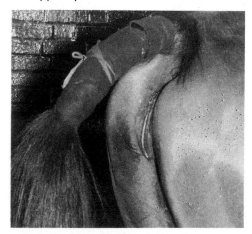

Figure 7.6 Lengthening of the vulva

Figure 7.7 Licking the coat is a sign of maternal instinct

ing from five to 60 minutes, with an average duration of 20 minutes. During this time the mare may repeatedly get up and down, changing from one side to the other (Figure 7.8). While straining usually occurs when she is lying flat, she may make some efforts when standing (Figure 7.9) or when lying on the brisket.

Between bouts of straining, the mare may lick or nibble at the straw around her, especially where the allantoic fluid of the placenta has fallen. While doing this she may retract her upper lip in the same way as in first stage labour. It is interesting to speculate whether the taste or smell of the fluid may act as a stimulant to maternal behaviour once the foal is born and if it may have had some significance in ancestral behavioural patterns by, for example, fixing the area in which the mare would remain until the foal was born

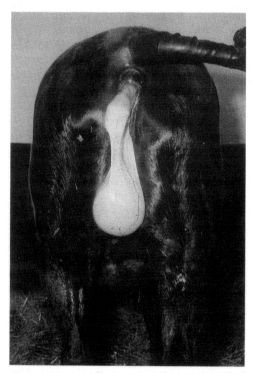

Figure 7.8 A small minority of mares may foal while still standing, or simply stand to alter their position

and capable of standing. Another interesting possibility is whether the mare can deliberately alter the way in which a foal is lying by altering her own position from side to side, or as sometimes happens, by rolling on her back during the course of delivery.

Third stage labour

The third stage of labour is concerned with the explusion of the afterbirth (placenta and amniotic membrane). At the end of second stage, the mare will normally remain lying down for anything up to threequarters of an hour. At first the umbilical cord remains intact; it is most important that this connection should not be severed artificially (see Chapter Eight). The cord breaks either when the mare gets to her feet or when the foal struggles in its attempts to stand. In either event it breaks at a natural point about 4 cm from the foal's navel (umbilicus).

The placenta separates from the wall of the uterus within an hour or two of final delivery. Once this separation has occurred, the afterbirth drops away and third stage is completed.

Management of the foaling mare

Up to this point we have been concerned solely with an explanation of the events as they occur during birth. It is now time to consider the significance of these events in relation to modern stud management.

Because of the great value of each individual Thoroughbred, we cannot leave these matters entirely to chance; it is true that 90 per cent of mares will foal without trouble whether or not attendants are there. In the remaining 10 per cent of births some assistance of a major or minor degree may be necessary.

Besides the considerable expense required to maintain a 24–hour watch on foaling mares, there is the additional burden of shelter which must be provided in areas of extreme weather conditions. The question of shelter is a particularly important one in view of the

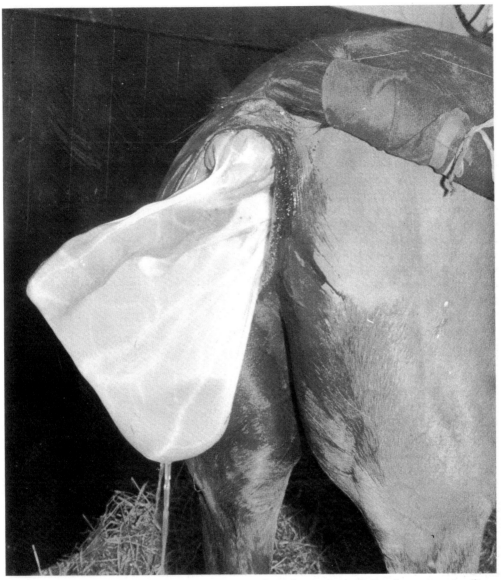

Figure 7.9 Mares may get up and down during foaling; here, the foal's forelegs are protruding, surrounded by the shiny membrane of the amnion

fact that Thoroughbreds are frequently foaled before the natural foaling season of April to July when the climate is more conducive to the event.

The essence of good management may be summed up in terms of watchfulness before and during birth, immediate provision of assistance when necessary to mare and/or foal, attention towards the feeding of the newborn and its protection against the elements.

Premonitory signs

Within about three weeks of foaling, the two mammary glands of the udder begin to enlarge and contain an increasing quantity of

71

Figures 7.10 to 7.13 After the foal has emerged (7.10) it may lie with its hind legs still in the mare's vagina (7.11). It is important that this close union (7.12) is not disturbed, as blood passes to the foal from the placenta (7.13) at this time

Figure 7.10

Figure 7.11

Figure 7.12

Figure 7.13

milk. Maiden mares may start to spring more abruptly and closer to the event than a mare that has previously had several foals. Beads of milk may form on the end of the teats within 24 to 48 hours of birth and dry into a wax-like substance which eventually drops off. This waxing-up is not an entirely reliable guide as to when mares are about to foal. Calcium levels in the milk rise at term (to 10 mmol/l) and give an early indication of when a mare is going to foal.

Many mares may run milk for several days before they foal. Hence, the first milk (colostrum) which contains the vital protective substances known as antibodies, is lost and the foal deprived of a substantial proportion of its resistance against infective diseases. There is much that still has to be learned regarding the causes of this loss of colostrum before birth. Udder development is linked, to an unknown extent, to the way mares are fed in the latter stages of pregnancy. Insufficient levels of protein in the diet will undoubtedly result in a poorly developed udder, while on the other hand steaming up might promote the loss of colostrum.

It is important to ensure that mares close to foaling should be subjected to a regular routine. Consistency in the timing of movements into and out of the paddock and contact with known attendants are factors which add to the stability of the environment and to the tranquillity which helps ensure a normal birth.

In the United Kingdom most mares are foaled (Figures 7.10 to 7.13) in specially appointed stalls. Looseboxes in which mares foal should be at least 4.24 m × 4.24 m and have suitable facilities for observing mares without the attendant having to enter the loosebox. This may be achived by windows placed on internal walls and/or television monitors.

The floor should be sloping to the drain and its surface roughened to prevent slipping. There should be a doorway placed so that people can enter and leave the loosebox from a neighbouring room or passageway in case of a veterinary problem to the mare or her foal.

Foaling boxes should be used as infrequently as practical in the context of the stud farm's number of mares due to foal. After each foaling they should be well cleansed and all straw removed so that a new mare may enter with fresh bedding and the minimal risk of infection being carried over from previous incumbents. Adequate lighting, electricity points and running water should be available for routine and emergency use.

When first stage signs become apparent, the 'sitting up man' calls the stud groom who has the sole responsibility of the 'midwife'. First stage signs may become apparent, then the mare may cool off to await another occasion for birth, some hours or even days later. These false alarms need not be regarded as abnormal although in certain instances, such as when they are associated with the running of milk, they are potentially harmful.

Duties during birth
When the placenta ruptures and the allantoic fluid escapes, the mare is said to have 'broken water'. In comparatively rare occurrences the membrane is so thickened by disease that it fails to rupture in the normal manner. In these cases it appears between the lips of the vulva as a red membrane, and should be artificially broken with the fingers or a pair of scissors.

The rupture of the placenta represents a critical point as far as management of the foaling mare is concerned, since it marks the beginning of the process of explusion of the foal. Once second stage has begun, it is essential to ascertain whether the foal is lying in the correct position. This can be done by inserting a hand into the vagina and feeling for the two forefeet and the muzzle of the foal (Figure 7.14).

The best time for this is while the mare is lying down and within about five minutes of the time that she has broken water. It should be remembered that during the last few months of pregnancy the foal has been lying in the uterus in the ventral position, that is,

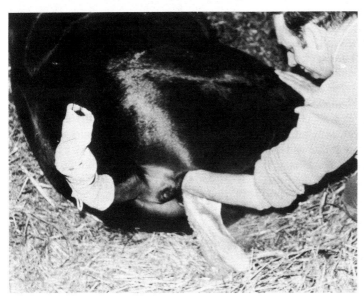

Figure 7.14 It is good policy to check that the foal is coming normally. Here, cleanliness is imperative

on its back, and that during the first stage and early second stage labour it rotates 180 degrees to lie in the normal dorsal position as described earlier. For this reason, if examined very early in the second stage the limbs may give the impression that the foal is lying upside down. Providing the muzzle can also be felt, this is unlikely to be the case and, anyway, the normal process of delivery will usually complete the transition from the ventral to the dorsal position.

It is customary for mares to break water when they are in a standing position, but having done so they will very soon lie down and the amnion should then appear between the lips of the vulva. If it does not, or if the mare ceases her efforts at straining, we must suspect that the normal passage of the foal is impeded, perhaps by a malalignment of its limbs or head. This condition (dystocia) must be corrected if the foal is to be born alive.

This is not the place to describe the various procedures necessary to solve the problems of dystocia; it is a subject which is best taught by working alongside experienced people.

If the mare has previously had a Caslick operation on her vulva, she should, at this time, be cut with a pair of straight scissors.

Once the amnion has appeared, the attendant should notice whether it has a normal, smooth shiny appearance through which can be seen a clear-coloured fluid. In certain instances this membrane may be thickened and/or the fluid it contains stained a brown colour. This denotes that the foal has been stressed in the later stages of development and may be unable to adjust properly once it is delivered.

Delivery should proceed steadily and it is by this estimation that we can judge whether or not help is required during second stage. It is helpful to note the time at which the water breaks so that at any given point of second stage one can judge accurately how long delivery has been proceeding. It is surprising how inaccurate a guess can be in this respect.

If a foal is positioned normally it is unnecessary to pull on the forelegs. As previously explained, the natural course of delivery is that the foal is pushed from behind by the combined forces of the uterine and abdominal muscles. The implication is, therefore, that any traction on the forelegs of the foal would introduce an unnatural force. Nevertheless it does appear helpful to apply gentle traction on one of the forelegs, especially if the foal's elbow becomes caught up on the mare's pelvis so that one foot is far in advance of the other (Figure 7.15).

Those attending the birth may have to get the mare to her feet if she is lying with her hindquarters so close to a wall that she cannot pass her foal. Apart from the actions described, it is preferable to watch second stage throughout its completion and interfere as little as possible.

The foal may be delivered retained completely in amnion and when it starts to breathe it will break this membrane by striking forward with its foreleg and arching its neck. It is only when the foal has been ill during the later stages of development or been seriously affected by the birth process that it is essential to break the amnion and raise the foal's head to make sure its nostrils are clear of the fluid when it starts to breathe.

Once the foal has been delivered, it will lie with its hind legs in the mare's vagina. Both mare and foal should, at this time, be left undisturbed. It is not advisable to sever the umbilical cord unless there are compelling reasons for doing so. Chief of these reasons is any evidence that the placenta or amnion are abnormal.

It is usual for those attending the birth to tie the amnion to the cord so that it hangs as a weight behind the mare. If the afterbirth is retained longer than a few hours, it is advisable to consult the veterinarian as to when it should be manually removed. If the afterbirth is left too long, it may set up infection in the uterus and perhaps even cause laminitis. Veterinarians differ as to the exact time they like to remove a retained afterbirth, but in general about 10 hours is the maximum allowed to elapse.

Once the afterbirth has come away, it is important to check that both horns are intact

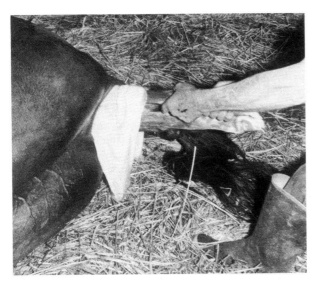

Figure 7.15 Some mares need help and the foal's forelegs may be grasped with both hands and pulled gently but firmly. Excessive or unnecessary traction should be avoided

and that a portion has not been left in the uterus (Figure 7.16). After the foal and its membranes have been expelled from the uterus the organ normally contracts quite rapidly. This process is often referred to as involution.

The mare may show signs of after-pains as her uterus contracts and especially before the afterbirth has been expelled. During these pains she may roll and sweat or look around at her flanks. There are a number of complications which can arise at this time and need a skilled diagnosis, so a close liaison between management and veterinarian is advisable.

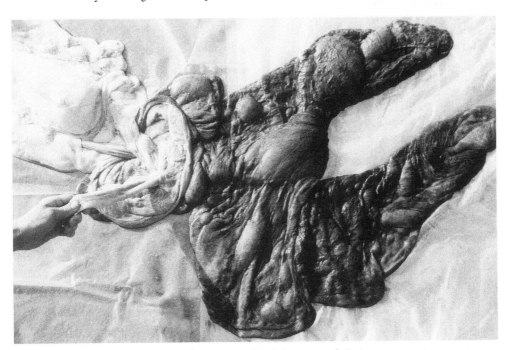

Figure 7.16 Checking the afterbirth to ensure both horns are intact

These complications include uterine haemorrhage.

Mares do not often bleed from the lining of the uterus after giving birth as may be the case in women. The difference is due to the fact that the placenta does not invade the uterine lining as it does in human beings. When it becomes detached the risk of bleeding is therefore less.

However, a quite common occurrence, especially in old mares, is for haemorrhage to take place internally from a branch of the artery supplying the uterus. This causes a great deal of pain and a haematoma (blood blister) forms between layers of the peritoneum (the lining of the abdomen which covers the walls and the organs). The mare may lose a substantial quantity of blood in this manner resulting in anaemia and pale membranes together with initial severe pain.

If the blood blister breaks through the peritoneum the mare bleeds to death as her blood escapes into the peritoneal cavity. If mares show evidence of severe pain following foaling veterinary assistance should be sought immediately.

A twitch should not be applied during the first three days after foaling as this will inevitably raise the blood pressure and may precipitate a haemorrhage.

Another complication of the after-foaling period is a prolapse of the uterus. In this case the organ turns itself inside out and protrudes through the vagina. In this event immediate professional attendance should be sought. While waiting for the arrival of the veterinarian, the mare should, if possible, be kept in the standing position and the organ held in a clean sheet to avoid it becoming damaged or contaminated. Massaging with warm soapy water may help. The longer the organ protrudes the more difficult it is to restore it to its normal position.

Successful replacement is usually followed by normal fertility although it may be necessary to rest the mare for a year rather than to attempt to get her to conceive in the months following prolapse.

CHAPTER EIGHT

THE NEWBORN FOAL

The act of birth delivers the foal into a very different way of life to the one it has experienced during the 11 months of development in the uterus of the mare. From the privacy of its own swimming pool, nurtured and nourished through the placenta, it moves into the hurly-burly of independent existence when it must feed, fend and forage for itself.

Period of adaptation

During the first few days of life the foal's body accomplishes the major changes of adjustment necessitated by the traumatic transition from intra- to extra-uterine existence. During this period any signs of failure to adapt will become apparent in terms of illness and disease.

There are two sides to the coin which require explanation: the way in which the foal responds to its surroundings and the associated physiological alterations in the body's functions. In the former category are the various behavioural patterns which can readily be observed by a casual onlooker and in the latter, the alterations in the organs and blood circulation.

The challenges of the environment

Survival of the newborn depends on successful adjustment; at no other period of life is the body expected to adapt to changes so dramatic, so profound and so sudden as those at the time of birth.

The challenges of the new surroundings include the immediate need to breathe air for the first time, to overcome the effects of gravity in standing, to keep the body temperature within normal limits despite the relatively low air temperature surrounding it and to evacuate waste material by defecation and urination.

These challenges can, of course, be tempered in minor ways by various methods of management. For example, foaling is often arranged in the comparative warmth of a loosebox, assistance may be provided with feeding and measures taken to facilitate evacuation of the first dung (meconium).

In general, however, a foal born normally and which has undergone a healthy development during foetal life will have no difficulty in adjusting and overcoming the challenges of its new surroundings.

Behavioural patterns

Essential information on the health and wellbeing of the foal is provided by the way it behaves. Those with experience can generally judge from its reactions whether the process of adjustment is normal or if there is cause for concern.

The patterns of behaviour are fairly stereotyped and for this reason they can be presented in the sequence in which they appear from the moment final delivery is complete.

The position of final delivery leaves the foal with its hind legs in the vagina of the mare and the cord intact (Figure 8.1). When its chest is passing through the birth canal the

Figure 8.1 The position of final delivery leaves the foal with its hind legs in the vagina of the mare and the umbilical cord still intact

foal may gasp (a breathing movement in which air is sharply drawn into the air passages through the mouth while the head and neck are arched) but regular breathing movements (a respiratory rhythm) are established within 30 seconds to a minute of final delivery.

As breathing begins so the lungs are expanded and filled with air for the first time. In consequence the concentration of oxygen in the bloodstream rises enormously and this enables the foal to exert the energy necessary for moving and standing in the world outside the uterus (Figure 8.2); inside the mare it had little or no need for any such activity.

Within two or three minutes the foal raises its head and then begins to right itself onto its brisket. This causes a reflex action – the hind limbs withdraw from the vagina so that they are underneath the foal's body in the preliminary position for getting up and standing.

Within five minutes of delivery the sense of suck develops and the foal shows typical sucking movements of the tongue. The sense of sight and hearing are also active, although at this stage the foal may not interpret all visual and auditory stimuli which it receives. It may, however, whinny and move its ears towards any sound.

Another feature is the way the foal uses its muscles for shivering. This is part of the mechanism for keeping its body temperature within normal limits.

As the foal becomes progressively stronger so it increases its efforts to stand. In the first instance it may have difficulty in getting to the starting position necessary for raising its body; that is, with the forelegs stretched out in front and the hind legs drawn underneath its body.

Its early struggles place an increasing tension on the umbilical cord (Figure 8.3) and eventually this ruptures at a point about 4 cm from the umbilicus. This is a natural breaking point and there is no need to sever the cord artificially or, apart from exceptional circum-

Figure 8.2 The amnion may remain intact until the foal is completely delivered when it breaks out of the membrane as it starts to breathe

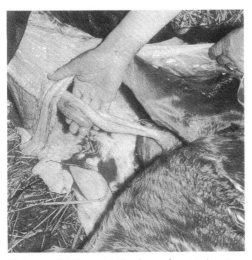

Figure 8.3 The umbilical cord contains two arteries and a vein. The vein is the large vessel close to the man's fingertips

stances, to tie it. Even if a small amount of haemorrhage occurs from the stump after rupture it is generally sufficient to pinch the vessels with two fingers for a matter of a minute or so and the bleeding will cease.

Many people still use iodine to treat the umbilical stump after the cord has separated. Others use antibiotic or antiseptic powder. However, the most important consideration is that the cord should be left and not severed artificially. Natural separation seals the stump more effectively than can be achieved with artificial severance with scissors or with any preparation to the outside.

Another way the cord ruptures naturally is by the mare rising to her feet (Figure 8.4). Most mares lie many minutes after they have delivered their foal and it is important to disturb them as little as possible at this period. It

79

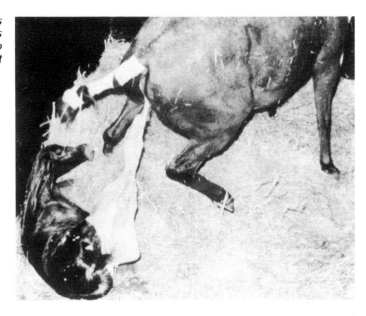

Figure 8.4 In some cases the umbilical cord is broken as the mare rises to her feet

has been shown that early severance of the cord may deprive the foal of as much as a third of its blood volume compared with severance in a natural manner some minutes after delivery (Figure 8.5). If the foal is so deprived then there may be few or no drastic consequences, but on the other hand the foal will suffer anaemia and disturbances in its circulation as a consequence of leaving part of its blood in the placenta. This may be of no consequence to a strong, healthy foal but may seriously affect one that has been weakened by illness while in the uterus or damaged by the birth process (see Chapter Nine).

After several unsuccessful attempts a foal will eventually gain the standing position about 50 minutes after delivery (Figure 8.6). The foal's ability to get to its feet for the first time gives us an overall indication of its health and wellbeing (Figure 8.7); any individual which has failed to stand within two hours of birth must be regarded as abnormal and possibly in need of veterinary attention.

Once on its feet a foal soon develops an affinity towards the mare and within about two hours of birth should have found the udder and sucked for the first time. In search for the teats a foal follows a well-defined pat-tern of behaviour. Contact with the mare's body usually begins in the forepart around the brisket and front legs and thence along the flanks to the stifle, at which the foal may suck quite vigorously for a time (Figure 8.8). Eventually it turns its attention to the region of the udder and then attaches itself to one of the two teats (Figure 8.9). Of course progress is not continuous and the foal may wander around the box and even suck at the walls or manger before eventually reaching the cor-rect position. The instinct for direction appears to be stimulated by shadow so that the foal is attracted by areas of darkness such as exist between the mare's hind legs.

The presence of attendants or other factors in the environment may disturb the mare and cause her to walk away from her foal, so delaying the time when the first suck is taken. By contrast, attendants may hold the mare and guide the foal directly to the udder which in many cases speeds up the process.

Young mares may be ticklish and instead of resting one hind leg to expose the udder, they kick or otherwise jostle their foals as they sniff round the mammary region. In these cases it may be helpful to hold the mare and perhaps raise one of her forelegs; where a

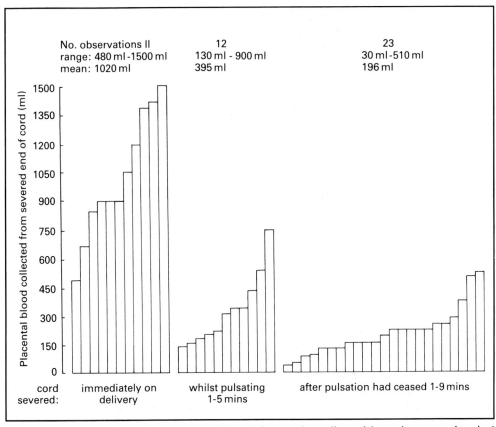

Figure 8.5 The chart shows the amount of blood that can be collected from the severed end of the umbilical cord at varying times after delivery is complete

Figure 8.6 Foals find it difficult to stand for the first time but once in the standing position they become increasingly strong until at three or four hours old they are able to run with their mother

81

Figure 8.7 The wellbeing of foals can be judged by the way they lie and the speed with which they can get up and suck

Figure 8.8 Before reaching the mare's udder the foal usually makes unsuccessful attempts to find it

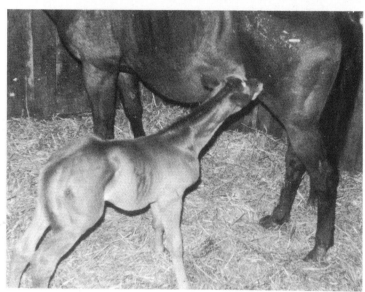

mare is particularly resentful of her foal it may be necessary to administer a tranquillising drug. It is not advisable to apply a twitch to the mare since this may raise her blood pressure and thereby increase the risk of post-foaling haemorrhage.

Once a foal has sucked for the first time it will seek the mare's udder at regular intervals and with increasing sureness (Figure 8.10). Bouts of sucking become longer and less frequent as the foal's age increases.

One of the best methods of observing the wellbeing of a young foal is to cause it to get to its feet; it should rise without difficulty and suck without undue delay. If it does not get up with ease and/or shows no interest in sucking we must suspect that all is not well.

Maternal instincts

The mare recognises her foal by its taste and

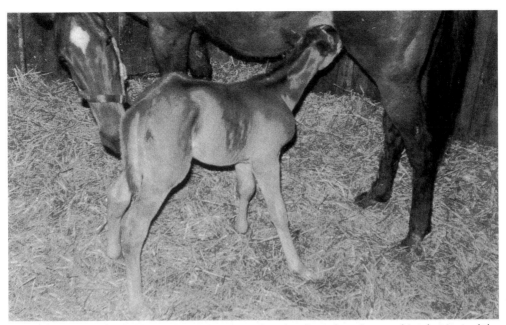

Figure 8.9 Within two hours after birth, the foal has developed mother-seeking habits and the mare has established her maternal instincts

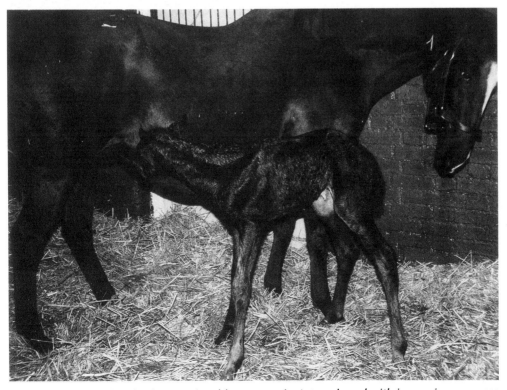

Figure 8.10 The foal seeks the mare's udders at regular intervals and with increasing sureness

smell. The foal's coat is saturated with amniotic fluid and it is contact with this which stimulates maternal instinct and provides the mare with a method of distinguishing her own foal from others. When a mare has recognised her foal, which normally she does within minutes of its being born, she will accept no other, unless there are special circumstances, e.g., where an orphan foal is introduced to a foster mother.

Fostering

An orphan foal is the result of a mare dying sometime soon after foaling or while she is suckling her foal. Alternatively, the mare may not have, or may lose, sufficient mammary development and milk production to maintain sufficient supply for her foal; or she may reject her foal and attack it so that the pair have to be separated.

In all these circumstances it may be necessary to foster the foal onto another mare. The need for fostering is proportional to the age of the foal and it is more usual to foster a foal under one month of age than when it is older.

In order to understand fostering one must understand the way bonding between the foal and mare develops from the moment the foal is born.

As far as the foal is concerned bonding depends largely upon the position of the udder, and the smell and taste of milk. A strong healthy foal possesses an almost irresistible drive to suck at the udder containing natural milk. It is only persistent and antagonistic attitudes on the part of the mare that will override the foal's motivation to suck. If the foal becomes frightened by being kicked it may become hesitant and reluctant to approach the udder.

Bonding of mare to foal is a more complicated and stronger union. A foal will suck from any udder, but a mare, once she has tasted the fluids around the foetal foal and smelt its skin, will rapidly come to recognise and accept only that particular foal. This recognition is accompanied by antagonism towards any other foal.

When we attempt to foster an orphan foal upon a foster mare, we have to take note of these behavioural traits that are instinctive and inborn. We have to take measures to overcome the foster mare's natural antagonism by the use of ruses such as confusing her pattern of recognition. This may be achieved by placing a high smelling ointment in her nostril and/or clothing the foal in the skin or amnion of the foster mare's foal, if these are available.

Nowadays, however, the use of tranquillising drugs together with other measures enable the foal to suck regularly from the mare's udder without her being able to retaliate. This may be achieved by restraining the mare in a loosebox alongside an opening through which the foal can reach the udder from an adjoining box.

Repeated enforced suckling under these conditions may bring the mare to acceptance of the orphan foal over a period of 24 to 48 hours. Once a successful fostering has been achieved, the mare will become firmly bonded to the new foal.

Establishing a steady state

The body is said to be in a steady state when its various parts function at a particular level and do not alter within certain small and well-defined limits. In general terms this means the limits of normality. For example we recognise normality through such indicators as the temperature, the rate of breathing, heart rate and so on; and internally by means of laboratory tests which provide information about the concentration of sugar, minerals, salts, acids of the blood, etc.

Whereas the foetus possesses a steady state at a certain level, the newborn foal has to establish one at a much higher level of activity. It achieves this state within 12 or 24 hours of birth and the intervening period must therefore be regarded as one of transition. Foals that do not successfully achieve this transition display signs of illness which are characterised by disturbances in their behavioural patterns.

Two particular functions by which the newborn steady state may be recognised are standing and sucking. There are others; for example the foal normally has no difficulty in maintaining its rectal temperature between 37.3 °C and 38.3 °C.

Although a foal breathes very rapidly in the first half hour after birth the rate falls so that once the foal has sucked for the first time the number of respirations is in the range of 30 to 40 per minute.

Heart rate can be felt quite easily on the left side of the foal's chest; at birth the beat is normally in the region of 80 per minute, rising to 140 per minute when the foal tries to get to its feet and returning to about 100 beats per minute by the time the foal is a day old. Of course, when both breathing and heart rates are measured we must be careful to distinguish those recorded while the foal is at rest from those recorded after exertion.

During the first 12 hours of life profound changes occur in the composition of the foal's blood. These are complicated and necessarily lie in the province of the veterinarian so only one of great practical importance need be mentioned. This is the increasing concentration of protein substances known as immunoglobulins (Ig) (antibodies). When the foal is born it lacks these substances and they are provided in the colostrum or first milk. The foal sucks for the first time at about age two hours and the protective substances pass from the milk into the foal's bloodstream after being absorbed through the stomach lining, thereby giving the foal a passive immunity (i.e. an immunity based on protective substances supplied from outside, in this case the mare, in contrast to active immunity in which the individual itself develops antibodies). The most obvious example of active immunity is that stimulated by vaccination.

There are a number of situations in which this passive immunity fails to develop (failure of immune passive transfer) and the foal has a reduced resistance to infection. This may happen if the colostrum is deficient in antibody because the mare has run milk prior to foaling. It may be that the foal does not receive sufficient quantity of colostrum or that it fails to absorb antibodies.

The antibodies are only absorbed from the lining of the intestines up to age about 24 hours and after this they will not be available to the foal however high the concentrations of antibody in the colostrum.

If it is suspected that the colostrum of the mare has been lost because she has run milk, donor colostrum may be given. On Thoroughbred stud farms small quantities of colostrum are taken from mares with surplus quantities and stored deep frozen for this purpose. The quantity that is necessary for such circumstances is about 400 ml. This must be administered from a bottle or via a stomach tube inserted by a veterinarian before the foal has sucked any other milk and before it is age 12 hours.

If there has been failure of passive transfer a condition that can be diagnosed only by measuring the Ig in the blood at age 24 to 48 hours, levels may be supplemented by intravenous serum therapy under veterinary supervision.

An important aspect of the steady state is the ability to pass meconium. This is the dung stored during foetal life as green, black or brown pellets. Except in abnormal circumstances it is not evacuated until after the foal is born, when it must be voided before the first milk can pass along the gut in the normal manner. All the meconium is usually expelled by the time the foal is two days old. Failure to pass meconium in the usual manner is associated with signs of colic.

Foals suffering from meconium retention can be helped with an enema of liquid paraffin (Figure 8.11). For this it is customary to use a can or syringe attached to a rubber tube. The tube, which should be soft and with the end well blunted, should be between 10 mm and 25 mm in diameter. The blunted end should be inserted gently into the rectum. It is inadvisable to administer large quantities of fluid at one time. As a rough

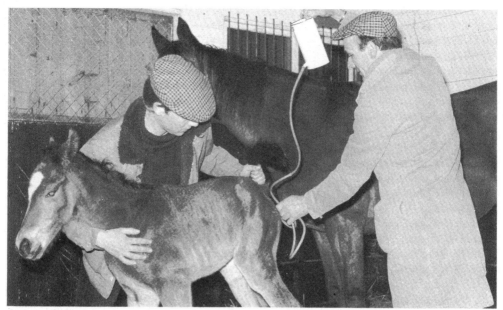

Figure 8.11 Enemas of soap and water or liquid paraffin can be administered when the foal is about eight hours old and repeated, if necessary, several hours later

guide about 50 ml can be used when the foal is about eight hours old and it may be useful to repeat the enemas every three or four hours until the meconium has passed and the yellowish 'milk dung' appears. Special enema packs available for human use may now be employed for foals.

Handling the young foal

In all circumstances young foals should be handled with care. Every effort should be taken to avoid rough handling in the early hours after birth when mare and foal are establishing a bond.

Young foals should be caught and handled with one hand placed in front and one hand behind (Figures 8.12 and 8.13). They should never be lifted with the hand underneath the chest as this will put pressure on the rib cage and possibly displace or even fracture a rib (Figure 8.14).

A headcollar may be placed on the foal when it is about one day old and it should be taught to lead at an early age. Initially a canvas headcollar may be used and later replaced by a leather one. Some mares may resent or even attack their foals if they smell a soiled headcollar so it is important to fit a clean collar which does not smell of other horses (Figure 8.15).

Newborn foals should be housed in stables as free from dust as possible, well ventilated and sufficiently insulated to prevent undue heat loss. It is not necessary to raise the air temperature above 4.3 °C. Normal foals can withstand zero temperatures quite easily, but it is a different matter if a foal is sick. They may then require special measures.

On establishments where many foals are born each year it may be necessary to give antibiotic injections during the first few days of life, to supplement the foal's natural resistance to infection.

Iron is also important if a foal has been

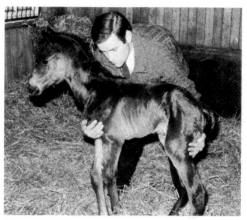

Figure 8.12 The correct way to handle a new-born foal . . .

Figure 8.14 The incorrect way to handle a newborn foal

Figure 8.13 . . . and to lay it on the ground

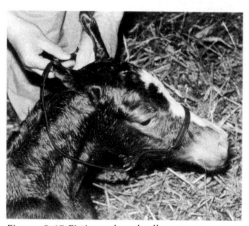

Figure 8.15 Fitting a headcollar

deprived of its placenta transfusion of blood, such as when the mare foals in a standing position or when the cord is severed immediately after delivery.

In addition, foals that are born early in the year so that they have to spend much of their time confined to a box will benefit from iron and vitamin injections.

CHAPTER NINE

THE FOAL'S STRUGGLE FOR SURVIVAL

The first four days of the foal's life represent a period of transition between intra- and extra-uterine life. If conditions in this transitory period become disturbed, for one reason or another, the foal may suffer illness or disease.

Prematurity and immaturity

During pregnancy the foetus develops to a state of maturity where it can adapt to, and successfully survive in, the environment outside the uterus. As previously explained, if birth occurs before 300 days gestation, the organs of the body are so underdeveloped

that the foal has little chance of survival and it is then described as non-viable; it is usual to describe such a birth as being an abortion. Foals born to a gestation of average length are said to be full-term (Figure 9.1).

A premature foal results when pregnancy falls short of the average duration of 340 days. The description of immaturity is frequently given to weak foals that are unable to stand for many hours or even days after birth; while capable of sucking from a bottle or when held under the mare, they have an underdeveloped suck reflex when compared with normal foals.

There is really no valid distinction between the states of prematurity and immaturity since

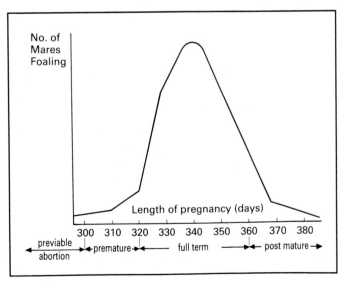

Figure 9.1 The normal length of pregnancy is 340 days. A foal is termed premature if the gestation period is less than 320 days. Prior to 300 days the foal is unlikely to survive and is said to be in a previable state. Although prolonged pregnancies are common, they cannot be titled 'post mature' until 360 days

the clinical signs are indistinguishable. Without skilled nursing many of these foals fail to survive the first three days of life.

A foal born at, say, 320 days, is usually described as being 20 days premature, but this definition is somewhat unsatisfactory as normal pregnancies last between 320 to 360 days. Therefore, as far as length is concerned, it is strictly correct to use only the 320th day as a line of demarcation between maturity and prematurity. The position is complicated by the fact that full-term foals may appear weak, while those born before time may be strong and healthy.

Some pregnancies may last beyond 360 days and in these cases we can expect a higher than average number of sick foals as a result.

Prolonged pregnancies are not, however, associated with foals that grow to an unusual size. More often the reverse is true, that is, the foetus is small and undernourished.

The birth-weight of the foal provides some indication of maturity. First foals usually weigh less than those foals produced by mares that have previously had a foal. In the normal course of events a wide spread of weights is found. The average in a Thoroughbred is about 48 kg for a first foal and 50 kg for subsequent foals, although the range varies considerably from 45 kg to 68 kg; colts generally weigh slightly more than fillies.

Thoroughbred foals weighing less than 40 kg at birth should be regarded as abnormally small. If they are the result of a pregnancy many days under 340 they may also be regarded as premature, irrespective of their capacity to establish normal behavioural patterns.

A more important consideration than the length of pregnancy *per se* is probably the type of development the foal has undergone while in the uterus.

Abnormal development within the uterus

There are many factors which may interfere with the normal development of the foetus and for our purposes they can be arranged in four groups (Figure 9.2). This is not the place

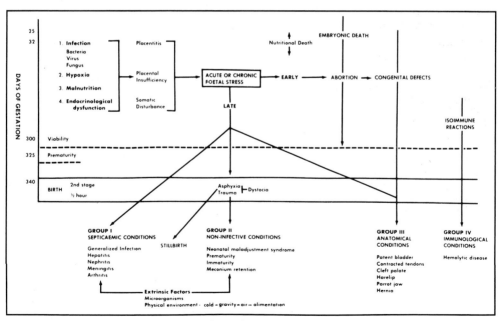

Figure 9.2 Summary of the factors which predispose to diseases of foals in the first four days of life following birth. Four groups of conditions are recognised

to consider these in detail because they lie mainly in the province of veterinarians, but a number of established principles should be mentioned. First of all, any deterioration in the environment will cause the foetus what we call 'stress'.

Stress can be the result of a disturbance in the normal placenta-maternal relationship. The foetus obtains nourishment from the mother through the close contact of the placenta with the wall of the maternal uterus. Interference with this normally harmonious arrangement may be caused by infective agents, such as bacteria or fungi, which enter the uterus at the time of foaling or mating, or are carried there in the bloodstream of the mare.

Infection may destroy large areas of the placenta, thereby cutting down effective contact with the uterus. Of course, infective agents may also enter the body of the foetus, so that when it is delivered it will already be suffering from an infective disease.

Perhaps the most common cause of stress to the foetus is asphyxia. Asphyxia (suffocation) is a process which deprives the body of oxygen and allows carbon dioxide to accumulate. Normally oxygen is inhaled into the lungs where it can easily pass into the bloodstream and carbon dioxide passes in the reverse direction. In the foetus the same process occurs without the use of the lungs because their function is taken over by the placenta. Although the foetus does not possess high concentrations of oxygen, its activity is such that it does not require large quantities of gas, while carbon dioxide is also eliminated through the placenta and never rises to toxic proportions in the foetal organs and tissues.

If, however, the blood supply to the uterus is reduced, the foetus may not receive sufficient oxygen or be able to get rid of its carbon dioxide. We do not know the exact circumstances in which this happens but the risks are very real; for example, even a change in the mare's position from standing to recumbency, or from one side to another, may affect the amount of blood being transported through the uterine wall. If a mare became cast against the wall of her stall she might inadvertently injure the foetus she was carrying by indirectly depriving it of oxygen.

Of course, in most cases any reduction in blood flow to the mare's uterus is temporary and the foetus comes to no harm; but to what extent modern management of broodmares may increase the hazards is something which only future research can establish. Transporting mares over long distances and interfering with their natural exercise may indirectly interfere with the foetal environment.

Other factors, besides infection, may reduce the placenta's efficiency and increase the risk of foetal asphyxia. Developmental faults may arise in the foetal circulation leading to insufficient exchange of gases by way of the blood circulating through the cord and placenta. If the asphyxia is acute and sustained, it will produce fatal results just as if we were to hold a pillow over someone's face. In practical terms, this means that we will be faced with an abortion (before 300 days' gestation) or with a stillborn foal (300 days or more). In many cases, however, the asphyxia is limited and its degree insufficient to cause death. The process may then cause damage to the foetal organs (especially the brain, heart and lungs) or, alternatively, may damage the placenta and thus further reduce its efficiency.

The net consequence of this damage is a check in foetal growth and development so that eventually the foal is born in a damaged state. This means the foal has a below-average chance of survival in the extra-uterine environment.

It should be made clear that asphyxia may occur at any time during pregnancy. A commonly encountered sequence might go something like this: a mare gets cast in her box after eight months of gestation and the blood supply to the uterus is temporarily disturbed so the foetus is subjected to a mild form of asphyxia which produces considerable stress. The episode being limited, the foetus survives and continues its development for a further three months. On the 340th day of gestation a weak foal is born which presents clinical signs of prematurity.

The hazards of birth

Normally, birth imposes a certain amount of asphyxial stress on the foetus as it passes through the birth canal, but the degree is not sufficient to cause any damage to the body tissues. In certain instances, however, the stress becomes unusually severe and the newborn foal suffers in consequence. For example, the cord may be compressed between the foal's body and the hard brim of the mare's pelvis. This is particularly likely to happen if the cord is prolapsed so that a loop comes in front of the umbilicus instead, as is normally the case, behind it. Compression of the cord so that blood cannot circulate between the foal's body and the placenta is most serious if it occurs before the chest has been delivered and the foal is able to use its lungs as the organs of respiration.

Another hazard of birth is that the placenta becomes separated from the uterus or that contractions of the uterus produce profound disturbances in blood flow to the foetus as it passes through the birth canal. As far as the foal is concerned, there is no difference in the results of asphyxia – however it is caused.

Finally, while considering birth, we must not forget the vulnerability of the chest which is exposed to compression on its journey through the maternal pelvis. The foal's chest is keel-shaped and the heart is extremely vulnerable to bruising and to pressure which may interfere with its normal function once the foal is born.

The newborn foal

At this point we must return to the newborn foal. From the description so far it should be clear that in certain circumstances the foal is born in a damaged state. The damage may be the result of malnutrition so that the various organs and muscles are depleted of their normal reserves of energy-producing substances, such as the carbohydrate glycogen. Alternatively, the tissues and cells of the body may have been selectively injured. For example, the brain cells are very vulnerable to damage from lack of oxygen. The damage usually takes the form of small haemorrhages among the nerve cells, with perhaps some seepage of fluid so that small areas of the brain become waterlogged. It should be realised that such a vital mechanism as the brain need be only slightly damaged to produce marked effects on the behaviour of the foal (Figure 9.3).

Convulsions, loss of the suck reflex or inability to get up or recognise the dam, are all signs of cerebral damage. Signs of irritability (wandering) or coma (dummy behaviour), grinding the teeth and blindness are other manifestations.

Haemorrhage and leakage of fluid can alternately occur and resolve in different parts of the brain, which explains why many newborn foals show a variety of symptoms depending on which area of the brain is affected; it is also the reason some foals may be normal after birth and then start to exhibit symptoms when they are several hours old.

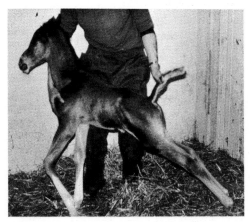

Figure 9.3 Foals with brain damage may convulse or suffer from increased extensor tone in their muscles. Note foal standing with head pulled back and hind limbs stiffly behind it

Asphyxia also produces an outpouring of lactic acid in the bloodstream and, in consequence, there is a marked increase in the acidity of the blood, which in turn reduces the efficiency of the lungs and heart. The blood will not then receive adequate amounts of oxygen nor will carbon dioxide be excreted in sufficient quantities to rid the body of this potentially poisonous gas. Cardiac failure adds to the complications so that the original asphyxia is superimposed by a chronic state consisting of a vicious circle in which lack of oxygen leads to reduced capacity of the heart and lungs, which in turn produces oxygen deficiency.

Meconium retention

Meconium is dung which the foetus stores in pellet form within the caecum, colon and rectum. The material is not voided until after the foal is born and then it must be evacuated during the first few days before colostrum can pass through the entire length of the gut. In some cases the meconium is retained, either because it becomes lodged in the rectum in a large mass close to the pelvic outlet or else the bowel itself becomes paralysed. In the latter event the condition is rather more troublesome and the foal suffers quite severe bouts of colic due to accumulating gas.

The foal shows signs of rolling, lying in uncomfortable positions (Figure 9.4), squatting and straining and perhaps going off suck. Usually, with the help of enemas and lubricants the meconium is successfully evacuated and the first milk passed. At this point the foal usually recovers and the signs of colic disappear.

Similar signs, however, may be exhibited by foals which have suffered from a ruptured bladder during the birth process. In these cases, urine escapes from the bladder into the abdominal cavity. Whereas perhaps one in ten foals may show evidence of meconium retention, fewer than one in 500 suffer from a ruptured bladder. In dealing with a case of meconium retention, the veterinarian will, however, bear in mind the possibility that he may be dealing with the rarer condition.

Infections or septicaemias

The possibility of infective agents such as bacteria and fungi being present in the foal's body at birth has already been mentioned. In addition, certain viruses which attack the foetus may cause illness in the newborn; the herpesvirus is an example.

After birth, infection may also enter the body through the mouth or the umbilicus. The signs exhibited by the foal will depend on the site of infection. For example, if the brain is involved (meningitis), the signs may

Figure 9.4 Foals suffering from meconium retention show signs of colic and roll or lie in awkward positions

be somewhat similar to those shown by foals that have suffered from an hypoxic crisis (i.e. convulsions and interference with normal behavioural patterns). Infection of the kidney (nephritis) may also cause convulsions but, more typically, the foal becomes comatosed (sleepy foal disease) and gradually loses its strength and power of suck. Infection of the liver will also produce coma and perhaps convulsions; illustrating how diverse causes may result in the same signs and symptoms from the patient.

Infection of the lungs (pneumonia), the peritoneum (peritonitis), or the joints (joint or navel ill) are other examples of predicted sites of infection which bacteria enter when the foal's powers of resistance are low. Resistance to infection is, in fact, the property of a system which includes:

1. The white cells of the blood.
2. The specific protection afforded by the antibodies of the colostrum. The antibodies are protective substances which are present in the mare's bloodstream and which become concentrated in the colostrum at the time of the birth of her foal. The foal takes colostrum into its stomach during the first few sucking bouts of its life and the antibodies are absorbed into its bloodstream. When the foal is about 24 to 36 hours old, the lining of the stomach and intestines ceases to allow the passage of the antibodies into the bloodstream so that the passive transference of immunity from the mare to her foal cannot continue.

Foals may fail to acquire sufficient antibodies if a mare runs milk prior to birth, or for some reason fails to develop a normal udder. In addition, the foal may not always be able to absorb the protective substances even though it has received them into its stomach.

Hemolytic disease

Hemolytic disease is an example of where, under special circumstances, natural mechanisms can have harmful effects. In this case, the foetus invokes an immune response from the mare, probably the result of a few red cells passing from the placenta into the mare's bloodstream. Normally, this happening would not provoke any response, but in rare instances the mare produces protective substances or antibodies against her own foal's red cells.

At the time of birth (parturition) these substances are concentrated into the colostrum and, after the foal has sucked, they pass into the foal's bloodstream. Here they destroy its red cells, causing a severe anaemia which, if not treated, is fatal.

Foals suffering from hemolytic disease may be recognised by the yellow colouration of their eyes and membranes of the mouth, the passing of red-stained urine, a fast heart rate and rapid breathing – especially on exertion.

Where there is reason to suspect a mare is going to have a foal subject to the disease (because she has had an affected foal before), tests can help. The mare's blood or colostrum is cross-matched with the foal's blood after birth and if the results are positive the disease is prevented by muzzling the foal for 36 hours. By this time the antibodies can no longer cross from the foal's gut into its bloodstream. During the time the foal is muzzled, it should be fed artificial milk or, ideally, colostrum from another mare.

Congenital abnormalities

In the intricate development and growth of the organs during foetal life, it is perhaps remarkable that in the great majority of cases the process is completed without any defects. There are, however, a number of well-recognised congenital (present at birth) defects. For example, button eyes, in which the eyeball is so small as to be virtually nonexistent, may occur on one or both sides; deformities of the head include twisted jaw (Figure 9.5) and cleft palate; the limbs may be unable to extend due to the flexor tendons being contracted (Figure 9.6). The latter condition may affect one or both forelegs as

Figure 9.5 Congenital abnormalities of the head include deformed upper jaw; as here, twisted to the left

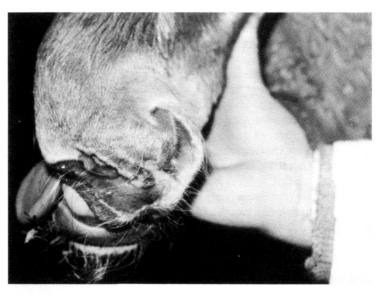

Figure 9.6 Birth defects of the limbs include contracted flexor tendons

well as the hind limbs. The foetal foal develops lying on its back or side with its legs flexed. The ligaments allow a degree of flexion of the joints which is exaggerated partly as a precaution against the limbs accidently causing damage to the mare. However, as full-term approaches these structures become firmer, and because of the pliability of the limbs during foetal development they may be shaped at odd angles which is apparent when the foal is delivered. Faulty development of the bladder and developmental failure of the gut, in which part of the colon or rectum is missing, may also be observed at this stage in newborn foals.

The causes of these abnormalities are generally unknown, but probably include such factors as:

a) viral infection and drugs received by the mare during the first few weeks of pregnancy at a time when the organs are being formed;

b) nutritional influences;

c) inheritance.

Nursing of sick foals

Treatment of the illness of newborn foals is primarily the responsibility of veterinarians.

But general nursing and handling (Figure 9.7) is a most important aspect and, in contrast, the prime concern of stud staff.

By nursing, we mean the measures which must be enforced to provide the foal with the necessary help for survival while therapeutic measures such as antibiotics and fluid therapy may be allowed time to act.

The administration of oxygen is an emergency measure which is necessary immediately after birth if the foal does not establish a respiratory rhythm in the normal manner. An oxygen cylinder is a must among the paediatric equipment kept at a stud farm. Artificial respiration can be administered through a rubber tube inserted into one nostril while closing the opposite nostril and mouth with the hand (Figure 9.8). The foal's chest can then be inflated and the nostril released at the appropriate moment when the natural recoil of the chest produces expiration. By this method alternate inflation and deflation may be achieved without difficulty. There are, in addition, specially developed masks and instruments which can produce a similar effect. Whatever method is used care must be taken not to overinflate the chest and the process should be maintained at the rate of about 20 to 30 movements per minute for as long as the foal does not breathe. This type of resuscitation is likely to be successful only if the heart is beating.

Oxygen may also be administered to a convulsing foal, although in many cases the

Figure 9.7 This sequence shows the correct technique for handling a sick foal

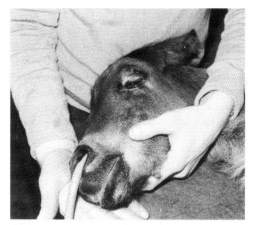

Figure 9.8 Artificial respiration, using a rubber tube inserted into the foal's nostrils

effects of oxygen therapy may be limited by the fact that the lungs cannot function in such a way as to make use of the additional gas provided.

Handling of foals, especially those which are sick, must at all times be carried out with care and using the correct technique.

The foal's body temperature may be judged by rectal temperature (Figure 9.9) and it is important to attempt to keep this within the normal range (37.3 °C to 38.3 °C). Foals suffering from convulsions tend to have ele-

vated rectal temperatures, but those that are weak or in a coma may fall towards room temperature. In the former event, it is necessary to avoid placing the foal in an overheated atmosphere, but in the latter case, it is essentail to raise artificially the surrounding air temperature. This may be done by heat lamps, electric fires, hot air blowers, electric blankets and/or placing some form of coat over the foal (Figures 9.10 and 9.11). In many cases where the foal is quite incapable of maintaining its own body temperature, it may be necessary to raise the surrounding

Figure 9.10 A coat placed over the foal helps maintain the correct body temperature; a soft covering below protects the foal's eyes from strain

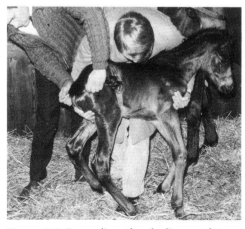

Figure 9.9 Recording the foal's rectal temperature. The thermometer is inserted gently into the rectum to a distance of approximately 75 mm

Figure 9.11 Soft material coverings reduce the risk of injury

temperature to as high as 26.5 °C. Frequent recordings of the rectal temperature must be taken to ensure that the foal becomes neither overheated or underheated.

Foals that are unable to stand will benefit from having some soft material placed under them to reduce the risk of injury to the eyes and the development of bed-sores, which may be brought about by straw or hard stable floors. It may be essential to have an attendant sitting with the foal to help it in attempts to stand and to restrain it from throwing itself about in vain efforts to get upright. These measures can be supplemented by various sedatives and anticonvulsant drugs administered by the veterinarian.

Regular feeds can be given by bottle if the suck reflex is present. If it is not then feeding by stomach tube is necessary (Figure 9.12).

Figure 9.12 Passing the stomach tube

Mare's milk should be provided in preference, but artificial milk is effective where the natural product is not available. The young foal requires fluid even more than nourishment and the quantities of fluid given in each 24 hours should be split into hourly feeds if possible. It is advisable to include some liquid paraffin emulsion in the feed (Figure 9.13) and also be scrupulously clean with all utensils. The feed must be administered at blood heat and certainly not above 37.8 °C.

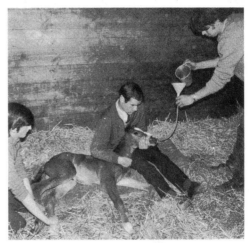

Figure 9.13 Administering milk to the foal

Quietness and patience are essential in the nursing of sick foals, especially where there is brain damage and the foal is incoordinated in its behaviour and subject to irritability which may herald the onset of convulsions. It should also be remembered that the foal's heart will be under great strain and that any excess struggling may make the difference between success and failure.

CHAPTER TEN

SCHOOLING FOR INDEPENDENCE

Once the foal is born and established in its new environment, the risks are considerably fewer, although there may be certain problems which still remain to be overcome if the breeder is to see a healthy and sound weanling.

Growth and development

The terms 'growth' and 'development' are really synonymous. There is perhaps room for distinction in that growth is concerned with size, and development with the conformation of the limbs, joints, etc.

The period of greatest intensity of growth is the first three months after birth. The rate slows down during the following three months and also again in the next six months. Earlier work by Colonel Denis Green of the Department of Animal Husbandry, Royal Veterinary College, London, found that gains in height and girth measurement during the first three months of life were only slightly less than the total increase during the following nine months. In this particular study, the average height at birth exceeded the girth but by approximately age six months the two measurements were equal and at 12 months the girth was greater than the height.

There have been a number of attempts to relate various body measurements to racing performance, including measurements of height, girth and distance from hip to hock. This and other systems have been concerned

with static measures and perhaps greater light could be thrown on the situation by those of function (such as length of stride related to age, height, etc.). There is obviously further scope for investigation of these aspects using modern techniques and apparatus not available to previous generations who set so much store on conformation *per se*.

Maturity is another facet of growth and development to which horse owners frequently refer. One has to define exactly what we mean by the term since, for example, a foal could be said to be mature at birth but immature some months later when reviewed in a different context. Likewise, the term may be used to denote sexual maturity or, in other words, puberty in either male or female. Strictly speaking, a horse does not reach full maturity of its skeleton until all the bones have finished growing which is at about five years old. To say that bone development in a foal is immature is therefore something of a misnomer, especially if, as is frequently the case, we are referring to the actual state of the growing ends of the bones (epiphyses) and whether or not there is an inflammatory process present (epiphysitis). It is in the limbs that we are most likely to find such a condition – at the lower end of the cannon and forearm bones and less frequently just above the hock. Another example of faulty development may be fractures which occur in the two sesamoids behind the fetlock joints of the fore limbs. In all these cases nutritional factors may be suspected and especially imbalance in the ratio of calcium and phosphorus in the soil or feed.

Other factors which predispose to epiphysitis are conformation of the limbs, the state of the hardness of the paddocks and interference with the amount of exercise that the young foal receives (perhaps brought about by confinement to looseboxes for several weeks after birth, before the weather is suitable for turning the mares and foals out to graze). In some instances the normal process of development of the fore or hind limbs becomes exaggerated and the limbs are contracted.

These angular and flexural deformities which are congenital or developmental become eliminated with time as the foal bears weight on the limbs. In some instances this may require veterinary attention such as the attachment of splints, severance of appropriate ligaments or corrective surgery to stimulate growth of bone at one side or other of the limbs.

The environment

The dictionary definition of environment is the sum total of all the conditions and elements which make up the surroundings of an individual. Regarding the environment in which young Thoroughbreds are reared, we are able to alter the environment but we cannot always control it to the extent of removing every adverse factor. All that we can hope to achieve is a balance in which the horse grows to full maturity in such a way as to remain healthy and sound, so that we can use it as we require.

The period covered in this chapter is a particularly vital one in this respect. Sometimes we try to tip the balance in favour of forced growth and development. We may even use means to achieve what must be considered somewhat dubious ends; for example, the habit of producing foals (and yearlings) for sale. For this purpose young horses are frequently given too little exercise and too much food so that they become overfat. The process may be exaggerated to the extent that bone structure is adversely affected; the environment is altered for short-term objectives, to the detriment of the long-term interests of soundness for racing.

A question which has to be answered is, just what is the ideal environment for a foal before weaning? One has to hedge to some extent by pointing out that it depends on climate and locality. In Europe the conditions are such that foals are frequently born into one extreme, that of wintry weather, and weaned in another extreme – that of summer. In the intervening period, there are fluctuations which make it impossible to be dogmatic on the correct type of management. Climatic conditions must decide whether it is preferable to have foals running out at pasture day and night or whether they should be confined to looseboxes. If the stud season coincided with the horse's natural breeding season, there can be little doubt that foals should be reared outside the stable – provided sufficient pasture is available to avoid the added dangers of parasite infestation in these circumstances. In fact, to rear foals out-of-doors it is implicit that pasture management should be excellent.

In principle, shade and shelter are essential to the wellbeing of sucking foals and in this regard stables have undoubted advantages. The disadvantages are, however, that they restrict exercise, subject the foals to draughts which may make them more susceptible to diarrhoea and other diseases, expose their lungs to the injurious effects of dust and, in hot weather, expose them to oven-like conditions, especially where there is insufficient insulation and ventilation of the building in which they are housed.

The foal starts its life on a non-fibrous diet of milk and some fibre is essential to the development of the gut and digestive processes. By the time the foal has reached the weaning stage, it will be capable of digesting a totally fibrous diet. The gradual introduction of fibre into the diet therefore plays an important part in the preparation of the foal for a life independent of its mother.

99

But confinement to looseboxes may mean the premature introduction of feeds of very high fibre content, such as when poor quality hay is fed and/or where foals consume quantities of bedding straw. The risks of digestive disturbances are therefore increased. A balance must be struck so that the foal has reasonable and increasing quantities of good quality fibre; grass and good quality hay are undoubtedly the best sources.

Nutrition is a vital part of the environment and the constituents of the diet must also be balanced according to strict principles both of levels and constituents of minerals, vitamins, carbohydrates, protein and fat (see Chapter Seventeen).

Rhodococcus equi infection is an insidious infection of foals aged from two to six months mainly, in which pneumonia and lung abscesses are commonly found. The disease has a significant environmental element attached to it in so much as the causal organism is capable of living in soil and dust and is not affected by direct sunlight. Infection may well be an expression of lowered immunity, as older animals seldom suffer from the disease.

Behaviour of unweaned foals

Foals will nibble at grass and other vegetation in the first few days of life and this habit increases with age, just as the amount of time spent resting gradually decreases throughout the first year. Likewise, from a very early age foals learn the various patterns of behaviour characteristic of adults, such as rubbing, rolling, nibbling, scratching, stamping and shaking. They also exhibit yawning and the flehmen posture.

Mares are usually aggressive to strange foals, biting and kicking them if they approach. Only occasionally will a mare allow a foal other than her own to suck from her (Figure 10.1).

Figure 10.1 Foals will approach any mare prepared to allow access to her udder

Management should be on the lookout for this situation, since it may be necessary to keep the offenders isolated. The foal appears to play a dominant role in this kind of poaching and may approach any mare kind enough to allow it access.

Foals usually go through a set ritual before getting into a sucking position. For example, they will move in front of their mother and if the mare does not then stop they repeat the process until she does. Mares also conform to fairly stereotyped patterns such as sniffing the foal when it is sucking, and biting the hind legs when it is too rough.

The older the foal the less frequently it will suck. Similarly, sucking bouts are ended by the mother, as opposed to the foal, with increasing frequency as the foal becomes older. All this leads up to the event of weaning.

Under natural conditions, weaning occurs at about one year, the mare repeatedly avoiding her foal and then threatening it on approach. Mares that do not have a new foal may allow their yearlings to continue feeding into their second or, very rarely, into their third year.

Weaning

On Thoroughbred studs, weaning is usually performed when the foal is about five to six months old.

There are two methods generally used; the first is when the foal is shut in a box on its own for several days after the mare has been removed to a far-off part of the stud. When the foal has become accustomed to its solitary state, it is then put into a paddock with other foals who have been weaned at the same time. Foals usually become distressed during this process and go partially or completely off their feed for several days.

The second method of separation is carried out in the paddock by removing one mare at a time from a group. This method is finding increasing favour with breeders and appears to cause the least disturbance to the foal which usually remains quiet and content, hardly noticing the loss of its mother.

Diarrhoea

A common condition in unweaned foals is diarrhoea. The causes are varied and involve those of dietary, bacterial, viral, fungal and parasitic origin.

Milk may precipitate scouring (diarrhoea) when the mare is in oestrus, probably as a result of certain chemicals which enter the milk at this time. The diarrhoea usually stops when the mare goes out of season but in some cases it is continued by other factors such as overgrowth of bacteria in the gut.

As already mentioned, the introduction of fibrous food when the young foal starts to eat grass, hay, or even straw, is necessary for the gradual development of the gut but it can present a digestive problem. This is especially the case where poor quality foods are provided. Rapidly growing herbage can also give rise to digestive disturbances, while mouldy hay is another example of how diet may be linked with diarrhoea.

Serious conditions of diarrhoea affecting an individual or developing into an epidemic are the result of infection with certain bacteria such as Salmonella, E. coli., or with rotavirus.

Rotavirus infection is the cause of an infectious scour in foals which has been a serious problem on some large stud farms in recent years. While considered to be on the wane at the moment, its importance cannot be discounted. Virtually all foals are affected, though the mortality rate is not high. The seriousness of the condition rises in the presence of secondary bacterial infection.

Other agents responsible for diarrhoea include the red worm (strongyles) and thread worm (strongyloides).

Diarrhoea is not a disease in itself but a sign of intestinal disturbance. It is not therefore always possible to differentiate between the various causes except with the aid of specialised laboratory techniques.

Signs associated with diarrhoea include fever (especially where infection is involved), loss of body fluid (dehydration), reluctance to suck from the mare, excessive drinking of water, and colic. The condition may be fatal although, if treated, the mortality rate is low, relative to the large numbers of foals affected each year. Cases that end fatally may do so because the germ causing the diarrhoea invades tissues and organs (septicaemia) or because of an imbalance of fluid and body salts as a result of the extreme loss (especially water and potassium) in the liquid faeces. In addition, it has been shown that foals with diarrhoea frequently suffer from an acidity of the blood after the loss of alkaline salts.

Foals suffering from diarrhoea should be examined by a veterinarian so that a proper diagnosis and balanced judgement can be made. On the other hand, many cases of diarrhoea are self-limiting and recover without the need of any treatment.

CHAPTER ELEVEN

THE WORM MENACE

The enormous dangers of parasite infection in horses cannot be overemphasised. We shall never know how many potential stakes winners have never even reached the racecourse because of the worm menace and it might astound us if we did.

It has been estimated that an adult horse may pass more than 10 million parasite eggs in its dung during every 24 hours. Many of these develop into young forms called larvae which are then capable of further development when eaten by horses grazing on the pasture.

This further development may involve migration of larvae through the blood vessels, peritoneum, liver and lungs before they return to the gut as adults (Figure 11.1); the females lay eggs and in this way the cycle is complete. During migration irreparable damage may be caused and manifested by colic, bronchitis, lack of stamina, unthriftiness and sometimes death. The younger the horse the greater the risk.

The figures quoted above refer to a horse with a faecal egg count of 1,000 eggs per gram, a count frequently found in horses at

Figure 11.1 White worms such as these may cause rupture of the gut and death of foals between the ages of two and six months

stud. Because young horses (i.e. 3-year-olds and under) are particularly vulnerable, it is here that we should concentrate our attention and efforts at parasite control; 4-year-olds and over develop a relative immunity through tolerance not possessed by their younger brethren and the consequences of infection are therefore not usually as disastrous.

First, let us examine the enemy. There are five groups of parasites which spend their adult life in the horse's intestines: three types of round worm and two types of tape worm, which are flat.

White worms

The large white worm (ascarid), *Parascaris equorum*, may reach 50 cm in length. The adult form lives in the small intestine and the females lay as many as 200,000 eggs per day. The eggs pass to the outside in dung and develop into an infective stage in about 10 days. The eggs are very resistant to drying or freezing and may remain alive for many years. Larval forms develop within the eggs and infection occurs when a horse consumes the eggs in food (mainly at pasture) or water. The larvae then hatch, burrow into the wall of the intestines and travel to the liver. From the liver they are carried in the bloodstream through the heart to the lungs, where they lodge in the small capillary vessels. Here they break into the air sacs, renew their development and travel up the windpipe to the pharynx where they are swallowed. In this way they pass to the intestine, become adults and thus complete the cycle of development. The period from ingestion of eggs to the adult form is approximately 12 weeks.

Ascarid infection affects mostly young foals and, to a lesser extent, yearlings and 2-year-olds. It appears that, as with other parasite infection, horses develop a resistance with age.

Red worms

Red worms (strongyles) include small and large forms and are really colourless. They appear red due to the blood they suck from the lining of the horse's gut (Figure 11.2).

The small strongyles consist of a variety of species belonging to the genera *Trichonema*, *Trichostrongylus axei*. The worms vary in length from 4 mm to 50 mm and live in the horse's caecum and colon. Their eggs are passed in the dung and hatch under suitable conditions with the liberation of larvae which crawl from the dung and collect on blades of grass. Here they feed on bacteria, developing by a process of moulting (i.e. shedding their outer coat) until the third larval stage is reached about five or six days later.

Infective larvae crawl up blades of grass which gives them a greater chance of being eaten. They are particularly attracted to mild, and repelled by strong, sunlight. For this reason they tend to crawl up the grass in early morning and again in the evening. Some moisture is necessary for these movements since the larvae are unable to crawl on a dry surface. Larvae are also more active in warm weather. Their life is prolonged by moisture, shade and relatively low temperatures but marked fluctuations in intensity of light, heat and cold cause exhaustion of food reserves and death. Larvae do not usually live longer than about three months.

They rely on reserves of food in their own intestinal cells. When these reserves are exhausted the larvae die, a fact of some importance when we come to consider methods of parasite control. Once eaten, infective larvae burrow into the lining of the animal's gut where they live.

The large strongyles include *Strongylus vulgaris*, *S. edentatus* and *S. equinus*, the latter being comparatively uncommon. They measure up to 5 mm in length and their larvae penetrate more deeply into the body than those of the small strongyles. *S. equinus* cross the peritoneal cavity and enter the liver. *S. edentatus* live in the peritoneal lining of the abdominal cavity where they may form nodules associated with bleeding (Figure 11.3). *S. vulgaris* is, however, the most dangerous because larval forms enter the blood

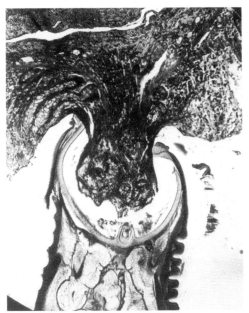

Figure 11.2 A highly-magnified view of red worm (below, centre) attached to the lining of the gut from which it sucks blood

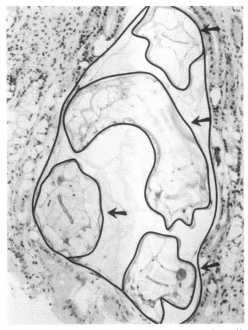

Figure 11.3 A view of the intestinal wall, highly magnified, showing encysted red worm larva which has been sectioned at four (arrowed) places

vessels that supply the small intestines. After crawling towards the aorta they develop in the arteries (Figure 11.4) and return to the gut some six months later. Depending on the species of strongyle, the period between ingestion of infective larvae and the reappearance of adult forms in the gut varies from two to 12 months.

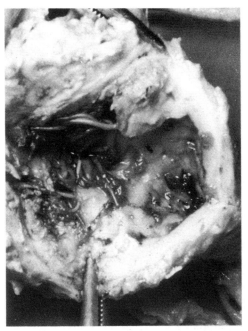

Figure 11.4 Red worm larvae (S. vulgaris) seen in the artery leading to the gut

Strongyloides westeri has a special life cycle in that it can be transferred from the mare in the milk or picked up from contaminated straw or hay. Unlike other red worms, such as *Strongylus vulgaris*, it does not require a stage of development on grass. It also has a very short life cycle between being ingested, becoming adult and passing its eggs in the faeces.

Pin worms

The pin (or seat worm), *Oxyuris equi*, measures up to 15 cm and lives in the large gut. After fertilisation by the male worm the

105

female passes to the rectum and crawls out through the anus where she lays eggs in clusters on the skin of the perineum. After about three days the eggs drop off and develop to an infective stage.

Tape worms

The tape worms *Anoplocephala magna* and *Anoplocephala pertoliata* live in the small and large intestines. They are up to 80 cm long and composed of segments which pass to the outside in the dung. The eggs that the segments contain are eaten by mites and develop into intermediary forms known as cysticercoids, which are found in the body cavity of the mites and which develop into adult tape worms after being swallowed by another host.

The ravages of worm infestation

Adult worms

Adult round worms damage the lining of the gut as they attach themselves to the mucous membrane and suck blood. White worms also irritate the gut wall although they lie free, feeding on the partially digested food of the small intestine. Pin worms irritate the anus and tape worms may injure the gut as they hang from its wall in the stomach or intestines. The damage caused by adult worms may be ulceration of the mucous membrane lining of the small and large intestines, bleeding and loss of blood, abnormally increased movement of the bowel (peristalsis) and in some cases, especially associated with white worms, rupture so that food escapes into the abdominal cavity causing peritonitis and death.

Most adult horses seem able to tolerate enormous numbers of parasites in the gut but it is the larvae which cause the most serious problems.

Larval worms

Wherever a larva travels it will cause an in-

flammatory response. Typical features include tracts lined by special cells which move to the area trying to seal off the parasite and repair the damage (minute haemorrhages and scarring). A few larvae do not evoke a significant reaction but great numbers invading the body in a short time may have a very damaging cumulative effect.

Bronchitis and liver damage is frequently associated with the passage of *Parascaris* larvae. Pea-sized nodules and haemorrhagic tracts in the peritoneum are associated with migration of *S. equinus* and *S. edentatus*. It is, however, *S. vulgaris* larvae which pose the most serious threat. They cause destruction of the inner lining and weakening of the blood vessel walls through which they migrate (Figures 11.5 and 11.6). The most common site of damage is at a point where the mesenteric artery to the intestines branches from the main blood vessel (aorta). The weakened walls of the artery become ballooned forming what is known as an aneurysm.

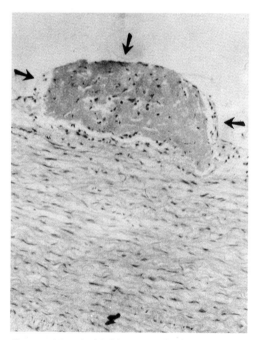

Figure 11.5 A highly-magnified view of an artery wall. On its surface a blood clot (arrowed) has formed as a result of S. vulgaris *larvae*

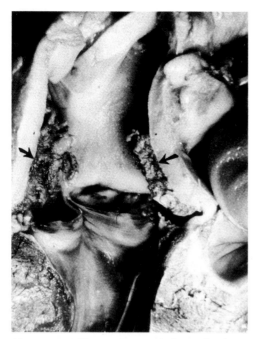

Figure 11.6 The main artery from the heart opened to show two valves and vegetative lesions (arrowed) caused by red worm

Wherever blood vessels are damaged, blood clots form. Parts of these may break away and block smaller branches. In this way portions of gut may be cut off from their blood supply and in consequence small sections of the wall die causing acute peritonitis (inflammation of the lining of the abdomen).

One of the purposes of the peritoneum is to allow loops of gut to move over one another and avoid friction with the abdominal wall. When the surface becomes inflamed two portions may stick together and in some cases fibrous adhesions develop forming a permanent union which seriously interferes with normal movement of the gut.

Symptoms

The symptoms of worm-infested horses vary according to the type of parasite, the migratory path of its larvae, the level of infestation and age of the horse.

Symptoms include diarrhoea, anaemia, retardation of growth and loss of bodily condition. Colic, due to migrating larvae, is associated with peritonitis, adhesions and twists of the gut. In the case of *S. vulgaris* infection, death may be caused by the rupture of a damaged blood vessel. In general, the older a horse the greater the burden of worms it can carry without showing symptoms. Owners are often surprised if they are told that their apparently healthy horse has a high egg count. The individual has acquired a tolerance to the parasites and with regard to worm control this type of situation poses a particular danger because large numbers of eggs pass unsuspected onto the pastures.

Adult white worms may cause colic, diarrhoea and anaemia while in foals the larvae may be responsible for bronchitis or pneumonia. White worms are not usually of any significance in horses over four years of age. In rare cases foals may die as a result of rupture of the gut caused by large accumulations of adult worms. Bronchitis may coincide with herpesvirus infection and therefore in foals it may be difficult to distinguish between the effects of white worm larvae and the snotty nose condition caused by the virus.

Tape worms are not usually associated with symptoms of any sort and pin worms only with irritation which causes a horse to rub its hindquarters.

Worm control

Worm control is one of the most important single aspects of stud management. Failure to implement a policy to control worm infection, especially that by red worm, undermines all other measures which we call good stud management. Ideally, fenced pastures, adequate diets based on scientific advice, warm stabling, intensive care of the newborn foal, sympathetic handling and lavish care can all be set at nought by the ravages of strongyle infection.

The aim of control is to prevent horses, particularly foals and yearlings, picking up

107

larvae from the pastures. We cannot prevent some infection taking place and it would be impossible to be 100 per cent successful whatever methods we employed in worm control. In fact, it is probably an advantage that some parasites should enter the body because in this way the individual develops a degree of immunity which enables it to tolerate the presence of worms without suffering undue damage.

Control is applied at two levels:

1. By various forms of pasture management.
2. By the administration of drugs to reduce the quantity of eggs passed onto the pasture.

Pasture control

As we have seen, each horse may pass enormous numbers of infective larvae. Control requires that these are killed as quickly as possible. This may be brought about by resting, deep ploughing and reseeding pasture, mixed grazing or the manual picking up of dung. Each of these measures is helpful but particular attention should be paid to those paddocks in which foals and yearlings graze.

Rest

The length of time a pasture should be left free of horses to effectively reduce the worm eggs and larvae there depends on the climate and the amount of shaded area. Moist, cloudy conditions alternating with sunny weather will tend to exhaust the larvae more quickly than cool shaded conditions such as under trees. In practice it is reasonable to suppose that if a pasture is rested through a hot, dry summer and the following winter the parasite burden is reduced to a minimum. Six months rest makes a useful contribution to the problem but anything less presents proportionally increased risks of serious contamination remaining.

Ploughing and reseeding

Ploughing to a depth of at least 26 cm and then reseeding relies on the principle that the

parasite eggs and larvae will be deeply buried and not able to survive. In fact, it is unlikely that this will completely free a pasture once it has been severely contaminated and the advantages come more from the rest than the reseeding. For this reason ploughing is not a policy which should be adopted purely for worm control.

Mixed grazing

Mixed grazing relies on the principle that sheep and cattle parasites do not infect horses and that larvae able to live in one species will be killed in the alimentary tract of the other. There is one exception and this is *Trichostrongylus axei* which is able to live in horses and cattle. However, it is a worm of little pathological significance and therefore need not be taken into account as far as mixed grazing is concerned.

Picking up dung

The manual picking up and disposal of dung is a simple although time-consuming method but of the utmost importance in pasture control. Dung should be removed from the pasture *at least* once a week. The strongyle eggs take about 10 days to hatch and develop into infective larvae so that if the dung is picked up within this period pasture contamination is reduced. Harrowing pasture is not to be recommended since it spreads larvae as well as tending to upset the selective feeding habits of horses who like to graze away from where they place their dung.

The proper disposal of manure from stables, yards and paddocks is obviously an essential part of good management. It should never be spread on horse pastures because it will infect these with eggs and larvae. It should be stored and allowed to ferment so that the heat destroys the larvae. If manure is stored in the open then the outer part of the exposed pile must be turned inwards every week so that it too becomes heated. It has been shown that horse manure may be sterilised by keeping it for two weeks in wooden boxes with double sides and floors. As a general rule, horse manure should only be used on fields which are grazed by animals other than horses.

Foal and yearling paddocks

The importance of all the measures described above cannot be overemphasised for the paddocks in which foals and yearlings graze. If it is not economic to carry out measures on all the pastures of the stud farm, then it is essential to concentrate on those in which foals and yearlings are to graze and to give these the fullest possible treatment. Mares are the chief source of infection as far as foals are concerned. Those with foals at foot must obviously be grazed on the same pastures; but barren, maiden and pre-foaling mares should be kept off paddocks reserved for foals and yearlings. It is also important that foals should not have access to the paddocks used for foals the previous year because of *Parascaris* contamination.

Control of worms in the horse

Methods of pasture control involve measures taken against a dispersed worm population; by treating the horse itself it is possible to kill large numbers of mature worms concentrated in the gut and so prevent their subsequent reproduction. Mares harbour in their intestines many parasites with a tremendous potential for egg-laying. This egg production increases markedly during the spring, reaches a peak in late summer and falls off in winter. It is important to take note of this variation and further reference will be made to it when we come to consider the usefulness of egg counts. It should also be emphasised that the period of maximal egg production coincides with the months that mares are on the paddocks with their foals at foot; they may even be turned out day and night during the summer.

Anthelmintic drugs – controlling parasites

Perhaps one of the most outstanding advances in veterinary medicine during the last two decades has come about by the development of Ivermectin. This drug is highly effective against most parasites. It was first introduced into cattle practice as an injection but following some problems associated with administration by this route, oral dosing has become routine in horses.

Ivermectin scored two double firsts because it could:

1. Kill a wide range of parasites from bot fly and warble fly larvae to the highly destructive red worm, *Strongylus vulgaris* and from the small strongyles to the large white worms, *Parascaris equorum*.
2. Destroy migrating larvae of red worms wherever these occurred, in the blood vessels or wandering through the nervous system or kidney, etc.

The first and second generation drugs, such as Phenothiazine, Piperazine and, more latterly, Benzimidazole drugs and Pyrantel compounds, are effective against some, but not all parasites.

A major problem has been the development of drug resistance against, especially, the Benzimidazole drugs. For this reason a rotation of the type of drug used for treatment and control is advocated.

Worming protocol

Worm control programmes should extend throughout the year and consist of regular administration of a drug selected on the basis of cost versus efficacy. The most effective is Ivermectin but it is also the most expensive and it may be reasonable to use less expensive compounds but include at least two administrations of Ivermectin per year. In general, drugs are administered monthly in the feed or, perhaps more conveniently, in the many preparations now available in paste form. Readers should refer to their own veterinary surgeon for advice on the exact programme required for their particular circumstances; and the manufacturer's instructions for each drug should be read carefully and taken into account.

All stock should be treated because the aim

is to prevent eggs reaching the pasture. All individuals arriving on a stud farm should be tested and treated before they are turned onto grazing. It is rarely necessary to treat the individual for worm damage unless symptoms are present and the drugs are prescribed by a veterinarian, providing reasonable parasite control is practised on the premises.

Mares should be treated in the months before they foal in order to reduce the risk of *Strongyloides* being passed to the foal.

Monitoring worm control programmes
There are three essential elements to the anthelmintic control programme:
1. Choice of anthelmintic.
2. Timing of treatments.
3. Monitoring of the control programme by faecal egg counts.

This third component is equally important as the first two because it reaches an endpoint which can be used to determine whether the first two measures are effective.

The number of eggs in a gram of faeces is measured in the laboratory. Although these counts do not provide an indication of the severity of the infection (a small number of females may produce a large number of eggs or conversely a large number of females a small number), they provide an assessment of the degree of potential pasture contamination.

Egg levels should be kept as close as possible to zero. Even a few eggs per gram represents a substantial contribution on a daily output of several kilograms of faeces. Counts should be made just before the routine dose of anthelmintics is due and carried out three or four times a year. The number of

occasions on which the count is monitored depends to some extent on the results obtained. If high counts are recorded in a substantial number of individuals on the farm, measures should be taken to reduce the problem on veterinary advice, and the intervals between monitoring should be increased. Conversely, if consistently low counts are obtained, monitoring need occur less frequently.

Conclusion

The worm population of the foal and yearling requires a special consideration. Foals are born free of worms but as soon as they are turned onto pastures they start to graze and to pick up infective larvae. These undergo their migration and return to the gut where they begin to lay eggs in the manner already described. The first worm to reproduce in foals and give rise to eggs is *Strongyloides westeri* which is mainly gained through milk rather than grazing. It is not one of the most harmful red worm species, but it does cause diarrhoea in foals. The eggs of these parasites will be found in the faeces when the foal is about one to four weeks old.

At about eight weeks the first eggs of true red worm and other white worm infection appear in the faeces. In practice, foals are therefore able to contaminate pasture from the second month onwards and should be treated from age about six weeks, preferably with Ivermectin so that the migrating red worm larvae are dealt with. For this reason, Ivermectin is the drug of choice for nearly all stock up to the age of two years.

Part II

CHAPTER TWELVE

THE HORSE ON TIPTOE

Those who work with horses should know something of the species' evolutionary history. The subject is by no means one of academic interest alone; we cannot hope to tackle successfully the problems which beset us in the care and management of the horse unless we are aware of the fundamental properties of structure and function contained within its body.

In essence the horse has a body which combines size and speed; other animals may be as fast or as large, but in *Equus caballus* (the modern horse) the dual combination has been brought to near perfection. It is, of course, this feature which has gripped the imagination of man and for centuries he has used the horse for transport as well as his military ambitions. Nowadays its use is confined mainly to the pleasures of riding and racing.

To a certain extent the horse's body has been modified, by careful selection in breeding, to meet particular requirements such as pulling heavy loads in agriculture or for racing, polo playing, etc. The fundamental structures of its body have not, however, been affected; the modern horse is a creature whose bones, muscles and organs conform to a plan which is common to all breeds whether they be Shires, Thoroughbreds, Standardbreds or Shetland ponies.

Changes in body structure

Because of the horse's grazing habits and its tendency to live in large herds, it has been buried and fossilised in large numbers. The horse's evolutionary history is therefore the most well-known of any species. The sequence from Eocene times to the present day is recorded from fossils discovered in North America. This story is well known and many books have appeared on the subject so that it is not necessary to repeat it in detail. Here we are more concerned with presenting changes in body structure which have occurred between the earliest-known horse called *Hyracotherium* (*Eohippus*, the dawn horse) and the horse we use today, in terms of their relevance to the problems of management in the twentieth century.

The dawn horse was a small creature about the size of a fox, possessing four toes on its front limbs and three on the hind limbs. The limbs were slender and some authors claim that this horse, which lived 40 million years ago, may have been nearly as fast as the modern racehorse.

Limbs

The evolution of the horse has seen a remarkable lengthening of the legs and a reduction of the side (lateral) toes with increasing emphasis on the middle toe. Humans have retained the five-toed condition which was the original plan in the ancestors of both horse and man; when we run we raise ourselves onto our toes, but at rest we stand flat on our heels. The modern horse stands virtually on the tips of the middle fingers and toes of the fore and hind limbs, and thus its stride is lengthened and it is permanently raised into the position of running on tiptoe (Figure 12.1).

A specialist structure, the hoof, has been

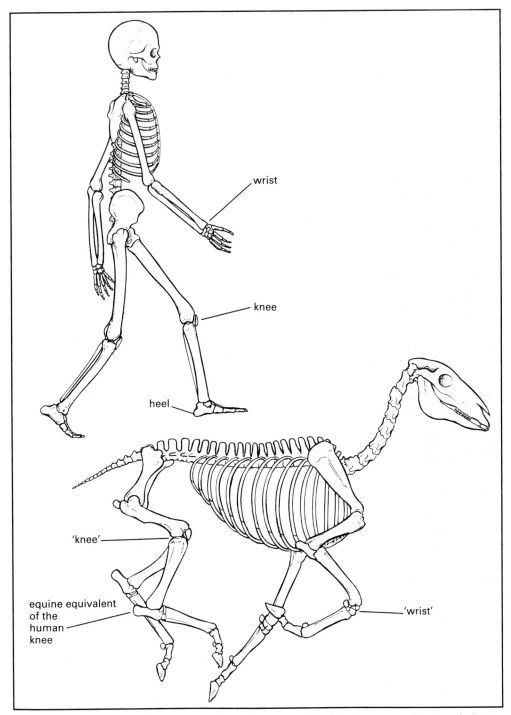

Figure 12.1 Diagram to show a comparison (not to scale) of the human and horse skeleton. Except when running, humans remain flat on their heels. Unlike humans, the horse is permanently raised on its toes

113

developed at the tips of each limb for protection of the extremities. This may be likened to the nail of our own fingers or toes and serves not only to protect the deeper structures against injury, but to absorb shock as the limb strikes the ground.

A number of bones in the horse's limbs have been reduced during evolution. The reduction has involved a simplification in the bones of the forearm and shin or gaskin (i.e. those between the stifle and hock). The dawn horse possessed two separate bones in the forearm (the ulna and radius) and two in the gaskin (the tibia and fibula); this is the arrangement still retained in our own bodies. In the modern horse these bones have become fused, with the result that horses have lost the capacity to rotate their limbs in the

same way that we can. They have, in addition, lost the power of grasping. In consequence, the muscles which carry out these processes have been discarded in favour of tendons to reduce the weight below the knee, and if we examine the body of the modern horse we will find no muscles below the carpus (knee) or tarsus (hock) (Figure 12.2). The equivalents of these joints in the human body are the wrist and ankle (Figure 12.3).

It is obvious that the development of the limbs has achieved its evolutionary object – the horse has been able to use its speed to evade its enemies. The horse has also become useful to man, who would otherwise undoubtedly have become its most deadly predator. The associated modifications of body structure have meant, however, that we

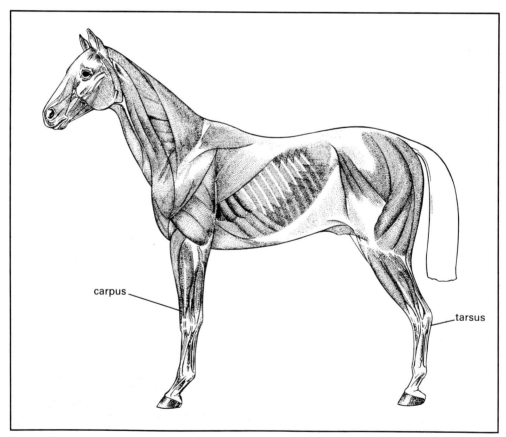

Figure 12.2 Diagram showing that, in the horse, muscles of locomotion are bunched above the carpus (knee) and tarsus (hock)

114

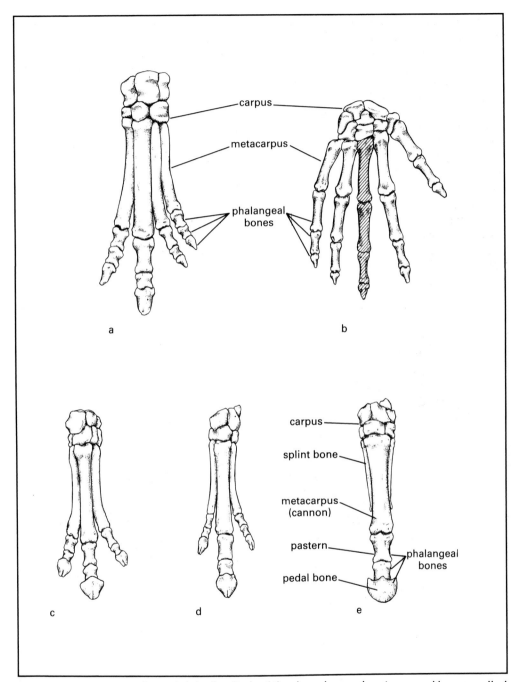

Figure 12.3 Diagram to show: (a) the forelimb of the dawn horse showing carpal bones, called the knee and equal to the human wrist, and the four metacarpal bones, equivalent to those between the human wrist and knuckles, to each of which are attached first, second and third phalangeal bones; (b) the five-digit plan has been retained in the human hand, whereas only the middle one (shaded area) remains for the horse; and (c), (d) and (e) the intermediary forms between the dawn horse and the modern horse

are presented with certain potential weaknesses which may lead to unsoundness.

For example, the practical implication of the enormous lengthening of the horse's limb below the knee and hock is that the tendons are correspondingly elongated and susceptible to injuries. The residual third and fourth metacarpal and metatarsal bones, usually referred to as splint bones, are another source of trouble. Injuries to the first phalanx (pastern bone), the sesamoid bones behind the fetlock joint, and the pedal bone are frequent causes of unsoundness as are various inflammatory conditions of the bones and joints (osselets, ringbones, carpitis) from which horses suffer. The foot is particularly exposed to risks of injury and the old saying 'no foot, no horse' is a truism many a horse owner has learned to his cost.

Back

Significant changes have also occurred in other parts of the horse's body. For instance, the back has become straightened and stiffened while a relatively heavy head is supported on the end of a long and flexible neck. The extension of the neck was, of course, necessary as the horse grew taller and at the same time adopted grazing habits. The condition of the vertebral column (spine) was an essential consideration for a species used to carry a rider but, in placing weight on its back, we have exposed the structures of the back to the risks of trauma (especially as it does not finish growing until the horse is five years old), many of which are a direct result of the way horses are ridden. In particular, causing the horse to jump subjects the ligaments and bones of the spine to unnatural stresses. It is not surprising, therefore, that many unsoundnesses are associated with inflammatory reactions of the back which may be of a temporary or permanent nature.

Neck

Injuries to the neck are another common source of trouble and lead to damage to the nerves which pass down the spine (from the brain) to the body, including its extremities.

The condition known as 'wobbler' disease, the signs of which include incoordination of the hind limbs, is such an example. This may have an inherited basis and if so it is interesting to speculate whether, in fact, horses suffered from the disease during their evolutionary history or whether it has been brought into the modern horse by untoward selection of breeding stock.

Head

As the horse grew in size, the weight of its head must have presented a problem (Figure 12.4). To a large extent this was solved by the development of large cavities of air within the bones of the skull. These cavities are called sinuses and occasionally we find that they become infected; since they communicate with the nasal passages the affected horse then suffers from a purulent discharge of the nose.

The enlargement of the skull has also caused the eye sockets to become raised so that they are well placed to observe the surroundings for the approach of danger while the horse is grazing. Natural selection would also have allowed those with better vision (i.e. those with the eyes set in higher eye sockets) to see predators, and thus escape. These survivors would pass on their genes, unlike those with inferior vision.

As the head became larger so it was able to accommodate teeth that were adapted to meet the special requirements of the diet. The earliest horses browsed on succulent foods which they found hanging on bushes, shrubs and trees; alterations in climate necessitated a change to grazing and the digestion of hard, fibrous grasses. To meet the demands of this diet, the cheek teeth became broader and their crowns were increased in height and complicated by patterns or ridges ideally suited for grinding food (Figure 12.5). As the teeth increased their size, so it was necessary for the skull to become deeper and the lower jaw broader to accommodate them. In the modern horse the front teeth (incisors) are designed for cutting grass so that it can be pulled into the mouth by a mobile tongue and then brought to the

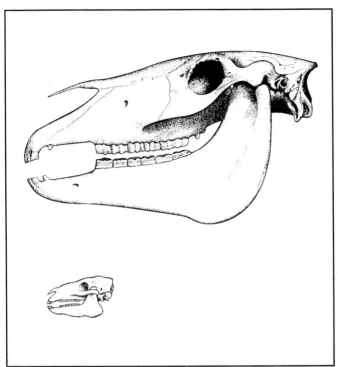

Figure 12.4 Diagram showing the skull of the modern horse (top) contrasted with that of the much smaller dawn horse (below). Apart from the size increase, the modern horse has the eye socket placed relatively far back and the jaws have become deeper to house more substantial teeth

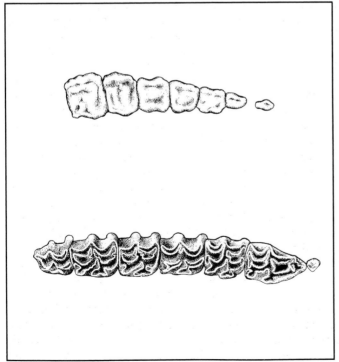

Figure 12.5 The dawn horse had teeth (top) with simple crowns adapted to eating soft food; the modern horse (below) has teeth suited for grinding hard fibrous foods, and crowns that are complicated by ridged patterns

molar teeth to be ground between their surfaces acting like a mill. It is perhaps fortunate that there is a gap between the incisors and the molars into which a bit can be conveniently placed! The grinding action of the jaws tends to produce sharp edges along the inside of the lower and the outside of the upper molar teeth. These sharp edges may be removed by rasping, a procedure which is usually carried out routinely about once a year or when there are indications that the horse is not chewing normally.

Alimentary canal

Although the soft parts of the body cannot be traced through the course of evolution there is no doubt that changes in the gut have occurred which paralleled those in dietary habits.

We should not forget that certain behavioural patterns, including the sexual aspects of behaviour, have become established during the course of evolution. There is also the equally important consideration of social and herd behaviour. The behaviour of the individual is based on a series of instinctive reactions; these instincts have developed to meet a way of life which is very different from being confined to stables or placed in paddocks at the whim of man.

CHAPTER THIRTEEN

ANATOMY OF LIMBS

The limbs

Jargon

The jargon of horsemen covers all aspects of the horse's anatomy. For example, 'cannon' and 'coffin' bones are terms frequently used in preference to metacarpal and pedal bones, more commonly employed by anatomists. Abnormalities have likewise received labels such as 'splint', 'spavin', 'curb', 'ringbone' and 'osselet', depending on the part of the body where they occur; they fail, however, to provide a precise definition of the trouble.

There is an increasing need to rationalise jargon and to introduce scientific terms rather than to rely on traditional terminology, although the latter may have served veterinarians and lay persons for many years.

The pros and cons of change may be summarised as follows:

1. Scientific terms are usually understood on an international basis whereas the horseman's jargon may be parochial or national in its origin. A common language helps to reduce any confusion when horsemen and veterinarians are gathered together from different parts of the world.
2. Anomalies are associated with certain anatomical descriptions of the body; for example, the horse's 'knee' is in fact that joint of the forelimb which is the equivalent of our own wrist and as such it should be described as the carpus. The true knee (genu) of the hind limb is actually described as the 'stifle'. Although it may be unlikely that horsemen will readily come to change this approach, they should appreciate the existence of the discrepancy if

they are to understand the structure of a horse's body.
3. Scientific phraseology is concerned with fundamental principles and it more aptly describes the various injuries and abnormalities. In this respect all concerned are able to gain a better appreciation of what has gone wrong in a particular animal and the best therapy to employ, than is the case with some of the more general terms of the horseman's vocabulary.

For example, it is sometimes customary to say that a horse has a 'joint', thus implying that there is an injury and an unsoundness in a particular part (the racing definition of a 'joint' is the fetlock joint). Since, however, a joint is composed of many different structures (articular cartilage, bone, ligaments, capsule, etc.), it would seem preferable to try to define a 'joint' according to the nature of injury and tissues involved.

In recent years there has been a definite shift towards a scientific approach. For instance, it is becoming more common to refer to inflammation of the horse's 'knees' as carpitis; a bone injury is referred to as periostitis and its location designated according to anatomical position. A ringbone, therefore, may nowadays be referred to as a periostitis affecting the second or third phalanx according to the bone affected; splints are now diagnosed either as fractures of the small metacarpal bones or inflammatory reactions of the ligament which binds these bones to the main metacarpal (cannon) bone.

4. It is true that scientific jargon may be difficult to pronounce; this can be off-putting to the lay person, but since diagnosis and treatment is nowadays often a matter of highly sophisticated scientific processes, these difficulties are small compared with the advantages gained if modern terms are grasped. In fact, old styles may well retard progress by the confusion that they can create in the minds of horsemen and veterinarians alike.

So much for terminology. It is also important to correlate the anatomy of the limbs with function and to appreciate their minute structure as an integral part of the system as a whole. Put another way, function can be observed as the horse moves at various paces, whereas on dissection we find that the limbs are composed of bones, muscles, tendons, ligaments, blood and lymph vessels and nerves. The bones are arranged so that they move upon one another at places of union known as joints or articulations. A practical knowledge of the limbs requires an understanding of the whole as well as individual components.

Bones

The framework of the limbs is formed by the bones. These are arranged as a series of struts and levers and where they meet, the joint forms a hinge. Each of the front and hind limbs contains 20 bones. Some of these are large (such as the shoulder blade, pelvis, humerus, femur, etc.) and some comparatively small (carpal bones, patella, sesamoids, etc.). Whatever their size, every bone plays some part in the total make-up of the limb. The larger bones form a scaffolding to which the muscles, tendons and ligaments are attached, thus providing mobility through their action, which is to produce movement. It is not difficult to appreciate the essential properties of the skeleton if one visualises a limb without the hard structure of the bone, or at the other extreme one that was composed only of bone, without any articulations. Small bones such as those in the knee (car-

pus) or at the back of the fetlock joint play their part in completing joints formed by larger bones. They may also act as semi-movable attachments onto which tendons and ligaments may be joined, as in the case of kneecap or patella.

Joints

A joint is composed of the ends of two or more bones which are capped by articular cartilage. Cartilage is somewhat similar to bone except that it is softer, possesses greater elasticity and is able to replace by growth any loss of its surface. These properties enable it to provide a joint surface of minimum friction. Wear and tear is further limited by the presence of joint oil (synoval fluid) which is normally found between the opposing cartilages in the joint cavity (Figure 13.1). The fluid is secreted by a membrane (joint capsule) which is attached around the edges of

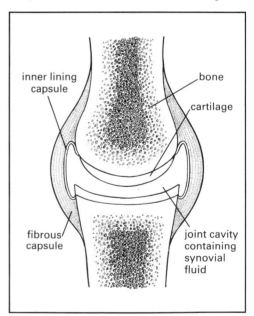

Figure 13.1 Structures forming a joint. A joint is a meeting point between two bones. Each bone is capped by cartilage and the space between is the joint cavity which is filled with synovial fluid (joint oil). The oil is secreted and kept in position by the joint capsule. This consists of a thin lining and a thick outer fibrous part. In many joints the fibrous part is strengthened by ligaments

the bones that form the joint. The joint capsule has a thin inner lining and, in most limb joints, a thicker outer fibrous part strengthened by bands of strong tissue known as ligaments.

Just as the bones of the limb have different shapes and sizes, so the joints vary in their structure according to their position in the limb and the way in which they move (ball and socket, hinge, etc). Every joint, however, will conform to the basic pattern described.

The moulding of the joints and ligaments, and arrangements of the muscles, allow for only a limited amount of rotation of the limb and most of the movement is in one plane (i.e. forwards and backwards). In the carpus, for instance, the surfaces are practically flat and allow only gliding movement largely restricted to a forwards and backwards plane.

Movement is similarly restricted in the elbow which is a hinge joint. Here, the end of one bone is in the shape of a cylinder or cone and is received by a corresponding cavity. By contrast, considerable freedom of movement is possible in ball and socket joints such as the

hip and shoulder. In these the prominence of one bone is received into a corresponding cavity on the other. In the case of the hip, the head of the femur fits into the socket of the pelvis (Figure 13.2).

In Chapter Twelve we saw how, during the course of evolution, the number of bones in the limbs has been reduced; the power of grasping and the flexibility so pronounced in our own limbs has also been lost. Of course, horses do not depend for their survival on the ability to manipulate with their limbs but only on their capacity for fast movement, so that the loss of flexibility in movement is quite logical.

Muscles and tendons
Movement of various parts of the body is brought about by the action of muscles. A muscle is made up of millions of small fibres, each of which is capable of shortening its length. The sum total of this ability to contract represents the power of the muscle.

The muscles are placed high up in the limb and there are none below the level of the

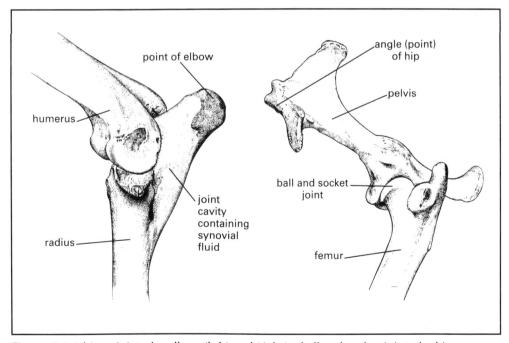

Figure 13.2 A hinge joint, the elbow (left) *and* (right) *a ball and socket joint, the hip*

121

carpus or hock. The reason for this becomes clear when we consider the fact that any muscles below these joints would be concerned with grasping and rotation. The muscles are attached above to various bones of the limb and body (ribs, spine, etc.) and below to the part of the limb on which they exert their action. The attachment of a muscle at its upper end is usually referred to as the origin; and at the lower end as the insertion. The latter is by means of a tendon and it is through this that the power of the muscle is translated into the force necessary for movement; (i.e. galloping, trotting or simply the lifting of a limb). Some muscles, such as those between the ribs, do not have a tendon but are attached at both ends directly onto bone.

In the limbs nearly all the muscles have a tendon, the insertion of which is at a point below the origin of the muscle. In two cases the muscle itself has disappeared during the course of evolution and only tendinous structures remain (Figure 13.3).

These are:
1. The suspensory ligament which extends from its attachment behind the carpus to insertions onto the sesamoid bones and the front of the second phalanx.
2. The check ligament which is inserted at

one end to the bones of the carpus and at the other joins the tendon of the deep flexor muscle in the upper third of the main metacarpal. Comparable structures exist in the hind limb. They form part of the 'stay apparatus' which supports the fetlock joint and prevents it becoming overextended.

Special structures known as synovial membranes are found where muscles or tendons pass over points of particular friction, such as bony prominences or joints. These represent accessory structures and are composed of thin-walled sacs similar to the joint capsules and they also produce a fluid. Two forms are recognised – a bursa, which is a simple sac, and a tendon sheath, which is composed of a tube enclosing a tendon. Examples are the bursa situated under the tendon as it runs over the point of the hock, and the tendon sheaths of the deep and superficial flexor tendons of the forelimbs which are behind the carpus and the fetlock.

Both sheaths and bursae normally contain a minimum of fluid sufficient to provide lubrication and they cannot therefore be felt or seen in the living animal. In certain circumstances, however, excess fluid collects and the sheath bulges from below the skin.

Figure 13.3 Dissection of the tendons behind the cannon bone shows the position of the check ligament, attached at one end to the back of the carpus and at the other to the deep flexor tendon

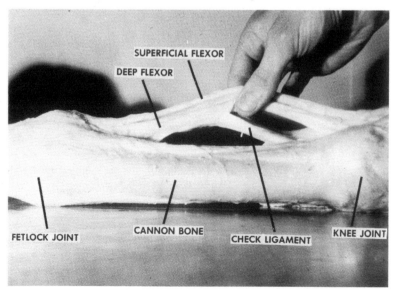

Each muscle may act in one or more of three ways:

1. By contracting it causes movement of the part to which it is attached.
2. By relaxing it allows an opposing movement.
3. By exerting a steady tone it enables the body to maintain a state of posture at all times.

The muscles of the limb are usually classified according to whether they extend or flex the limbs (i.e. extensors or flexors, respectively). When a flexor muscle contracts, it is necessary for its opposite number (extensor) to relax and vice versa. In standing, both groups will exert a mild force to counter the effects of gravity; if this force were not present the horse would collapse under the weight of its own body.

The actions described are all controlled by nerves, the trunks of which leave the spinal cord at various points along the backbone and convey messages to and from the brain or directly from one muscle group to another.

To illustrate the system of muscles and tendons let us consider the origin, insertion and action of three muscles of the forelimb (Figure 13.4).

The superficial digital flexor muscle has its origin on the humerus and radius. It is inserted into the first and second phalangeal bones and its action is to flex the toe and the carpus. It also acts to extend the elbow, but it is nevertheless defined as a muscle of flexion since this is its main action. This muscle is fused with its tendon just above the carpus. The tendon runs behind the joint and is enveloped by a sheath which extends downwards to the region of the middle of the main metacarpal bone. At the fetlock joint the tendon becomes flattened and broader and forms a ring through which the tendon of the deep flexor passes. A second sheath encloses the tendon as it passes behind the fetlock. The deep digital flexor has similar origins to the superficial flexor muscle, is inserted into the third phalanx and flexes the joints of the distal limb.

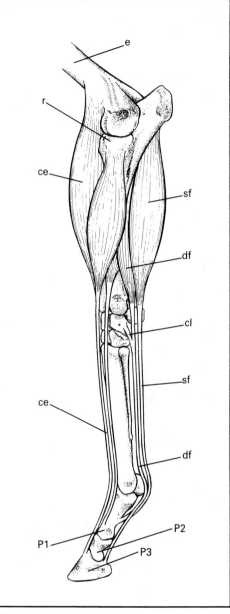

Figure 13.4 Arrangement of two flexor and extensor muscles in the forelimb of the horse. The common extensor muscles (ce) have their origin on the humerus (e) and the radius (r) and are inserted through their tendons to the pastern and pedal bones (P1, P2 and P3). The deep and superficial flexor muscles (df and sf) have similar origins and insertions on the posterior aspect of the limb. (cl = check ligament)

123

The common digital extensor has its origin on the lower end of the humerus and the upper end of the radius. It is inserted through its tendon to the front of the first, second and third phalanges. Its action is to extend the toe and the carpus and to a minor extent to flex the elbow joint. It has a synovial sheath where the tendon lies over the front of the carpus and a bursa between the tendon and the joint capsule of the fetlock.

Nerves, blood and lymph vessels

The various structures of the limb are nourished by oxygen-rich blood brought to them in the arteries. The blood returns to the heart by way of the veins and in so doing it has to travel against the force of gravity. It can do this partly through the pressure created by the pumping action of the heart and partly through the movement of the muscles and tendons which massage the veins as the horse moves its limbs. In fact, the veins possess valves which allow the blood to flow only in an upward direction. The lymphatic system is also concerned in the drainage of fluid from the limbs. It is this particular system which is involved in conditions known to horsemen as 'filled legs' and lymphangitis.

The limbs also contain nerves which control and coordinate the movement of the muscles as well as supplying a means by which the horse can appreciate sensations such as pain and the position of its limbs.

Finally, reference must be made to the feet, the structures which have been developed during the course of evolution to protect the tips of the limb. The horse's foot is an excellent example of the way in which nature adapts the structures of the body to meet its particular needs.

The foot

In most species the weight of the body is borne through several digits; the horse, however, stands on the tip of a single toe on each of its limbs and there is, therefore, a need to have some special structure to protect against

wear and tear. Nature has provided the ideal answer in the form of the hoof (or foot).

The hoof may be likened to a box, the outer casing of which is formed by a hard substance known as horn. Besides being hard, horn has elasticity and is capable of growing so that it is continually replaced as it becomes worn. The function of the foot is to support a body weighing some 500 kg at speeds of up to 64 kph over possibly rough ground. Obviously, the horn must withstand considerable friction and rough usage which would shatter many a hardened alloy composed of non-living substances; that the horn rarely breaks is indeed a tribute to its natural efficiency. The foot must also serve against concussion (jar) which is associated with the sledgehammer-like action recurring many hundreds of times per kilometre at the gallop. The structure of the foot is arranged so that, despite the mechanical stress to which it is subjected, the outer casing is fixed firmly to the contents by an interlocking of layers and is in no danger of flying off the end of the limb.

The pedal bone and the lower part of the second phalangeal bone occupy the centre of the box (Figures 13.5 and 13.6). These bones form an articulation commonly called the corono-pedal (or coffin) joint, at the back of which lies the navicular bone. The deep digital flexor passes over the navicular bone to its insertion on the back of the pedal bone and the tendon of the common digital extensor is inserted onto the front of the pedal bone.

The caudal aspect of the box is formed by a fibro-fatty pad which lies immediately above the frog and which, together with the lateral cartilage attached to the wings of the pedal bone, represents the shock absorbing mechanism of the foot. It is these structures which provide sufficient elasticity and movement so that the foot is not entirely rigid and unyielding when it meets the ground.

Horn

Horn is made up of cells somewhat similar to those found in the skin. They are, however, firmly cemented together with a hard sub-

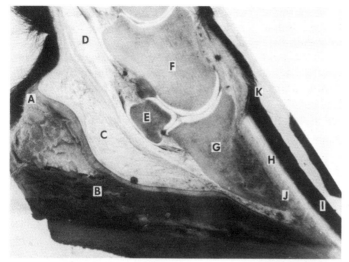

Figure 13.5 Cross-section of the foot showing: (A) bulb of heel; (B) frog; (C) fibro-fatty pad; (D) deep flexor tendon; (E) navicular bone; (F) second phlanx; (G) pedal bone; (H) white line (insensitive laminae); (I) wall composed of horn; (J) sensitive laminae; (K) coronary band

stance known as keratin. The horn grows from a special area around the coronet, in a way which may be likened to the growth of nail in our own fingers or toes. Just as our damaged nails can be made good only growing down from the nail bed, so the wall of the horse's foot can be replaced only by growth from the coronet. Horn is composed of three layers, the outer one helping to prevent evaporation of water so that the horn does not become brittle and crack (dryness may result in sandcracks); a dense middle layer which, if the feet are coloured, contains pigment; and an inner layer composed of a large number of fine, leaf-like filaments. This layer is often referred to as the insentitive laminae since, like the rest of the horn, they do not contain nerve endings.

The insensitive laminae fit into corresponding leaves which project from a velvet-

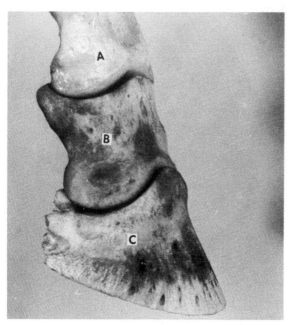

Figure 13.6 The bones forming the end of the limb comprise (A) first phalanx (long pastern bone), (B) second phalanx (short pastern bone, half of which is in the foot, and (C) the pedal bone (or coffin) bone also known as the third phalanx

like membrane covering the pedal bone (Figure 13.7). These are abundantly supplied with nerve endings and blood vessels and form the sensitive laminae. The two layers of filaments keep the hoof firmly attached to the skeleton and, in addition, the sensitive laminae nourish the horn.

The horn can, for the purpose of descrip-tion, be divided into the wall, bars, sole and frog (Figure 13.8). The wall comprises the front and sides of the foot, merging at the heels with the bars. The wall grows at the rate of about a centimetre per month and at this rate it would take about 12 months for complete growth to occur from the coronary band to the toe. The sole is composed of horn

Figure 13.7 The horn which forms the outer casing of the box, or foot, seen from above and with the contents removed. Note the insensitive laminae (X) which in life would be beneath the bulb of the heel

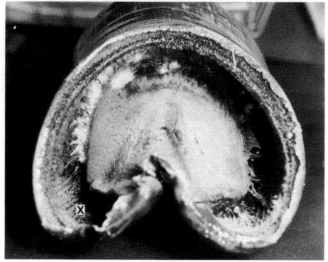

Figure 13.8 The front foot: (a) bulb of the heel; (b) bar; (c) sole; (d) wall; (e) frog

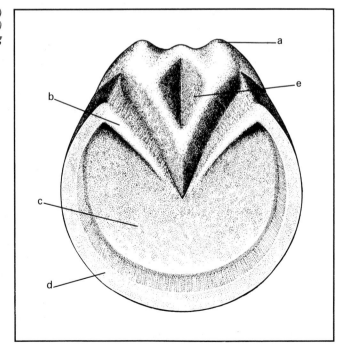

126

which is softer than that found in the wall since it contains a higher percentage of water. The inner or insensitive laminae of the wall can be seen as a white line where the sole meets the walls. The sole is usually concave and is divided into two by the frog which forms a wedge-like projection of a very pliable type of horn. Weight is normally borne by the lower part of the wall, bars and the frog.

Conformation

If the shape of the foot differs in any way from the normal conformation then that individual may be particularly susceptible to injury in the foot, as well as in the joints, ligaments and tendons farther up the limb. This is because faulty conformation may interfere with the main functions of the hoof (i.e. protection of the contents and reduction of concussion as the foot strikes the ground). It should be stressed that a foot of abnormal shape may *cause* unsoundness to develop farther up the limb, but also that the abnormality may be *the result* of faulty limb action.

The ideal foot is one in which the axis through the pastern and front of the foot make an angle of approximately 47 degrees with the ground. The sole should be slightly concave so that it does not protrude lower than the weight-bearing structures of the wall and bars and it should be divided by the frog into two equal halves.

The front feet should be rounded and wide in the heels, and the bars well developed; the hind slightly more sloping, narrower and more pointed with their soles more concave than those of the front (Figure 13.9).

The weight, whether at rest or in action, should be borne through the centre of the coffin joint and the column of bones which form the limb. In other words, it should be shared equally by each half of these bones on either side of their centre. The more pronounced the shift of weight to either side the greater will be the stress. This imbalance may be caused by a misshapen foot, or it may be the result of faulty action and conformation in parts above the pastern. In this case the shape

of the foot will be secondarily affected as one area becomes excessively worn compared with others which do not bear an equal share of weight. For example, an individual who has a base-narrow and toe-wide action of the hind limbs will bear more weight on the inside aspect of the foot. If we examine the sole of such an animal we will find that it is not equally divided by the frog but that the inner half is small compared with the outer half.

Diseases of the foot

There are various terms used in describing faulty conformation of the foot. 'Dropped sole' for instance implies that the sole is flat and therefore bears greater weight than it should. In these cases the foot is more susceptible to bruises, corns and other injuries. 'Contracted heels' means that the foot is narrow at the heels, while 'club foot' is a very upright hoof with the toe making an angle of perhaps more than 60 degrees with the ground.

These faults can be the consequence of inherited structural defects, faulty shoeing or disease. We saw earlier the results to the foot of defective action higher in the limb and this may result in any of the conditions just mentioned. For example, a yearling that suffers from contracted flexor tendons will place most of its weight on the toe; the heels will then grow unduly in length since the horn is not worn away in the normal manner and the individual will develop a tendency toward a 'clubbed foot'.

When horses go lame, veterinarians usually start their examination at the foot, because a substantial proportion of lamenesses occur here. One of the most common conditions is an abscess (collection of pus). This usually develops between the hoof and the pedal bone where it presses on the sensitive laminae. An abscess in this position is as painful to the horse as it would be in the root of one of our own fingernails. It is not surprising, therefore, that the horse is reluctant to place weight on the affected limb.

An abscess in the foot may start because

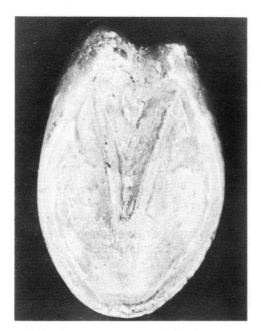

Figure 13.9 Dried specimen of the hind foot from three different angles showing the outer casing of the 'box' formed by the horn. The rather narrow pointed shape indicates that this specimen belongs to a hind limb

infection enters through a penetrating wound made by a nail or sharp stone, or it may be the result of the sole becoming bruised. People often talk of 'gravel' working its way into the foot but in many cases the grit probably finds its way in because the horn is already damaged.

Wherever an abscess forms, the pus it contains will eventually work its way to the outside in whichever direction there is least resistance. It may therefore burst through the coronary band, the sole or the heel depending on the original site of the abscess. Wherever it occurs an abscess should be drained by an opening from its lowest point and for this reason it is important to cut the horn immediately below. It is also necessary, as with all wounds, to give tetanus anti-toxin serum unless the individual has already been vaccinated against this disease or tetanus (lockjaw).

Bruising of the sole is another common injury and may result from a shoe which has been badly fitted or left on too long. The most usual site of bruising or corn, is between the bars and the wall. The horn becomes moist and reddened and the condition is associated with pain, especially when the horse is turned so that it throws more weight onto the affected side.

The bruise is frequently associated with a small haemorrhage in the sensitive laminae.

In some cases the sole will be tender to pressure but the discoloration of the horn may not appear for several days or even weeks. The condition may then be difficult to diagnose at the first signs of lameness; some indication of the cause may be found when the horn above the haemorrhage is cut away.

Fractures of the pedal and navicular bones are also very painful. The pedal bone may be broken at almost any point and a complete diagnosis can only be made by X-ray examination. Some fractures may take a considerable time to heal and will often cause permanent unsoundness; however, many horses will return to peak performance.

Laminitis is a condition in which the sensitive laminae become inflamed. The feet – it is unusual for only one foot to be affected – become hot and tender so that the horse tries to shift its weight. It may, therefore, adopt extraordinary stances. For example, it may bunch all four feet close together under its body, or alternatively stretch them as far in front and behind as possible; when walking it will snatch up the limbs like a cat on hot bricks!

Laminitis may be followed by disruption of the laminae followed by the rotation of the pedal bone as the laminae fail to fix the bone to the horn (Figure 13.10). The bone may even descend through the sole of the foot. Horses that have suffered from laminitis will often have feet with concave walls and may suffer from a condition known as seedy toe. In this the horn of the sole and wall at the white line becomes dry and crumbles. If a foot thus affected is struck with a metal instrument it will sound hollow.

A great deal has been learned recently about the true nature of laminitis, although the actual cause of the condition is still unknown; it may follow an acute illness involving diarrhoea, infection of the uterus after foaling, or as a result of nutritional disturbances, especially those associated with pasture management and the feeding of high-protein diets.

Navicular disease is a condition of the bone of that name situated behind the

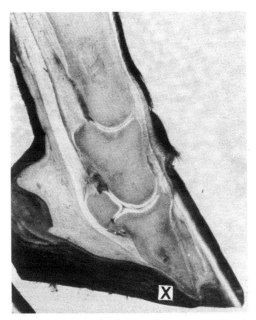

Figure 13.10 In laminitis, the sensitive laminae separate from the insensitive laminae and the pedal bone rotates downwards. In severe cases the bone may penetrate through the sole (X)

corono-pedal (or coffin) joint. Signs shown by affected horses include pointing of the limb at rest and lameness which usually has an incipient onset; in the early stages they warm up with exercise, perhaps starting out lame from the box but returning sound after exercise. On X-ray examination diagnosis is confirmed when cavities and new bone on the wings can be observed in the navicular bone.

Many horses previously diagnosed with navicular disease are likely to be suffering from poor foot conformation (i.e. long toe, low-slung heel; sometimes called caudal foot syndrome). If the foot conformation is corrected over several months, then the lameness may diminish as well.

An experienced observer may, by watching a horse's action, often suspect that the seat of lameness is in the foot. Confirmation is available through such clinical observations as the presence of heat and signs of pain when pressure is applied to the foot. In addition, the nerves leading to the foot are easily

129

accessible as they pass beneath the skin behind the fetlock and here they may be infiltrated by local anaesthetic and the foot desensitised. This technique, commonly referred to as a nerve-block, will cause the horse to go sound if the seat of pain is lower down the leg below the block. The foot may also be viewed by X-ray examination and this will indicate any alteration in the structure of the bones.

CHAPTER FOURTEEN

LAMENESS

Inflammation

When a horse feels pain, it alters its behaviour. Thus, in lameness the disturbance in gait is the result of the horse attempting to keep its weight off the affected foot. In these circumstances pain is part of the body's local response to injury. To understand lameness the reader must know something of the inflammatory process.

Inflammation is the body's reaction to injury in the broadest sense (e.g. wounds, abrasions and burns; foreign bodies, such as splinters of wood beneath the skin; infection with bacterial, viral or fungal microorganisms).

There are two main types of inflammation; acute and chronic.

The signs of acute inflammation are pain, redness, swelling and heat, and changes during the process are the same in horses as in other animals and in ourselves. There may also be limitation of movement (e.g. of an inflamed limb). Although redness cannot always be seen in horses, since the skin is usually covered by pigmented hair, the other signs are present.

Chronic inflammation is the term used for persistent lesions in which fibrous tissue formation is a prominent feature.

Before describing the differences between inflamed and healthy tissue we will refer to conditions in which the reader may have seen inflammation. For example, when a tendon is sprained, some of its minute fibres are torn. This represents an injury to the tendon, an inflammatory response takes place and the condition is referred to as tendonitis. If the interior of a joint is damaged, we use the term 'arthritis'; where the outer lining (periosteum) of a bone becomes inflamed, the condition is known as periostitis.

So far examples have been used of inflammatory processes found in the structures which make up the limbs, but there are numerous occasions when the process occurs in other tissues or organs. For instance, peritonitis is inflammation of the outer lining of the gut (peritoneum), hepatitis is associated with damage to the liver (perhaps by virus or bacteria) and similarly, pneumonitis is used if lung tissue is involved. Meningitis is an inflammatory reaction of the outer lining of the brain called the meninges, whereas nephritis follows injury to the kidney by infective or toxic agents. Finally, an abscess is a rather specialised type of inflammatory reaction which may be found in any part of the body but which frequently occurs just beneath the skin.

So much for examples; the reader will probably have realised that all the conditions mentioned, apart from abscess, end in '-itis'. This suffix denotes that an inflammatory process is involved.

To understand the changes which occur in the tissues during inflammation, let us consider the signs of heat, redness, swelling and pain, since these will be the most obvious to the reader in his or her everyday experience.

Heat of the affected part is due to the increase in blood flow which ensues once the tissues have become damaged. This extra blood is the direct result of the arteries in the area increasing their size; not only do the associated blood vessels dilate but blood may be diverted from its normal course toward damaged tissue. The very fine vessels known as capillaries open up to receive the additional volume of blood.

The sign of redness is also due to the increase in blood flow and, in particular, to the dilation of the capillaries. Similarly the throbbing often felt in an inflamed area is a consequence of pulsation transmitted by the heartbeat to greatly enlarged vessels. The phenomenon may be likened to the pulse wave normally felt where an artery lies close to the surface, such as a third of the way along the lower jaw in the horse, or on the inside of our own wrist. In an inflamed part the whole area appears to be pulsating.

The swelling of inflammation is due to excessive accumulation of protein-rich fluid which passes out of the blood vessels as their walls become more permeable. This fluid, which may be known as inflammatory oedema, comes to lie in the tissue spaces (i.e. between the layers of cells of which the body is composed). The lymphatic vessels normally drain away this fluid but it collects in inflammation.

Pain is the result of the stretching of special nerve endings through which the brain appreciates this particular sensation. Pressure on the area heightens the pain because of the increased tension on the nerve endings.

We have been concerned with the changes that take place during an inflammatory reaction. Now we must consider the purpose or function of the process. The blood flowing to the damaged area brings with it substances which neutralise toxins and combat microorganisms by collecting them together, or in other ways preparing them for ingestion by specialised white blood cells (leucocytes). These cells have the power of engulfing the bacteria and thus destroying them, although in the process they may themselves be killed. When large numbers of white cells are destroyed an abscess may be formed, the pus being made up mainly of an enormous number of dead white blood cells.

White cells also remove the debris tissue cells which have been destroyed by the injury. Once the cause of the damage has been dealt with, the inflammatory response is then concerned with repair. Excess fluid drains into the lymphatic vessels. Specialised cells capable of dealing with the problem are brought to the area in the blood. These cells, called fibroblasts, are spindle-shaped and provide a scaffolding to replace tissue. In this way they knit together the injured area. Two examples of this type of repair process are recognised in scars which form after a wound, or in a horse's tendon following sprain.

Once the repair has been achieved, the amount of blood entering the part is reduced and eventually inflammation subsides and the signs disapper. The extent and intensity of the process will depend largely on the nature of the damage and the area involved. To make this point clearer, one may compare the effects of a burn with a clean cut made by a knife. The amount of tissue damage associated with a cut is small compared with an area affected by a burn – which will usually be greater and, therefore, the nature of the inflammation is likely to be more wide-ranging.

The type of tissue also has to be considered. For instance, a tendon, with its poor blood supply, is often associated with a chronic inflammatory reaction whereas in a muscle the response is most frequently acute.

The inflammatory process may be likened to a fire in a town centre; the police, fire and ambulance services travel to the spot from near and far depending on the severity of the fire. Once the fire has been extinguished, demolition experts and builders follow.

In certain circumstances the inflammatory response of the body may bring its own problems. For example, when a horse's tendon is sprained, blood flows to the damaged part and there may be insufficient drainage away from the area, causing congestion. In the terms of the analogy, the roads are blocked by ancillary services and a traffic jam forms. We shall see later how treatment for leg inflammation is concerned with the problem of drainage of blood and fluid.

Another situation in which the inflammatory response is provoked by natural mechanisms getting out of hand is where the body becomes sensitive (allergic) to certain substances. These may be proteins, antibiotics, dust, etc. In these conditions the foreign substance enters the tissues through the routes of injection, inhalation or ingestion and stimulate the tissues to produce protective substances (antibodies). Antibodies are normally produced to combat infective agents. For example, a horse is vaccinated against the influenza virus and thereby the body is artificially stimulated by the vaccine to produce antibodies which neutralise the influenza virus, thus protecting the horse.

But in the case of allergies, the process gets out of hand and there is a violent local reaction when the invading substance is met by antibodies; the inflammatory response is initiated. We may see this in the form of wheals or spots on the skin as a result of the animal coming into contact with plant pollen or fungus. Other examples of allergic reaction are those associated with asthma in horses with broken wind.

However, the inflammatory process is normally associated with healing and without such a response by the tissues the body would not be able to combat or repair the injuries it is bound to sustain during a strenuous life in an environment containing many potential dangers.

Unsoundness in joints

Joints may become injured if they are subjected to unusual stresses (e.g. by over flexion or extension; by exaggerated pressure in a direction not normally undertaken, such as any sideways movement of the fetlock joint; by direct trauma resulting from a kick or brushing action, or by infection). The terms 'sprain' or 'strain' also may be used and occasionally a horse is said to have 'twisted' its joint.

These stresses may be sudden, as when a horse makes a false step, wrenching the joint and causing damage to one or more of the retaining structures; or they may be brought about by faulty action which causes slight but repetitive stress. We shall see later that treatment of parts damaged by faulty action is much less likely to be effective where the predisposing cause remains.

When any of the structures forming the joint are injured, an inflammatory reaction occurs. As previously explained, this represents the body tissues' response to damage. The signs of inflammation are heat, swelling, redness and pain. The area of heat and swelling may be localised or involve the whole joint, depending on the actual structures that are damaged and the amount of trauma sustained. For instance, if fibres of one of the ligaments supporting a joint are torn, this may cause a restricted reaction within the ligament. Alternatively, if the sprain is more severe, the inflammation may spread outward toward the skin and inward to affect the joint capsule so that the signs of inflammation will be correspondingly more severe. Likewise, the more intense the pain the greater the chances that the horse will go lame as it attempts to keep weight off the affected part.

We can roughly divide joint injuries and their associated inflammatory reactions into two categories: intraarticular and periarticular.

In the former category the interior, and in the latter category the outer, structures of the joint are involved.

Inflammation affecting the interior of the joint is called arthritis. The condition may be simple (serous type) and characterised by an increased amount of synovial fluid. The joint cartilages are not usually involved. On the other hand, osteoarthritis (degenerative joint disease) is a more advanced condition affecting the cartilages and the synovial membrane.

Degenerative joint disease
The term 'degenerative joint disease' (DJD) has been used with increasing frequency in recent years as our understanding of the

nature and growth of cartilage has improved with scientific knowledge.

Cartilage is a skeletal or connective tissue which is firm, flexible and slightly elastic. It consists of specialised cells (chondrocytes) enclosed in a matrix of collagenous fibres and firm jelly. It is found in all areas throughout the body.

DJD is considered by some to be a generalised condition of deficiency which may effect any one or more joints at differing stages of development and athletic usage. This concept will explain why defects may occur in the fetlock joint of one horse, the hock joint of another and in both in a third individual.

Degeneration of the cartilage surface may also be described as 'decay' or 'excessive wearing', but, whatever it is called, the essential process is that the surface of the cartilage loses its normal smooth, resilient surface and becomes granular with loss of substance and cells. This process starts in the form of a small ulcer and then extends more deeply so that more cartilage is lost.

The underlying bone then becomes inflamed and starts to proliferate (i.e. develops outgrowths of bone that develop into spurs). Two consequences follow this development:

1. As in all cases of inflammation the condition is painful.
2. The tiny projections of bone (spurs) may fracture off and become loose in the joint, thereby causing further damage to the joint surface as they become crunched when the joint moves.

DJD starts therefore as one condition and then develops into a cycle of events involving pain, further damage and extending degeneration. DJD is a disease of cartilage but the health of cartilage is closely associated with the joint oil (synovial fluid) that is secreted by the joint capsule and which lubricates the joint. The products of inflammation change the composition of joint oil which further disturbs the health of the surface of the joint. However, knowledge of this relationship has placed a means of assisting repair of the joint surface or, at least arresting further destruction by injecting substances known to be necessary for the health of cartilage. These substances are known as glycosaminoglycans.

Osteochondritis dissecans

As with DJD, osteochondritis dissecans (OCD) affects the cartilage. Some authorities believe that it is a form of DJD, but its development and symptoms are somewhat different and hence it is usually considered separately. OCD is confined mainly to the hock, stifle and fetlock joints. It takes the form of roughness developing on the surface of the joint cartilage. The area of roughness then develops into a surface flake, parts of which may crumble and become detached and fragments break loose into the joint cavity.

Though OCD affects horses of all ages its symptoms are seen characteristically in foals or yearlings when the joint becomes filled and a stilted gait develops, especially in those cases where the stifle joint is affected.

OCD may be treated surgically. The damaged cartilage is scraped away and this allows a healthy cartilage to develop. This procedure is now performed quite simply through the technique of arthroscopy.

Arthritis

Arthritis can also be caused by infection. Bacteria may enter through a wound or in the bloodstream as one happens in foals, a condition known as joint ill (infective arthritis). In advanced cases the joint surfaces are destroyed and become adhesive so that the cavity is obliterated and there is a complete loss of mobility. This situation is described as ankylosing arthritis.

The signs of arthritis include distension of the joint capsule due to increased synovial fluid, a thickening of the capsule itself and pain elicited by pressure over the area or on flexion and extension of the joint. Pain in movement will result in lameness. X-ray examination is essential to a diagnosis of arthritic changes and to differentiate between the various types and degrees of damage in the joint. Radiography is particularly important in establishing whether or not a fracture exists. Fractures that involve joint surfaces are particularly common in the small bones of the carpus, the pastern bone and the sesamoids of the fetlock joint.

When the joint is filled by an excess of synovial fluid, the distended capsule may be felt as a soft swelling at points where the capsule is free of overlying ligaments, tendons, etc. (Figures 14.1 and 14.2). For example, the capsule of the fetlock joint may be palpated between the cannon and the suspensory ligament (swellings referred to as articular windgalls); the carpus consists of three joints. The capsule of the middle one may be felt on the front of the joint and that of the upper on the outside of the forearm, immediately above the knee; distensions of the hock joint (bog spavin) appear on the inside and at two places on the outside of the hock. These fluid swellings may be distinguished from those caused by oedema

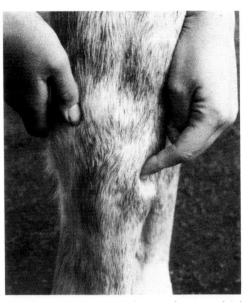

Figure 14.2 The right knee photographed from the side illustrates positions where the capsule of the upper joint may be felt. In cases of distension, fluid waves may be transmitted from finger to thumb

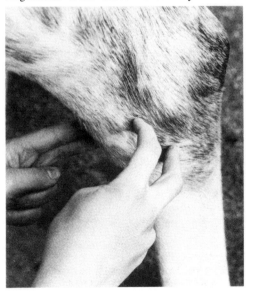

Figure 14.1 Positions in which the capsule of the joint may be felt. The two fingers on the left hand are pressing into the medial aspect (site of bog spavin) and those of the right hand rest on positions where the capsule is free to bulge if there is excess fluid in the joint

fluid and fibrous tissue by transmitting pressure waves through the fluid. For instance, if the capsule of the hock is pressed on the medial aspect the fluid waves can be felt on the outer aspect of the joint. In oedema, when the tissue is pressed, an impression of the fingerprint remains.

A filled joint does not necessarily mean it is affected by arthritis since it may be caused by humour (passive fluid accumulation). In borderline cases the two conditions may be differentiated only by laboratory analysis of the synovial fluid.

Periarticular injuries

Periarticular injuries can involve the ligaments or fibrous layer of the capsule (Figures 14.3 to 14.5). These structures are composed of numerous small fibres, a number of which become torn when a sprain occurs. This may happen at a point some way between, or actually at, the insertion onto the bone. In the latter event, the bone lining (periosteum) may be affected. The resulting inflammation causes an outgrowth of new bone (exostosis)

135

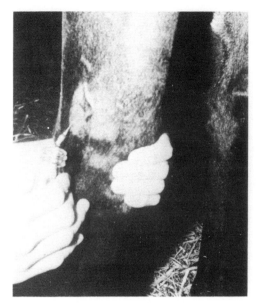

Figure 14.3 Synovial fluid being drained from the upper carpal joint of the right knee

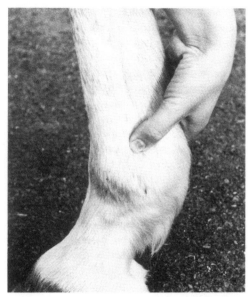

Figure 14.4 Position of joint capsule in the fetlock joint at the site of articular windgall

and the hard swelling can be seen radiographically as a roughened area on the bone surface. Certain types of ringbones and osselets are examples of the reaction of bone to a tearing of the periosteal lining at the places of attachment of ligaments and joint capsule. Periarticular injuries, inasmuch as they do not affect the joint surfaces, are less likely to cause lameness.

It should be emphasised, however, that there is often no clear demarcation between intraarticular and periarticular injuries.

The joints most commonly affected in young Thoroughbred racehorses are the carpus, fetlock and hock. With the carpus, it is the radial carpal bone, one of the small bones on the medial side of the joint, which is the most frequent site of arthritic changes. The hock, stifle and fetlock joints are those most frequently infected in cases of joint ill. Older horses may suffer from arthritis of the joints between the vertebrae.

Bones and their injuries

Bone is the hard substance of which the

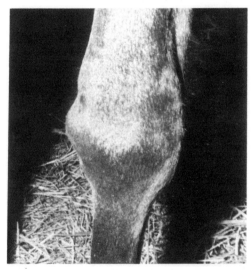

Figure 14.5 Excess fluid, due to arthritis (in this case) in the lower carpal joint of the left knee, is causing the capsule to bulge on the front and inside

supporting structure of the skeleton of the body is composed. It consists of a system of concentrically arranged cells (osteocytes) surrounded by a hard substance containing a high proportion of minerals, especially calcium and phosphorus.

The horse's skeleton is made up of 205 bones: spine 54, ribs 36, skull 34, limbs 80 and one sternum.

During the time a horse is growing, the bones become longer and thicker but on reaching maturity they do not alter appreciably.

Many bones have a new bone-producing area called the epiphysis which is composed of cartilage possessing the special property of being able to increase in size (Figure 14.6). Cartilage is a substance somewhat similar in structure to bone but not nearly as hard. There are other types of carrtilage besides that responsible for growth – that found in joints (hyaline) and that containing a high elastic content such as in the nose and in the discs between the vertebrae of the spine.

The cartilage at the end of the long bones, such as the cannon, forearm and second thigh, is often referred to as the growth plate. It grows toward the main shaft of the bone and is converted into bone at the place of union between the two. This process continues until maturity and the plate closes, becoming fused with the main shaft of bone. Closure occurs at different ages depending on the position of the bone. For example, in the lower end of the cannon bone it takes place between nine and 12 months and in the forearm between 24 and 30 months.

On the outer surface of all bones (except the joint surfaces) there is a membrane known as the periosteum, which is a fine sheet of specialised tissue. The periosteum is responsible for the health and shape of the bone and contains cells capable of laying down new, or destroying old, bone. It should be pointed out that bone, like other tissues in the body, exists in a dynamic and not a static state. Put another way, the cells and matrix are regularly replaced in a continuing process of exchange between blood and bone. The vitality of bone depends on remodeling by deposition and removal of the constitutents over periods of several months.

The inner surfaces of bones are lined by a membrane called the endosteum. This has a similar function to the periosteum and it also

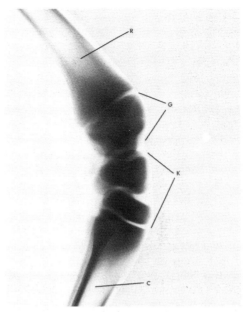

Figure 14.6 An X-ray photograph of a foal's knee joint (K) showing the area of growth (G) at the lower end of the radius (R). C = cannon bone

lines the central cavities of the long bones which house the blood-forming tissue known as marrow.

There are several types of diseases and injury which affect bones. Those of particular interest to horsemen are:
1. Periostitis (i.e. inflammation of the periosteum)
2. Osteitis, an inflammation of the bone substance itself due to infection or injury.
3. Disorders of the growth plate (epiphysitis).
4. Degeneration of articular cartilage (OCD).
5. Fracture.

These conditions all involve an inflammatory reaction familiar to the reader in splints, osselets, ringbones, curbs, etc. The swellings may vary in form depending on whether they are the result of inflammatory fluid, fibrous tissue or bone. They may be painful on pressure and/or during movement. In the latter event the horse will go lame.

The periosteum becomes inflamed due to tearing of fibres at the place of insertion of the joint capsule or ligament onto the bone. The same situation arises where tendons are joined onto bone. In all these cases small haemorrhages and fluid may collect beneath the periosteum, raising it from underlying bone. New bone is formed as a direct consequence of the inflammatory reaction and the outgrowth is usually described as an exostosis. Examples of exostoses at the site of ligament capsule or tendon insertions include ringbone and osselets (Figure 14.7).

Ringbones may be classified according to their position or whether they affect joint surfaces. They are generally designated as high if they occur on the lower part of the first phalanx and low if they are found on the lower part of the second phalanx. The term articular is used if they form in the proximity of the joint surface and periarticular if they do not. The term false ringbone is sometimes given to a periarticular (outside the joint) exostosis appearing in the middle of the second phalanx. The lump of new bone may be seen as an enlargement at the site of ringbone although in the early stages of inflammation there may be little or no swelling.

Osselets are associated with a periostitis resulting from a sprain in the insertion of the capsule of the joint at the front of the fetlock. They may also be related to injuries at the point of insertion of the extensor tendon and to arthritis due to concussion. Signs include a thickening on the front of the first phalanx which in the first instance is formed of oedematous fluid and fibrous tissue but which may subsequently consist of a bony outgrowth or exostosis.

Curbs are the result of an inflammation of the plantar ligament on the caudal aspect of the hock. This may be associated with a periostitis of the bone but it is more often confined to the ligaments and tissues immediately beneath the skin.

Sesamoiditis or inflammation of the sesamoid bones is a further example of inflammation at the surface of a bone due to a tearing of the insertion of a ligament, in this case the suspensory ligament.

Sore shins are another example of periosti-

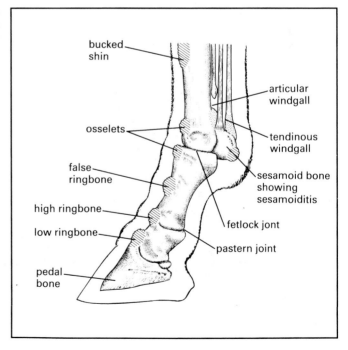

Figure 14.7 Positions where enlargements due to periostitis and exostosis are common

bucked shin

articular windgall

osselets

tendinous windgall

false ringbone

sesamoid bone showing sesamoiditis

high ringbone

fetlock jont

low ringbone

pastern joint

pedal bone

tis but in this case the inflammation is not associated with the insertion of a ligament or joint capsule. The signs may be confined to soreness in a localised area on the front of the cannon bone (Figure 14.8), or if the periosteum becomes lifted from the bone, new growth is stimulated and the shin becomes 'bucked' (Figure 14.9). In some cases of sore

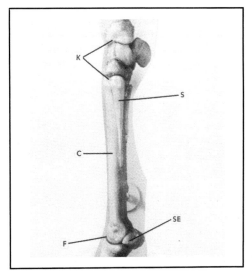

Figure 14.8 The cannon bone (C), knee joint (K), splint bone (S), fetlock joint (F), and sesamoid bones (SE)

Figure 14.9 'Bucked' shins may be the result of an inflammatory fibrous reaction or the formation of new bone following periostitis

shins the inflammatory reaction affects the subcutaneous tissue between bone and skin so that fluid collects and the swelling may then become firm and fibrous. It is not often possible to distinguish this swelling from one caused by an exostosis on the cannon bone except by X-ray examination.

The same distinction has to be made in the case of splints (Figure 14.10). These bones represent the remnants of the second and fourth metacarpal bones and their slender stalk is bound to the third metacarpal (cannon) by a ligament. An enlargement at the seat of splint may be the result of a periostitis of the cannon bone or an inflammation of the ligament. In both cases the inflammatory reaction is likely to spread into the tissues

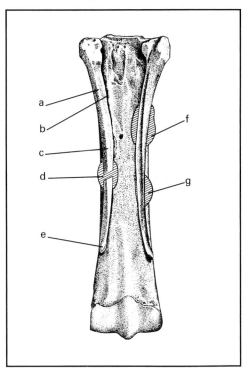

Figure 14.10 Various types of splint. The splint bones (a) are bound to the cannon bone by a ligament (b) and consist of a shaft (c) which ends in the button (e). Enlargements may be due to a callus (d) forming round a fracture, and inflammation of the ligament causing a periostitis and a fibrous reaction (f). Splints may also be the result of periostitis of the cannon bone (g)

139

THE HORSE FROM CONCEPTION TO MATURITY

around the splint bone so that a fibrous lump is formed.

An even more common cause of splints is fracture of the shaft of the bone resulting in callus formation. Whenever the continuity of bone is broken, the fractured edges react and form a fibrous union which becomes converted into bone (callus). In this way the fracture ends become permanently united and the strength of the part is restored. Once a callus is formed, the periosteum reduces any excess of new bone which it contains. In the case of a fractured splint bone, the callus projects from beneath the surface of the skin and it is only on viewing a radiograph that this type of splint can be differentiated from purely fibrous reactions.

Although the majority of fractured splint bones are successfully united by callus there are occasions when movement between the fractured ends provokes an exceptionally large amount of new bone. In these cases the callus may press on the suspensory ligament and tendons behind the cannon and these structures may become inflamed.

The healing process of bone that has been fractured (Figure 14.11) depends, as indicated, on immobilising the fractured ends. This is not usually a problem in the case of a

pastern bone (Figure 14.12), if the fracture is a simple one. Several months' rest and a supporting banadage are all that is required for succesful union and for the horse to go sound. Other fractures may be serious because they are comminuted (i.e. the bone is shattered into many fragments) (Figure 14.13). Alternatively, the blood supply may be poor, as in the case of sesamoid bones (Figure 14.14), so that effective union by callus formation may not occur; or the position in the skeleton is such that the part cannot be immobilised. The latter is the case in

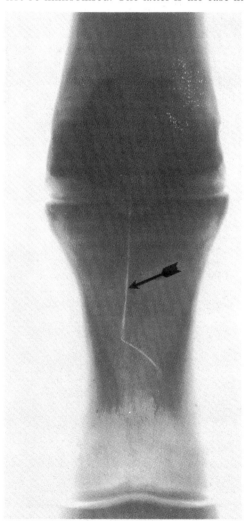

Figure 14.12 Simple fracture (arrowed) of the pastern bone

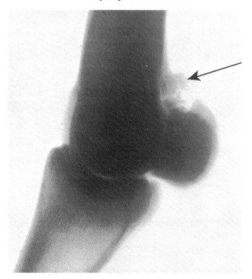

Figure 14.11 Radiograph of fractured sesamoid (arrowed)

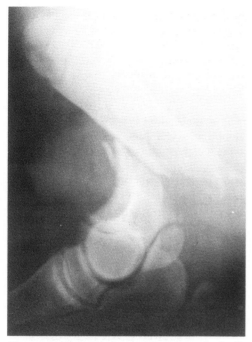

Figure 14.13 Comminuted fracture of a foal's humerus

weight-bearing bones high in the limb, such as the femur and humerus. In these, plaster casts are not practical and surgical support may be difficult because of the tremendous forces exerted on screws and plates.

Inflammation may also affect the growth plates in young horses, especially those at the lower end of the radius just above the knee, at the lower end of the cannon bone above the fetlock joint and at the lower end of the second thigh bone (tibia), just above the hock. This inflammation, or epiphysitis, may be the result of dietary factors such as excess protein or an imbalance in the ratio of calcium to phosphorus. A firm, painful swelling appears, usually on the medial aspect of the limb (Figure 14.15). The condition is often referred to as rickets but is probably not identical to that in other species. Signs are most commonly seen sometimes before closure of the particular epiphysis involved, that is, in the regions of carpus and hock in individuals 18 months old and in the lower end of the cannon at six months.

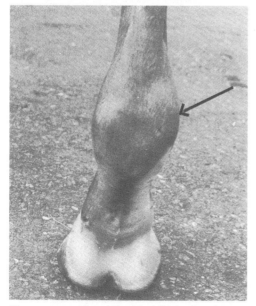

Figure 14.14 The right hind limb showing an enlargement (arrowed) behind the fetlock joints due to a fractured outer sesamoid bone

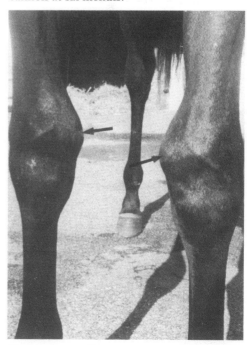

Figure 14.15 Inflammatory reaction involving the epiphysis (epiphysitis) and causing painful lumps (arrowed)

141

The term osteitis indicates inflammation in the bone substance itself and osteomyelitis that it is also present in the central marrow cavity. These conditions are frequently associated with infection. In the foal, abscesses form and the disease is referred to as joint ill, since the infection most commonly spreads to the joints themselves. In older animals, infection may also complicate fractures especially if these are comminuted or compound (i.e. the bones project through the surface of the skin).

Pedal osteitis, as the name implies, is an inflammation of the pedal bones and may be caused by chronic bruising of the sole, laminitis, puncture wounds or unknown causes. Osteitis is usually associated with destruction of bone tissue and therefore the bone becomes less dense but the inflammation often spreads to the periosteum so that a periostitis develops and new bone may become laid down (Figure 14.16). Because of the unyielding structures surrounding the pedal bone, a small amount of new bone at the surface will cause considerable pressure on the sensitive laminae and the condition is therefore likely to result in lameness.

Injuries to the horse's limbs

The anatomy of the horse's legs is such that it should be clear that injuries affecting the units which produce movement may involve muscle, tendon or nerve. The nature and point of damage will depend on a number of factors. Muscle injuries are often the result of fibres being torn when the muscle contracts but the part on which they exert their force remains fixed. This might happen if a horse is cast in its box or if it slips so that the limb is held in, or forced into, an abnormal position.

Tendon injuries, on the other hand, are usually the result of strain produced by the forces of motion, especially when the muscle controlling the tendon is fatigued and therefore fails to support its tendon in the normal, resilient manner. Tendons may also be

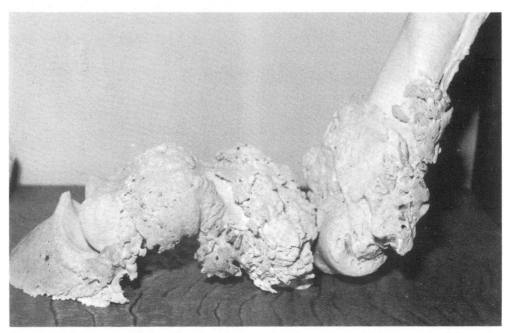

Figure 14.16 An extreme case of periostitis extending from the pedal bone on the left to the cannon bone on the right

injured by bruising as a result of a blow from the hind foot overreaching or through being struck into by another horse.

The essential ingredient of tendon or muscle sprain is the tearing of small fibres and the severity of the injury depends to a large extent on the numbers involved. The damage invokes an inflammatory response typical of the kind previously described. The part becomes swollen due to the increase in blood flow and to fluid which collects in the tissues adjacent to the site of damage. In addition, small haemorrhages may accompany the rupture of fibres.

Excessive bleeding into muscle may result in an enormous accumulation of fluid (mainly blood) finding its way towards the overlying skin where it causes a swelling, sometimes of massive proportions. This condition is known as a haematoma and the fluid is sometimes evacuated by lancing the skin with a knife or inserting a needle of large bore to establish drainage. Haemorrhages may also occur in tendons but are usually less extensive than in muscles and the fluid is contained by the much firmer nature of tendons. The changes associated with inflammation in both muscle and tendon are heat, swelling and pain.

The inflammatory response provides a way of removing injured tissue so that healing eventually takes place accompanied by the deposition of special cells (fibroblasts) which bridge the damaged area and form a scar.

In general, it is true to say that a sprained muscle heals faster than a tendon. The main reason for this is that muscle is well supplied with blood vessels, whereas tendon is relatively avascular. In addition, excess fluid is more readily drained from an area of muscle, by lymphatic drainage, and this helps to speed recuperation.

It is quite common to find that tendon sprains involve surrounding structures (e.g. blood may escape into the synovial fluid of the tendon sheath if there is one at the site of sprain). The sheath itself may be affected and can also receive a sprain separate to that affecting the underlying tendon. A further complication associated with tendon sprain is

that the inflammatory reaction may extend into the subcutaneous tissue (i.e. the layers immediately beneath the skin). Inflammation of the subcutaneous tissue is called cellulitis and is very painful.

Any muscle or tendon may be sprained but some are more frequently affected than others. The most common sites of torn muscles are the back and hindquarters and since most of these are painful it is not surprising they are associated with hind limb lameness. The muscles that move the shoulder are subject to sprains which result in forelimb lameness. Haematomas following a kick or other external injury are more often seen in the lower part of the hindquarters or between the forelimbs.

Nerves may be damaged as a result of trauma or by bacterial toxins. Nerves in exposed positions and those close to bone are particularly liable to direct injury; an obvious example is paralysis of the shoulder muscle following damage to the radial nerve as it passes over the front of the scapula immediately below the skin (Figure 14.17).

Radial paralysis of the forelimb can be an unusual consequence of surgical procedures

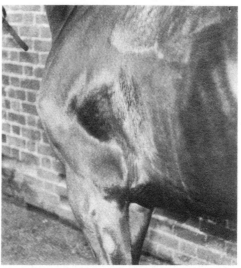

Figure 14.17 An injury to the radial nerve has resulted here in wasting of the triceps muscle which lies behind the line drawn from the point of the horse's shoulder to that of the elbow

where the horse has been cast and laid in a position which has damaged the nerve supplying the muscle concerned. The primary sign of radial paralysis is the horse's inability to advance its forelimb. Inflammatory lesions of the vertebrae which form the spinal column may indirectly cause damage to the nerve trunks as they leave the spine. Nerve injuries resulting in paralysis may be temporary or permanent, wasting of the muscles being most obvious in permanent paralysis.

Wasting also occurs when a muscle is not used because of pain arising from structures such as joints, bones and other muscle groups. To illustrate the point: a horse that has an injured hock joint might be prevented from using the limb so that the muscles of the hindquarters waste due to lack of use.

By far and away the most common site of tendon injury is in the region behind the cannon bones of the forelimbs. Here we may encounter sprains of the check ligament, the superficial and deep flexor tendons, or the suspensory ligament (Figure 14.18). The tendon sheaths enveloping the flexor tendons as they pass behind the carpus and the fetlock are frequently involved in sprains. Of the structures mentioned, the highest incidence

of injury occurs in the superficial and deep flexor tendons and most often in the region of the middle third of the cannon – a region devoid of tendon sheaths. In severe cases inflammatory reaction spreads to the subcutaneous tissue and the area becomes increasingly swollen due to the accumulation of fluid.

Sprains of the flexor tendons of the hind limbs are less common but the superficial flexor tendon which passes over the point of the hock can be dislocated.

Inflammation of tendon sheaths may be due to sprain or trauma from a blow (Figure 14.19). An invariable consequence is that there is an increase in synovial fluid which may become blood stained. Well-known examples are thoroughpins (Figure 14.20), swellings that involve the sheath of the deep digital flexor tendon as it passes behind the hock (Figure 14.21) and articular windgalls associated with the sheath of the deep and superficial tendons as they pass behind the fetlock joints.

The filling of tendon sheaths may also be the result of general reaction following periods of over-feeding and under-exercise, because of allergic responses to drugs or

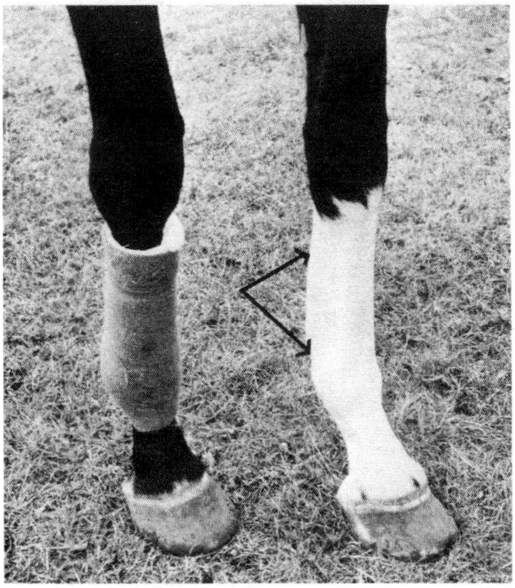

Figure 14.18 A swelling (arrowed) due to a sprain of the deep and superficial tendons of the near foreleg of a 3-year-old colt

Figure 14.19 A sheath may be injured by a kick; fluid escapes and infection enters causing acute lameness

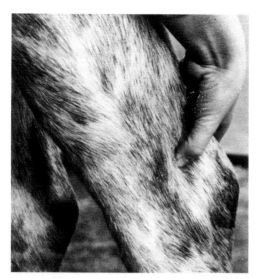

Figure 14.20 Palpating the area of thorough-pin

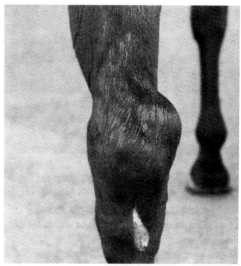

Figure 14.21 A bilateral swelling that has occurred as a result of excess synovial fluid in the sheath of the deep flexor tendon

infection. Unlike inflammatory reactions involved in thoroughpins, etc., these swellings usually subside once the condition is resolved. However, if the sheath becomes distended for any reason, it is more liable to fill again and in some cases they become permanently enlarged. This is particularly true of articular windgalls of the fetlock joints in older horses.

As already mentioned, a certain amount of scar tissue is formed during the healing of muscle and tendon and it is this which may cause further trouble when a horse resumes work. The scar may tear and cause inflammation similar to the signs of the original sprain. Successful healing implies that any scar tissue will be able to accommodate the strain of maximum exertion. A scar that is too short may cause the tissues to which it is attached to tear under the stress of exercise.

A further complication arises when the healing process involves different surfaces. For example, the superficial flexor tendon is sprained in the upper third of the cannon and a clot forms in its sheath. Eventually adhesions occur between the superficial and deep flexor tendon as well as in the sheath. After several months' rest the heat, swelling and pain of the original injury are no longer evident. The horse is then put back into work but the adhesions that have formed are torn and fresh inflammatory reaction takes place.

CHAPTER FIFTEEN

DIAGNOSIS OF LAMENESS

Lameness is a disturbance of gait, in most cases the result of a painful limb lesion, which upsets the horse's normal rhythm of action as it attempts to keep weight off the injured part.

Causes other than pain include paralysis due to nervous disorders when terms such as 'wobbler', 'shiverer' and 'stringhalt' may be used. Poor conformation can predispose to lameness by creating conditions which make the limb structures (i.e. ligaments, joints, bones, etc.) more susceptible to injury.

We have seen that any injury or damage is accompanied by an inflammatory process, the signs of which are heat, redness, swelling and pain. It is for these signs that we must look in our search for the site of any lesion causing lameness.

To diagnose lameness we must discover the site of pain and nature of the lesion involved. As a horse is unable to talk, veterinarians are faced with a problem in detection. Like a detective they must seek clues and assess their significance, persevering until they unearth the final solution. A methodical approach yields best results and investigations fall into the categories of visual inspection, physical manipulation and pressure, appraisals of swelling or heat and the application of special techniques such as nerve blocks, radiography and bone scanning.

A joint may be affected by a sprain, trauma, infection or from a process of degeneration of the cartilage forming the joint surface. Each of these conditions requires expert diagnosis and it is not the place here to describe these in detail.

The methods used to diagnose the exact nature of injury include a clinical evaluation by manipulation and palpation, radiography, ultrasonography (scanning of tissues with diagnostic ultrasound) and needle puncture to obtain synovial fluid (joint oil) for laboratory examination.

Looking for signs of pain

The cornerstone of lameness diagnosis is the visual examination (i.e. the interpretation of signs exhibited by the moving horse whether walking and trotting or moving over in its box).

An alteration in gait, which is the horse's way of keeping weight off a painful part, illustrates pain just as much as rolling does in an individual with colic; both are a matter of cause and effect.

Signs of pain depend on its severity and its site. For example, severe pain resulting from an abscess in the foot or a fracture of the pastern bone will cause the horse to avoid placing any but the very minimal amount of weight on that limb. In both these cases the site of pain is in direct line with the weight-bearing column and the damaged part receives maximum pressure during movement. The disturbance in gait is therefore extreme and the horse may hop on three legs.

By contrast other lesions may be less painful or, to put it another way, painful only at paces faster than the walk when stress on the part is increased as in simple arthritis of the carpus joint or a damaged splint bone.

Sometimes the lesion may be sited so that it is painful only during certain movements, for instance, a horse suffering from a

146

sprained muscle in the hindquarters may go lame when it moves over in the box but not at the walk or trot.

In some conditions a horse may show signs of pain at rest (Figure 15.1). For example, one that is suffering from navicular disease will point its toe. Resting the affected limb for exaggerated periods may also be associated with lesions that are particularly painful or those that receive pressure or tension (as in muscle) when the limb is in the weight-bearing position.

The above examples emphasise the necessity of observing the horse at rest as well as in movement, both in and out of the stable.

In general, signs of lameness are most obvious when a horse is walking or trotting. At faster paces the eye cannot easily discern disturbances in gait, although they may be felt by a rider. The visual diagnosis of lameness is best learned by observing a horse in action either directly or on film in the company of an experienced person. Here it is possible to state some general principles.

The horse will raise the long axis of its body as the lame limb meets the ground and lower it as the opposite leg comes to bear weight. This means that a horse will show forelimb lameness by raising the head and withers as the lame leg meets the ground. In hind limb lameness the reverse occurs although to a lesser degree (i.e. the head drops as the unsound limb meets the ground in severe cases). A more frequent sign is increased amplitude of movement of the 'joint of the hip'. Normally asymmetric head movement is absent in a sound animal.

It may be difficult to distinguish between a hind and forelimb lameness simply by observing movement of the head since this will tend to be the same if the horse is lame on, for example, the right hind or the left forelimb. If, however, the observer stands to the side and lets the horse trot past it should be possible to detect a shortness in stride of the affected limb.

Some confusion may also arise if a horse is lame on more than one leg since the signs of lameness in one limb will tend to cancel out those in another especially if both forelimbs or diagonally placed fore and hind limbs are affected. In these cases special methods of diagnosis such as nerve blocks may be necessary. Nerve blocks are also needed when just one limb is affected.

Hind limb lameness can sometimes be best observed from behind. As a horse walks or trots away, the angle of the hip is seen to rise

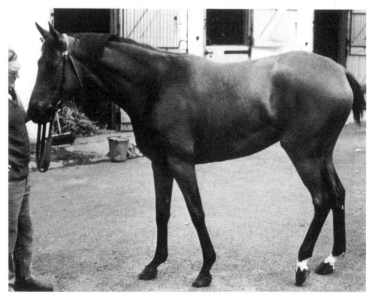

Figure 15.1 This horse is showing evidence, at rest, of lameness in the near hind

as the affected limb meets the ground and conversely to drop on the sound side. There is an increased range of movement in the *lame* leg.

Hind limb action can also be tested by causing the horse to turn in a tight circle to the left and right, making it move over in the box while the head is held, by causing it to walk backward – wobblers that are special cases of lameness may be most readily diagnosed when the horse is backed (Figure 15.2) or when made to pull up suddenly from a trot.

Notice should be taken of whether or not lameness is accentuated during any particular manoeuvre. For instance, if the site of the painful lesion is to one side, as in a bruised sole, lameness may be obvious when the horse turns and throws extra weight onto the affected part. Signs of lameness may vary over hard or stony ground compared with turf. In certain cases of lameness affected horses warm up with exercise; that is, the signs temporarily diminish. Navicular disease is an example and also sprained muscles which become less painful as they are brought into use and conversely 'seize up' when the horse is 'cold'. However, exercise tends to exacerbate bone and joint injuries.

It should be possible to identify the lame limb by watching a horse move in these different ways. We may be in a position to speculate on the actual part which is the site of lameness, but this must be confirmed by other procedures.

Manipulation

The object of manipulation is to elicit a response to pain caused as pressure is brought to bear on the damaged part (Figure 15.3). Joints may be tested by forced flexion and extension or by rotation in a clockwise and counter-clockwise direction. These manoeuvres tend to stretch the joint capsule and its ligaments, as well as causing movement over articular surfaces so that the horse feels pain if any inflammatory lesions are present on these structures. Only a moderate amount of force should be used since exaggerated stress may cause pain whether or not the joint is in fact injured.

Manipulation of the lower limb joints is comparatively simple but surrounding muscle limits complete manipulative examination in the case of the hip and shoulder joint and, to a lesser extent, the elbow and stifle.

Certain joints such as the hock, carpus

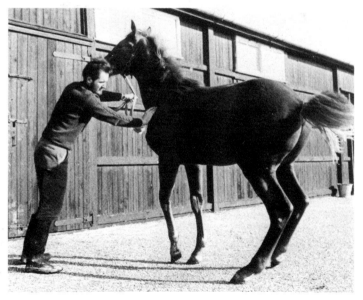

Figure 15.2 Horses that are incoordinated behind (wobbler disease) may show it when backed up, but be able to use their hind limbs in actions such as rearing and cantering

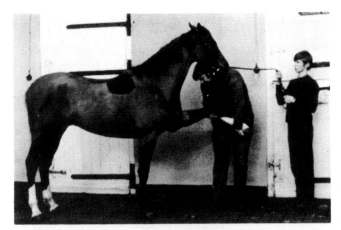

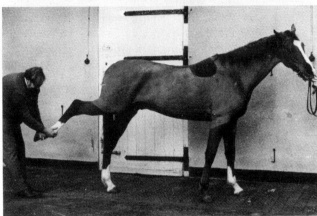

Figure 15.3 The veterinarian manipulates the horse's front limb (top) and hind limb (centre and below) for evidence of painful lesions in the outer part of the limb

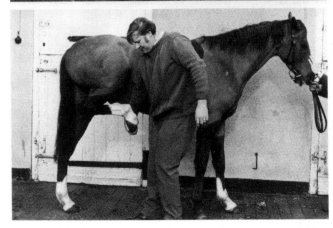

(Figure 15.4) and fetlock (Figure 15.5) can be stressed by flexing for several minutes and then observing whether or not this subsequently causes an increased degree of lameness as the animal trots.

Testing of muscle for a painful lesion is made difficult by the fact that it is not often possible to stretch the muscle sufficiently to cause pain. In addition the neighbouring muscles will reflexly guard the injured muscle

149

Figure 15.4 Manipulating the carpus for evidence of pain

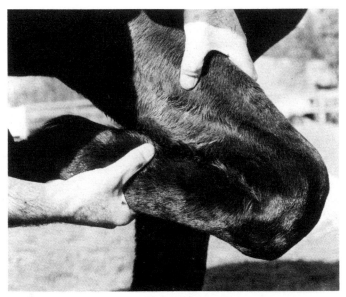

Figure 15.5 Manipulating the fetlock joint

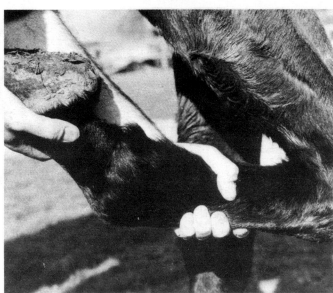

during manipulative procedures. A more efficient method of diagnosing injuries in muscle is that of Faradism which is described later.

Pressure

Signs of pain may be exposed by exerting pressure over areas in which injury is sus-

pected. Sore spots on the splint, cannon, pastern bones and tendons are best examined by pressing on them between thumb and first two fingers; investigation of areas higher in the limb can be made by probing with the finger tips (Figure 15.6); and pincers should be used on the foot in view of the relatively unyielding casing of horn (Figure 15.7). If a fracture of the shaft of the ilium (pelvis) is suspected, the point of the hip may be hit

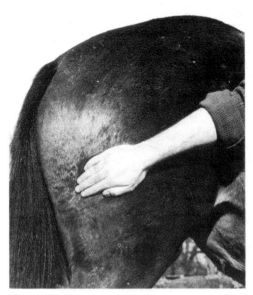

Figure 15.6 Testing the thigh for sore spots

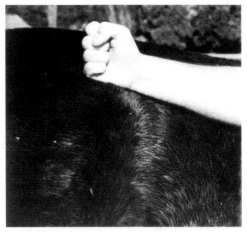

Figure 15.8 Using a clenched fist on the outer angle of the pelvis

Figure 15.7 Using pincers

Figure 15.9 Pressing the back with the thumb to diagnose the presence of painful lesions on the spinous processes of the backbone

firmly with the outside of the clenched fist (Figure 15.8). The back may be tested by pressing on the tips of the bony processes in the midline under the saddle region (Figure 15.9) and by observing any evidence of a 'cold back' reaction when the rider mounts.

The demeanour of the horse under investigation should be carefully noted. Signs of pain include withdrawal of the part, putting the ears back, jerking the head and grunting.

Examinations should always be carried out quietly and with patience so that false reactions are avoided. To ensure that the horse is not reacting as a result of apprehension or resentment, it is essential that the opposite limb should be checked in an identical manner. Certain cautionary comments are necessary if we are not to be misled by the patient, for instance, some parts of the body may be sensitive to pressure whether or not

151

they are injured (the coronet and back for example). Then, horses may become nervous about being felt and flinch in anticipation due to previous experience of a painful injury in that region.

Swelling

Swellings frequently accompany injuries and can usually be seen or felt at the skin surface. They may be described as splints, curbs, ringbones, osselets, bowed tendons and so on, although these terms do not provide any indication of their nature. Essentially they consist of an inflammatory reaction (Figure 15.10) in underlying structures (such as bone, periosteum, ligaments and subcutaneous tissue) which is fibrous, bony or oedematous. It is often necessary to employ X-ray examination to determine if a hard swelling is composed of fibrous tissue or new bone.

Oedematous swellings may be recognised by the fact that they pit on pressure; the imprint of a finger will be left after the area has been gently squeezed. Oedema usually accompanies acute inflammation of ligaments and tendons and may also be associated with bleeding from small blood vessels that have become fragile due to the damage caused by

sprain. The swelling around a sprained tendon may therefore consist of blood and oedematous fluid extending from the centre of the tendon to the underlying tissues of the skin.

Heat

The traditional method of search for the site of lameness is to feel for areas of heat. In some cases this sign is obvious and when accompanied by pain and swelling a conclusive indication of the area involved. In the absence of swelling the detection of heat is a rather more subjective matter and care has to be exercised that the difference in temperature in two parts is not the result of the horse standing with more or less weight on that particular limb. The development of electronic techniques for measuring skin temperature may, in the future, give greater objectivity to this aspect of lameness investigation.

Special techniques

At present there are a number of special techniques used by veterinarians. Nerve blocks can be very helpful where anatomically

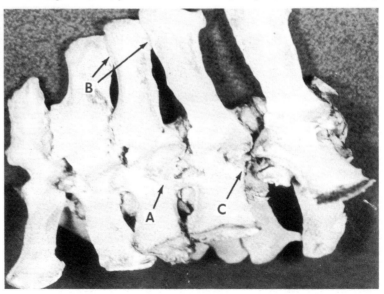

Figure 15.10 Five of six lumbar vertebrae from a horse which in life was going to be lame behind because of inflammatory lesions (A) between the joints; (B) between the spinous processes. Note (C) is a normal joint

possible. Small amounts of local anaesthetic are injected over a nerve trunk so that the part it supplies loses sensation (Figure 15.11).

An example will help to illustrate the point: a horse is suspected of being lame in the foot or lower part of the pastern so the two nerve trunks on either side of the leg are blocked at the level of the fetlock joint. If the block is successful (this can be tested by pressing on the skin around the coronet), any pain coming from a point below the block will not be felt so long as the effects of the anaesthetic last (usually about two hours) and the horse will go sound as a result. If, however, the pain is coming from above the block then the anaesthetic will make no difference to the lameness. Nerve blocks can be carried out at points below the knee or hock but above these joints the distribution of nerves is such that they are not always practical.

Anaesthetic solutions may also be injected into joints to 'freeze' them so that any difference in lameness before and after administration can be assessed. Anti-inflammatory drugs such as cortisone may also be used for this purpose.

Diagnosis of muscle injuries presents a special problem because, as already mentioned, it is not usually possible to passively move the limb so that the injured muscle is stretched sufficiently to make the horse feel pain. A technique is available which overcomes this limitation. When an electric current is passed through a muscle it causes it to contract. This principle is invoked in a form of therapy and diagnosis commonly referred to as Faradic stimulation (after English physicist Michael Faraday, 1791–1867). Two pads are placed on the horse and an alternating current of low voltage fed between the two. The muscle under the smaller of the pads contracts at each make or break of the current. In this way individual muscle groups may be tested for evidence of pain. Normally the horse shows no resentment at having its muscle made to contract by Faradic stimulation but if a lesion is present the horse will flinch and show by its behaviour that it is feeling pain. This method of diagnosis requires some experience on the part of the operator before it can be used successfully but once mastered it is a helpful aid for diagnosing injuries to the muscles of the back and limbs (Figure 15.12).

In many instances, radiography, that is, examination by X-ray photograph, is essential to a full understanding of the case, particularly where bone or joints are involved. X-ray examination of soft tissues such as tendon,

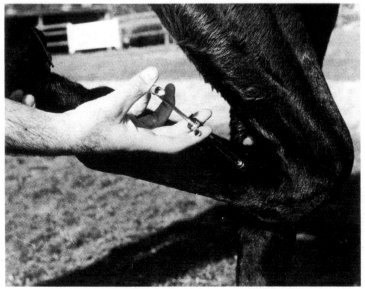

*Figure 15.11
Anaesthetic being
injected over areas of
nerves to cause nerve
blocks*

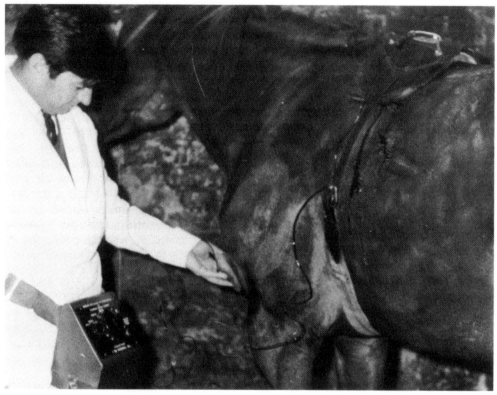

Figure 15.12 Faradism is being used here to test muscles around the shoulder by causing them to contract

muscle or ligament, except where attachments to bone are involved, is not usually helpful. It is hard tissue only which shows on the photograph. Another of this technique's limitations is that it is difficult to obtain photos of the bones and joints such as the hip, pelvis or back, because they are buried deep in muscle. Radiographs above the hock and carpus require machines of greater power.

Lesions on bones may become apparent only some weeks or even months after the original injury – another reason to limit X-rays. A fracture, except in rare cases, will show immediately but early arthritic or periosteal lesions may cause pain and lameness before evidence of their presence appears on the X-ray photo as a roughened edge or darkened area on bone or joint surfaces.

Gamma scintigraphy has greatly assisted diagnosis of fractures in the acutely lame performance horse where there may be few obvious clinical findings.

The horse is injected with a small amount of a radioactive substance – techniform MPD – which has a high affinity with areas of bone activity. The compound bonds to such areas, 'hot spots', and these are found several hours later by means of a hand-held probe, or gamma camera, which is sensitive to the low-grade radiation emitted by the substance within the horse. Areas of high activity such as fractures (and the growth plates) give an increased reading on the measuring instrument.

It is usual practice to scan the other leg of the pair (i.e. left and right fore, or left and right hind). In rare bilateral cases, both front legs, for example, there will be hot spots at the same site in both forelegs.Once a hot spot has been identified, the area is then radiographed with high-detail film and multiple views until a fracture is found.

Gamma scintigraphy has played a very significant role in the diagnosis of fractures in racing Thoroughbreds by pinpointing the area where radiography should be concentrated. It is of less value in low-grade, long-standing lameness.

The pelvis and to some extent the back can be explored by means of the rectal examination. The veterinarian can press on the pelvis or the muscle lying on the underside of backbone in order to elicit any signs of pain. The major arteries running to the hind limbs can also be felt for evidence of aneurysms of thrombosis which are sometimes the cause of hind limb lameness.

Arthroscopy is a technique that can be used to diagnose, as well as treat, joint injuries.

Conclusion

Most cases of lameness can be diagnosed, although some require a lengthy and painstaking investigation before the injured part can be identified. In comparatively rare instances veterinarians must admit defeat; perhaps the techniques required to confirm the presence of injury are not available.

CHAPTER SIXTEEN

TREATMENT OF LAMENESS

Because pain is the actual cause of lameness, so relief of pain must form the basis of any cure. An extreme illustration is the act of denerving a part, such as the foot, by cutting its nerve trunks so that all sensation is lost. In this case the lesion remains but soundness of action is restored. Most therapy does not rely on this drastic and irreversible alteration but is aimed at alleviating the inflammatory reaction and speeding repair.

The veterinarian, by contrast to his medical colleague, is expected to restore his patient to full physical fitness in the shortest possible time; in human medicine a cure may be claimed if pain is removed. Therapy which enables a racehorse to canter but not gallop might be likened to an opera singer who is cured to the extent of being able to appear on stage but not to sing.

Treatment of injuries depends upon their nature and the structures that have been damaged or inflamed. With injuries of bones, joints and ligaments, box rest is often the central avenue of approach to restoring normal function. Physiotherapy, antibiotics and anti-inflammatory drugs may also form part of therapy depending on the nature of the injury.

The restoration of complete fitness is the consideration above all others that dictates the methods used in treatment and which represents the greatest single obstacle to success. It is also the reason why, over the years, so many techniques have failed to satisfy the requirements of veterinarians and trainers and why there is a perpetual search for new skills.

We will approach treatment under the following headings: control of inflammation; arthroscopy; and management of scar tissue.

Control of inflammation

The extent of the inflammatory process must be controlled so that sufficient blood flows to the injured part, bringing with it the cells which are vital to repair. But too much blood will produce congestion causing minute blood vessels to rupture and allowing blood to escape into the damaged area together with excess oedematous fluid. This delays healing and results in excessive scar tissue or adhesions which, in practical terms, means the injury is more severe, its effects more lasting and complete recovery less sure.

Control of inflammation is essential from the moment an injury takes place and often insufficient attention is paid to early warning signs. Let us consider various methods by which inflammation can be made to work to our advantage so that the horse is restored to function in the shortest possible time.

Cold therapy
Cold therapy and drugs represent the spearhead of attack. In the former category, continuous flow from a hosepipe applied over the injured part is effective and simple. Standing the horse in a stream of running water or attaching a rubber tube with holes in it around the part are variations of cold water treatment which may be used on legs. Cold water bandages require constant changing to ensure that the cooling effect is more than transitory and ice applied by bandage or

packed into plastic boots are other methods favoured by many trainers and veterinarians. In addition, cooling lotions based on lead acetate and zinc sulphate and a number of proprietary solutions have their advocates and varying degrees of success.

Cold therapy is particularly important in treatment of sprains of the deep and superficial flexor tendons of the forelegs. Lowering of temperature of injured tissues prevents the inflow of blood to those parts where draining is relatively poor. The process of control may be aided by anti-inflammatory drugs. Corticosteroids have nowadays lost their popularity; the drugs known as NSAID (Non Steroidal Anti-Inflammatory Drugs) are now most commonly used – for example, phenylbutazone. They act primarily by suppressing the inflammatory process and in general are more effective the earlier they are used; another reason for applying treatment at the first signs of an injury (Figure 16.1).

Certain substances (e.g. hyaluronates) may assist in the healing of damaged joints.

Heat therapy

Once inflammation has been controlled other measures may be considered. Alternate hot and cold therapy promotes the passage of blood through the part by stimulating inflow and promoting drainage. Heat may be applied in a poultice form of bran, kaolin or boracic acid-impregnated gauze. However, experiments measuring the temperature of skin and underlying tissues by means of thermocouples show that heat does not penetrate far and that the poultices themselves soon lose their heat.

High-energy waves

Because poultices soon lose their heat, high-energy waves produced by various machines, similar to those used in human physiotherapy, have been used on horses. In summary these are:

Ultrasonic

Ultrasonic therapy is where ultra high-frequency sound waves are passed into the tissues and converted into heat. This treatment appears most beneficial when used on soft tissue injuries such as those in muscles. The heat penetrates deeper than in other forms of therapy and also the pulsating quality of the waves has some massaging effect. The sound waves are transferred from electricity by a machine possessing a metal head. This is placed over the area of treatment, but because the waves do not pass through air it is

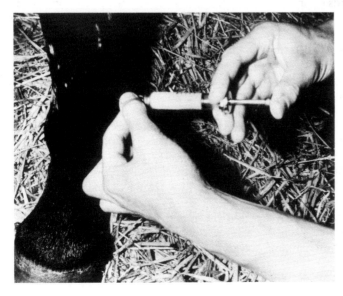

Figure 16.1 Certain drugs may be injected into a fetlock joint

necessary to use a substance such as mineral oil or water to establish contact with the skin.

Diathermy

Diathermy consists of passing into tissues short waves or ultrashort waves, in which the current oscillates at several million cycles per second. The depth of penetration will be in the order of 5 cm and the waves may be applied from a single electrode or by including the part within the circuit. Short waves are particularly useful in the treatment of injured joints and other associated structures.

Counter irritation

Another old-fashioned approach to therapy and one that might be held to be opposite to those already described was the use of counter-irritation. This is a term used to describe the action of blistering. A substance is rubbed into the skin that causes superficial inflammation. Blisters have now largely been replaced by more modern approaches to the treatment of injuries.

Rest

Whatever therapy is chosen, a most important consideration in healing is that the part should be at first rested and then gradually returned to full use. Equine patients are, unfortunately, not very cooperative in this respect. Once the pain has diminished they tend to make violent movements which undo much of the progress achieved. Although we would like to restrict some of our patients to many months of inactivity to give the best chance of complete healing, time is a commodity in short supply and commercial interests usually deem otherwise. In general, tendon and joint injuries require rest or relative inactivity for weeks or even months depending on their severity, while those affecting muscle are, on the whole, best treated by continued use although on a controlled basis. Faradism is the optimal therapy for treatment of muscle injuries because by this means it is possible to exercise artificially the injured muscle through daily treatment.

Faradism

This technique has already been mentioned but its principles should be summarised. The therapy is based on the passing of an electric current through muscles in the area of injury. The current is a rhythmic surged Faradic current at a frequency of 80/100 per minute. This produces rhythmic muscular contractions which are not usually resented by the horse and, providing their strength is regulated, even painful parts can be made to move. In this way the circulation is augmented and the effect is much the same as massage. In addition the process helps to limit the formation of adhesions or shortened scar tissue which, if allowed to develop, may result in further tearing of adjacent muscle fibres during exercise once healing has taken place.

The apparatus is run on batteries contained in a small box and carried on a belt around the operator's waist. The control panel regulates the strength of the current and number of surges produced beneath the active electrode which is a small pad held in the operator's hand. The indifferent electrode covers a much larger area and contractions do not occur at its site of contact – usually the horse's back. Contact is facilitated by saturating the coat in water and movement of the active electrode is facilitated by a lubricating jelly.

Muscle injuries are treated daily and the horse gradually returned to full work while still receiving treatment. In some cases that do not respond to other forms of therapy, Faradism achieves dramatic results.

Arthroscopy

When a joint is damaged medical treatment may be sufficient to alleviate suffering and even restore function. However, direct intervention to remove a chip or to scrape a degenerated area of cartilage may be an essential course of action. Opening a joint poses the risks of introducing infection and/or creating a necessarily penetrating wound of the joint capsule and its membrane which may fail to heal, thereby creating an open joint with consequent loss of joint oil and further risks of infection entering the joint.

These risks can be avoided only by very strictly controlled conditions of surgery. Asepsis is absolutely essential and the patient must be completely immobile during the operation. These conditions have been met for many years in equine and human orthopaedic surgery. With the horse, the advent of modern anaesthetic drugs and techniques together with special surgical facilities reaching standards found in human hospitals, enables surgeons to enter joints and perform appropriate surgery with minimal risks of contamination and maximal chances of uneventful healing of the wound.

Nevertheless in exposing the joint surfaces it was necessary to make fairly substantial wounds, perhaps 3 cm or 4 cm long. The introduction of arthroscopy enabled the surgery to be performed without the need for large wounds but with two portals of entry no more than 1 cm length at the most.

Arthroscopy means literally scoping (viewing) arthros (a joint). The procedure is still performed under general anaesthesia in order to ensure complete immobility for the surgeon. All that is required is a small incision to pass a tube through which the surgeon may view the interior of the joint.

Another small incision is made on the side of the joint opposite to the place of entry for the viewing instrument (endoscope) in order to pass an appropriate instrument for removing chips of bone or to scrape the joint cartilage. Following the operation the wounds require only one or, at the most, two stitches compared with maybe 10 or more in the performance of the old style approach.

This keyhole surgery is very successful in achieving its objective both in surgical terms and in rapid healing. It does not in itself lead to a more rapid recovery of the joint injury but its simplicity allows for and encourages much more frequent use of surgical correction of injuries to racehorses. The more frequent use in itself has provided surgeons throughout the world with more experience and therefore better techniques which in themselves lead to impoved results.

Scar tissue

The length of the healing scar is one of the major problems of treating lameness. To produce a complete cure the healing process must end with the formation of scar tissue, the strength of which is sufficient to avoid a recurrence of the injury. Weak scars may lead to tearing of healthy tissue to which they have become attached or they may not themselves be strong enough to withstand the full pressure at exercise.

Two examples will help the reader to understand. A muscle is sprained (i.e. some of its fibres become torn and an inflammatory process is provoked). The damaged tissue is removed by specialised cells brought to the area by the bloodstream and healing is completed by the laying down of a small amount of fibrous scar tissue. Consequently, signs of heat and pain disappear and the horse is restored to soundness at slow paces. However, when it gallops the area is again subjected to maximum stress; if the healing scar is too weak it results in further tearing of muscle fibres so that the injury recurs and the horse again becomes unsound.

The same thing happens in a tendon and in addition the surface of the tendon may become inflamed and adhesions form between it and the sheath. Then, when the horse goes back into full work, these adhesions tear and signs of sprain recur.

Finally, when we consider success or failure of treatment we should distinguish between the causes of injury. Some injuries are caused by a once-and-for-all happening (e.g. a stumble or false step) and some by a predisposing factor. This means conformation in action is such as to place undue strain on a particular part, thereby making it more sus-

159

ceptible to injury. Treatment in the latter event does not remove the underlying cause and is, therefore, never likely to be completely successful.

Greater emphasis should be placed on functional rather than static conformation. For example, a horse that is back at the knee may for this reason place greater strain on the check ligament and tendons behind the cannon and these will become more susceptible to injury. But many horses with this conformation stand training and it is sometimes those that tend to stand over at the knee which become involved in sprains of the structures mentioned. This illustrates the point that injuries depend not on how the horse stands but rather on how it uses its limbs when galloping.

We are unlikely to make great advances in treatment of lameness until we have discovered more about predisposing causes. There is an increasing need to apply modern photographic, electronic and physical techniques to the investigation of stresses imposed on particular parts in galloping. Not until we have achieved a better understanding of these shall we be able to assess the success of any particular line of physiotherapy.

CHAPTER SEVENTEEN

THE FEEDING PERSPECTIVE

Feeding is a subject so important to the health and normal development of horses that it deserves special study. Unfortunately, relatively little is known compared with the wealth of data available for other species. Many of our feeding practices are based on knowledge of the requirements of farm animals and often there is no way of knowing whether or not they are applicable to horses.

The reason for this lack of information is that the horse is too valuable an animal to investigate *en masse* for the serious study of nutritional problems. To illustrate the sort of approach required, we can take the case of an experiment to investigate the need for a particular element in the diet of sheep. Four hundred sheep are divided into two groups, one fed normally and one on a diet deficient in the element. At the end of the experiment all are slaughtered and the carcasses examined and compared. The cost of such an experiment is relatively small but the expense would be enormous using horses.

Paradoxically, despite the horse's value, the species is not considered sufficiently important to justify the allocation of government funds for research into nutrition. Therefore, nutritionalists and other scientists have devoted their energies to food-producing animals.

Horses are fed for performance, a nebulous consideration compared with quality of weight-gain. The effectiveness of a diet in terms of live-weight gain per kilogram of food – so important for stock farmers – does not matter where horses are concerned. In fact, the dangers of overweight, including limbs filled by humour, tendon sprains and exaggerated reactions to injuries and infection are constant hazards of which all stable staff are aware. Growth is important in young horses but genetic variation within breeds is so great that it is difficult to measure results against the type of diet that is fed. Diets which are grossly imbalanced in certain nutritive materials such as phosphorus, protein, etc., cause abnormalities during the growing period. It is quality rather than the quantity of the diet which must be the prime concern of those responsible for the horse's diet.

Art or science?

Is the feeding of horses an art or a science? The question is frequently discussed. Certainly, there have always been people who, whatever the circumstances, appear to get better results as feeders than others. They may have an intuitive awareness of a horse's quantitative need and a shrewd insight into the benefits of other aspects of management. For example, one horse may require its grain ration to be split into three or four portions per day whereas another might do as well or better on only two feeds. Again, one individual may require more quiet, warmth, or fresh air in order to make most use of the diet. The type of food is, of course, an important consideration: some horses do better on mashes, some on pellets, some on hard and others on soft hay. How the food is presented is also a factor here; for example, is the hay to be fed in racks or loose on the floor? Successful feeding is certainly an art.

However, if the art is doing, then science is

knowing and here the veterinarian and nutritional scientist have their part to play. The science of feeding is particularly important where young stock are concerned; once growth has ceased the dangers of malnutrition are proportionately reduced. The intention of this chapter is not to enter into the details of different diets but rather to explain nutrition from the point of digestion and types of diet.

Digestion

Digestion is the process by which highly complex material is broken down by the body into simpler substances which are then absorbed into the bloodstream through the intestinal wall. It is the method by which hay, grass, oats, pellets, etc., are reduced to relatively simple molecular states of carbohydrate, protein, fat, minerals, vitamins. These are then carried in the bloodstream to the liver. This organ acts as a filter, allowing certain constituents to pass, changing others and storing some for future use. The nutritive material of the food is thereby made available to the rest of the body for energy, the building of muscles and local storage of fat. The liver also plays a major role in protecting the body against drugs and other noxious substances which may be eaten (or injected). It prevents them from accumulating in proportions which may harm the cells and tissues of the body.

Digestive system

Digestion is accomplished in a tube called the gastrointestinal (alimentary) tract (Figure 17.1). This extends from the mouth to the

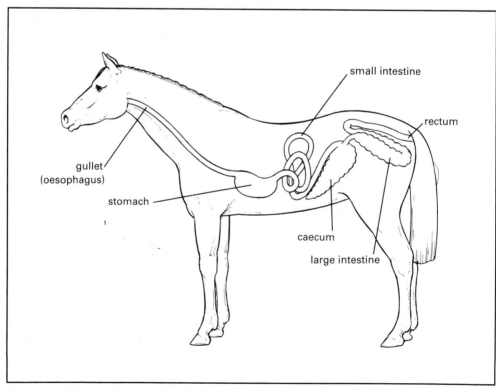

Figure 17.1 The gastrointestinal (alimentary) tract of the horse

anus and is adapted along its length for different purposes; thus we recognise the mouth and tongue for the collection of the food, the teeth for grinding, the gullet (oesophagus) for conveying food from the throat to the stomach and the stomach, small intestine, large intestine (consisting of caecum and large and small colon) for digestion.

The different size of each compartment is associated with the digestive function it performs (Figure 17.2).

	Litres	Length (m)
Stomach	8–15	—
Small intestine	40–50	21.34
Caecum	25–30	—
Large colon	60–70	3.66
Small colon	15–20	3.66

Figure 17.2 Chart to show capacities of the horse's digestive system

The stomach and small intestine are small, relative to the caecum and colon, compared with the cow and carnivorous animals.

The accessory organs, besides the teeth and tongue, include the salivary glands, and the liver and pancreas which, together with small glands in the inner lining of the tube, secrete fluids containing special substances known as enzymes. These mix with the food as it passes down the tube, breaking it down and preparing it for the major digestion in the colon and caecum.

Once food is swallowed, it is automatically conveyed along the tube by contractions of the muscles in the gut wall. The waves of muscular contraction are known as peristalsis and the sound of the movement, which can be heard if we listen at the horse's flanks, is called *borborygmi*.

Horses' digestion differs from other species because most of it takes place in the hind end of the tube (i.e. in the caecum and colon). Animals such as the dog digest most of their food in the stomach and small intestine.

The caecum and colon of the horse contain large numbers of bacteria which live on the fibre and cellulose in the horse's diet. They produce a by-product of fatty acids essential to the horse and which can be readily absorbed through the lining of the tube. The importance of these microorganisms can be illustrated by the fact that if we feed antibiotics to an adult horse we often change the bacterial flora so that digestive disturbances occur and the horse may suffer from diarrhoea.

The foal has a simple type of digestive system, similar to that of a dog, where most of the digestive process occurs in the stomach and small intestine.

During the first six months of life the colon and the caecum become increasingly important. This changeover from fore- to hind-gut digestion corresponds with the gradual change of diet (i.e. milk to highly fibrous grass, hay, etc). Foals may suffer from diarrhoea in the first three months of life as a direct result of fibre in the diet. Therefore, it should be emphasised that only the best quality food should be fed during this period.

Diets

Those who formulate diets for horses at stud have a particular problem. The variable access to the paddock pasture complicates the necessity for feeding hay, grain or pellets in the stable. The pasture itself will vary in nutritive value at different times and between different farms.

This means we need to reduce the protein given in processed feed in spring and early summer when the grass protein is highest and, conversely, to compensate for falling protein levels in autumn and winter.

Dry feed also varies in quality and it is difficult to know just what nutritive material a horse is receiving. This is where the art of feeding has the advantage over science; the good feeder relates the condition of a horse to the amount and type of its food. Only when the results are not satisfactory is the veterinarian asked for advice. The fault may not lie in the food but in other factors such as parasites or virus infection. However, these situations do call for a careful scrutiny of the diet to make sure there are no deficiences.

This brings us back to considering the nutritional needs against little background information. We have to consider these needs in relation to the type of animal: a foal, yearling or pregnant mare. Stabled horses present similar problems although the added variant of pasture quality does not affect the issue.

The following is intended as a summary.

Protein

Proteins are complex organic compounds made up of simpler substances known as amino acids and which are present in definite proportions for each particular protein. Proteins are essential to plant and animal life and form the basic components of every living cell. The total protein content of a horse's body ranges from about 10 to 20 per cent according to age and condition. Protein requirements are greatest during growth. Foals from two weeks to 10 months require about 21 per cent of crude protein in their diet compared with weanlings (14 per cent) and 3-year-olds and over (12 per cent).

The source of protein is important and it should be of high quality so that the all important amino acids are available. Although over 200 amino acids have been isolated from biological materials, only 25 of these are generally regarded as being components of proteins. To be sure we do not feed a deficient diet, multiple sources of protein should be included. Good quality hay and pasture are usually sufficient but for young animals a few tablespoons of dried milk in the feed may be advisable.

Carbohydrates

Threequarters of all dry matter in plants is carbohydrate (sugar) and since plants are the chief source of food, deficiencies are unlikely. There are, however, differences between the nitrogen-free extract and fibre. The nitrogen-free extract includes the more soluble and therefore the more digestible carbo-hydrates such as starch, glucose, fructose and hemicellulose. The fibre is the woody portion of plants which is not dissolved by acids and weak alkalis. It is harder to digest.

The digestibility of fibre varies according to the state of the plant. For example, it is more readily digested in growing pasture than in hay; early-cut hay is more digestible than that cut later or left on the ground for long periods.

Young horses require a ration which is low in fibre and high in nitrogen-free extract. For instance, very young foals require milk which is free of fibre. When they start to eat, the fibre content of their diet should be minimal (i.e. below 6 per cent). Yearlings can digest up to 20 per cent of crude fibre and older horses 25 per cent. As already mentioned, the natural development of the colon and caecum requires an increasing content of crude fibre. In general it is advisable to feed the best quality hay to young horses and to those on which we rely for performance.

Minerals

Horses require calcium, phosphorus, cobalt, potassium, sodium, chlorine, copper, iron, iodine, magnesium, zinc and manganese in their diets. Unfortunately, the exact requirements are often unknown. As we can rarely tell if a horse is suffering from a mineral deficiency it is advisable to depend on some form of comprehensive additive. Due regard must, however, be given to the fact that some minerals fed in high levels may be toxic. The soil in some areas may be deficient in certain minerals although, unlike cattle and sheep, horses are not prone to mineral deficiency diseases. There are exceptions, such as in the copper-deficient areas of Australia and in parts of South Dakota and Wyoming, or where poisoning by excessive amounts of selnium occurs.

Calcium and phosphorus are the mineral elements required in highest quantities because of their importance in bone formation. They exist in the body in a ratio of 2 calcium: 1 phosphorus. Although it would appear rational to feed these minerals in the same ratio, it is known that many natural sources of phosphorus are poorly absorbed from the intestines. It is generally recommended, therefore, that calcium/phosphorus ratio in horse rations should be within the range of 1.1 to 1.4. The absorption of these minerals from the intestines depends on factors such as the presence of vitamin D, quantity of protein and other constituents of the diet. The problem is accentuated by the lack of control over content of all diets, especially those where pasture is included.

Vitamins

Information on the vitamin requirement for horses is extremely limited. All vitamins are necessary although the horse may be able to synthesise some in its intestines. It is particularly important to add vitamin A to the diets of pregnant mares, foals and yearlings. It is essential to horses stressed by the excessive demands of performance as well as by natural events such as gestation, but amounts over 100,000 international units daily are to be avoided because they may be toxic.

Vitamin D is essential for the proper utilisation of calcium and phosphorus while Vitamin B deficiencies are said to cause horses to become nervous and suffer from intestinal disturbances. Vitamin B_{12} deficiencies may occur in stabled horses and cause anaemia. However, all horses should receive additives of a wide range of vitamins.

Pelleted feeds

Pelleted rations have much to recommend them. They are less bulky and therefore easier to store, transport and feed. The ingredients may be selected on a scientific basis and therefore deficiencies or excesses avoided. Further, they reduce wastage and eliminate dust, thus reducing the risk of respiratory problems.

Pellet feeding is increasing in popularity but there are certain dangers. Whatever we feed to horses, it is likely that the intestinal bacteria will be altered; horses have evolved a digestive system to deal with natural foods such as grass and dried plants. Hay and corn

is as near to the natural diet as we can get, which is one reason why good quality hay and oats produces horses in good condition. If, by feeding pellets, we produce a theoretically balanced diet but fail to provide a vital factor such as sufficient bulk of fibre, we may be faced with a digestive upset or even fatal autointoxication, that is, where the bacteria in the gut become harmful. Extreme care is required until we understand more of the relationship between dietary contents and the digestive process.

Diets according to class or stock

Comment has been made in previous chapters on the special needs of particular conditions and class of stock. These may be summarised as follows.

Barren mares

In the summer, barren mares should be kept in good condition on a basic ration of grass. In autumn they should be given a small quantity of good quality hay. About December they may be brought into boxes and given a concentrate ration to coincide with artificial lighting to stimulate their oestrous cycles (see Chapters Two and Four). At the same time the protein content of the diet may be increased although it should be recognised that this 'forcing' may affect follicle development, increasing the risk of a twin conception (see Chapter Two).

Individuals that become over-fat may be difficult to get in foal although it is not clear if this is because they are fat or because their glandular system is out of balance and the fatness is therefore a symptom, rather than a cause, of endocrinological problems. Large fat deposits in the body may absorb a naturally produced hormone such as progesterone and so interfere with normal oestrous behaviour.

Pregnant mares

The in-foal mare usually finds ample nourishment from pasture but towards the end of

August a supplementary feed becomes necessary. The diet should then contain about 14 to 15 per cent crude protein and a calcium/phosphorus ratio of about equal parts. Concentrate rations should be fed to Thoroughbreds at about the rate of 3.64 kg per day and gradually increased to about 6.82 kg at foaling time. During the last three months of pregnancy the mare's protein requirement is particularly heavy.

When the foal is born the demand for protein and other nutrients becomes even greater and the mare's diet should be increased to about 9 kg of concentrates per day with good quality hay to appetite (Figure 17.3). This should provide for her milk production which reaches its peak at about two-and-a-half to three months after foaling.

Newborn foals

Newborn foals must receive colostrum during the first six hours following birth. It is advan-tageous to allow the foal to eat solid food as early as possible and all feeds should be of the highest quality. At first the foal should be encouraged to eat by letting it have access to the mare's manger (Figure 17.4). Once in the habit of nibbling it can be introduced to a 'creep' feeding system by which it may eat freely at any time without obstruction from the mare (Figure 17.5). An advantage of this system is that the foal can receive a higher protein feed than the mare and the feeder knows how much the foal is consuming. A foal's diet should be in the region of 18 per cent crude protein, with a calcium/phosphorus ratio of nearly 2:1. By weaning time the foal is usually consuming 3 kg of concentrate feed per day, plus hay. This should be increased steadily to about 5 kg by the yearling stage. The protein in the diet should then be reduced to 14 per cent because growth in the yearling stage slows down. Allowances must be made for the protein content of grass

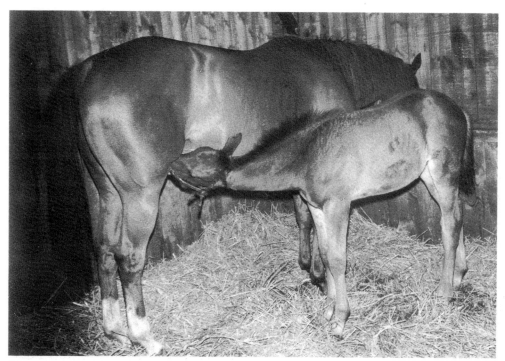

Figure 17.3 The foal's demands on the mare should not lead to a deterioration in the mare's condition. Her diet may need to be increased

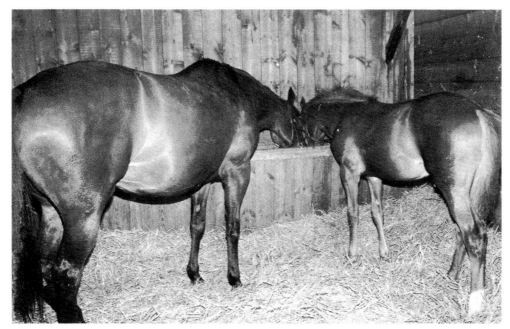

Figure 17.4 Letting the foal have access to the mare's manger encourages it to eat solid food

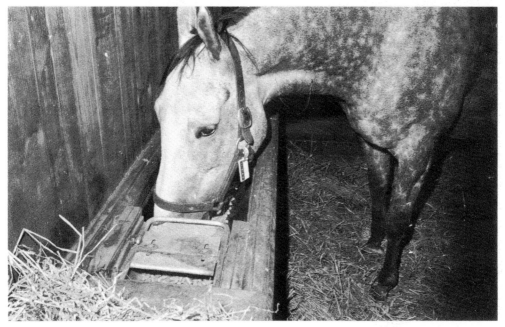

Figure 17.5 A special 'creep' feeding bowl placed in the manger enables foals to feed without interference from the mare

167

and the protein of all diets correspondingly reduced.

Orphan foals

Orphan foals for whom a foster mother is not available can be reared with a bottle and artificial teat or, preferably, by teaching them to feed from a bowl. There are a number of proprietary dried milk substitutes available and these should be mixed according to the manufacturer's instructions. In the first week of life, and following the provision of colostrum (a most important proviso), a foal weighing 50 kg should be allowed about half a litre per feed every 1½ to 2½ hours depending on its appetite.

It is essential that the milk should be fed at blood temperature or below and never above 38 °C.

All utensils should be kept scrupulously clean. The quantity of feed should be increased with age and the foal should be encouraged to eat solid food at an early age. Pelleted feeds containing milk powder, linseed and vitamin additives are particularly useful. The dried matter of liquid diets should be between 15 to 20 per cent (approximately double that of cows' skimmed milk).

It has been found that digestive upsets associated with the explosive growth of pathogenic bacteria in the gut is inhibited by frequent small feeds and the early introduction of dried food.

Horses in training

Energy rather than growth is the consideration here. We also have to remember that horses are usually confined to stables for many hours at a time. They may become bored and eat their bedding or, because they do not have access to pasture, suffer from dietary deficiencies. Folic acid and salt are examples of substances which may become deficient. Care should be taken to ensure that adequate vitamins and minerals are incorporated in the diet.

Horses that have not finished growing, that is 2-year-olds and, to a lesser extent, 3-year-olds, require a higher level of protein than mature horses.

Blood tests

The examination of the blood for such factors as haemoglobin, red cell and mineral content may give some guide to particular deficiencies, although they are far from being specific (i.e. anaemia may be related to a mineral deficiency but it is not usually clear which mineral, and other factors such as parasite infestation or bacterial infection may be involved).

INDEX

Page numbers in *italics* refer to illustrations

Stifle 119, 134
Stillborn foal 90
Stomach 163
Straw ix
Stress 90
Stringhalt 146
Stroma, ovarian 2
Strongyles 101, 104–7, 109
Strongyloides 101, 109–10
Subcutaneous tissue 144
Subfertility 36–7, 44
Suck reflex 78, 84–5, 91, 93, 97
Sucking 101
Suffocation 90–2
Surrogate mothers 47
Swab test 39, 42
Swelling 152
Synovial fluid 120, 133–6, 143–6
Synovial membranes 122, 133
Synovial sheath 124

Tape worms 106–7
Tarsus *See* Hock
Teaser stallion 9–10, 13–17
Teasing 13
Teats 80
Teeth 91, 116–18
Temperature of foal 85, 96
Tendon sheaths 122, 143–4
Tendons 116, 121–4, 132, 138, 144
  bowed 152
  contracted 93–4
  injuries to 142–3
  sprained 144, 157
Terminology 119–20
Testes 23–5, 28
Testosterone 24, 28, 44
Tetanus 128
Thoroughpins 144–5
Thread worms 101
Tibia 114, 141
Training, horses in 168
Tranquillising drugs 18, 82, 84
Transitional oestrus 13
Triceps *143*
Trying 13
Tumours, ovarian 43
Twins 21–2, 52–3, 55–7, 60
Twitch 18, *30*, 34, 76, 82

Udder 71, 80, 82–*3*
  See also Mammary glands
Ulna 114
Ultrasound 20–2, 47, 52, 55, 146, 157–8
Umbilical cord 47, 49, *54*, 70, *78–81*, 91
  severance of 74, 87

United Kingdom 56, 58, 72
Unsoundness 116, 127, 133–6
Urachus 48–9
Urethra 23, 25, 42, 45
Urination 10
Urine 23, 47, 52
Uterine haemorrhage 76
Uterine horns 27
Uterine infection 9, 28, 39, 60
Uterine prolapse 76
Uterine wall 5, 20, 48, 66
Uterus 2–*4*, 8, 28, 39, 47

Vaccination x, 85
Vaccines 58, 62
Vagina 2–5, 20, 39, 40–2, 54
Vas deferens 23, 25
Venereal infections 42
Vertebrae, lumbar *152*
Veterinary examinations 18–22, 52
Viral infection 57–8, 62
Viruses x, 62–3
Vision 116
Vitamin injections 87
Vitamins 165
Vulva 2–4, 10, 40–2, *69*

Wall of hoof 126
Wandering 91
Warble fly 109
Wasting of muscle *143*–4
Waxing up 72
Weaning 101
Weight of foal 89
White line 129
White worms *103*–4, 106–7, 109
Windgalls 135–*6*, 114
Winking 10, *16*
Wobbler disease 116, 146, *148*
Worm egg counts 110
Worms 103–110
  control of 107–110
  pin 105–7
  red 101, 104–7, 109
  seat 105–6
  symptoms of 107
  tape 106–7
  thread 101
  white *103*–4, 106–7, 109
Wounds 142
Wyoming 164

X-rays 153

Yellow body 2, 6–9, 22, 47, 50–1, 60, 64
Yolk sac placenta 47
Young horses 104, 164